Fusion

Fusion

A year's worth of teaching materials for 5–12s

- Useful Insights Into Reaching a Totally New Generation
- Over 100 Games • 52 Unique Stories, Bible Texts and Bible Lessons • Step-by-step Curriculum Guide
- Illustrations • Major Format Ideas
- Contemporary Magazine-style Programme
- The Curriculum That Really Works

Mark Griffiths

MONARCH
BOOKS

OXFORD, UK & GRAND RAPIDS, MICHIGAN, USA

First published in 2001 in the UK by Monarch Books, (a publishing imprint of Lion Hudson plc),
Mayfield House, 256 Banbury Road, Oxford OX2 7DH
Tel: +44 (0) 1865 302750   Fax: +44 (0) 1865 302757
Email: monarch@lionhudson.com
www.lionhudson.com

Reprinted in 2002, 2004.

Distributed by:
UK: Marston Book Services Ltd, PO Box 269, Abingdon, Oxon OX14 4YN;
USA: Kregel Publications, PO Box 2607, Grand Rapids, Michigan 49501.

ISBN 1 85424 526 0 (UK)
ISBN 0 8254 6026 3 (USA)

British Library Cataloguing Data
A catalogue record for this book is available
from the British Library.

Designed and produced by
Lion Hudson plc.
Printed in Malta.

Fusion (fu'sion), n. the coming together of energetic objects with the result of explosive power

Does this sound like
your children's projects?

It should do!

FOREWORD

'What we learn as children shapes the society we make when we become adults.'

Jonathan Sacks, *Chief Rabbi*

When the pressures of handling difficult children become too much for a brilliant and highly experienced head teacher, then you know that something is wrong. If our best professionals are struggling with very young children, it must be time to stop and ask what is going on in our homes and what kind of society these children will make when they become adults.

Governments are desperate to increase standards in education. They are constantly devising new schemes and promoting the latest 'best practice' to maintain progress. But how much of this is simply trying to hide the ever-widening cracks in the walls? I look forward to the time when all our strivings cease and we grasp the fact that without leading children to a knowledge of the Creator and his ways we are simply chasing the wind.

When *Fusion* first passed through my hands I realized at once that here was a programme – a curriculum – that could both hold and instruct the children we meet on our streets and in our estates. Mark Griffiths has a passion for the gospel and for children which communicates with an energy that ripples off the pages. But there is more than just enthusiasm here.

My work brings me into contact with many children's leaders who are very committed to what they do, but find the disobedience and defiance of some of their charges highly draining. In *Fusion*, Mark provides us with not just the content but – crucially – the structure of meetings which enables biblical truths to be taught in an atmosphere that is at once great fun and carefully controlled.

I would urge every children's leader to read and learn from the introductory section of this volume. The guidance given requires no special skills or resources to put into practice, but combine it with the detailed content of the following pages, add the richness of your own personality, cover the whole with prayer – and you could just find that your children's work takes off in a way you had hardly dared hope.

Chris Chesterton
Author of *77 Talks for 21st Century Kids* and children's work adviser

A FEW WORDS FROM THE AUTHOR

The vast array of curricula that exist are designed primarily for children from Christian homes. Twelve out of every thirteen children have no contact with church, or church programmes*. The Fusion Curriculum exists to fill this vacuum. It is designed to communicate the Christian message in a relevant and contemporary manner.

A battle is raging. The spoils of the war are the lives of countless children. If we are to win boys and girls for Jesus we must learn to communicate with them effectively and passionately. According to Winkie Pratney, 'He who learns to communicate to a generation ultimately has the power to control that generation.' This curriculum series is designed to enable you to communicate with a generation that desperately needs Jesus; to communicate the life-changing principles of God's word; to communicate with them while they are still young and untainted by the lies of hell. Why spend all our resources repairing men and women when we can build up boys and girls? Surely prevention is always better than cure.

I am not a theorist. This resource is not merely a collection of good ideas but a curriculum that is used week in week out. It has developed and changed as it has been used. It affects the lives of hundreds of children every week. You have in your hands a proven curriculum and structure.

This curriculum was designed for a specific audience: children from primarily non-Christian backgrounds. However, it will meet the needs of children from many different backgrounds. The uniting of energetic objects resulting in explosive power – does this sound like your children's projects? It should!

Yours committed to winning the battle for Jesus,

Mark Griffiths

---

* Child Evangelism Fellowship Statistics, 1998.

CONTENTS

INTRODUCTION

Useful Insights Into Reaching a New Generation

When we look at scriptures such as Deuteronomy 6 and 11 we are left in no doubt that the ideal setting for passing on godly principles is the daily life of the family. God instituted the family as the seedbed for Christian education. The God-given pattern is that of parents passing on living faith to their children. It was the ideal at the start of time and God's ideal pattern hasn't changed.

What has changed is society's understanding of God's pattern. In 1750 Robert Raikes launched the very first Sunday School. It became the pattern for a nation and for the nations. Thousands of children attended every week. Wesley and his contemporaries were great advocates. Lancaster and Bell took the idea and used it as a catalyst for what has now become the modern school system. The positive effects of Raikes' vision were great, but there were negative effects also. In the mind of the average person, Christian education became something that happened on Sundays for an hour or two. It became something which professional Sunday school teachers did. It moved the responsibility for Christian education away from the home and placed it in the hands of a chosen group of specialists.

Since the 1960s attendance at Sunday schools has declined steadily as their significance has become more and more devalued. In most cases home is no longer a place where godly values are kept or taught. We are now faced with an entire generation that doesn't know Jesus. An entire generation that doesn't have parents who can instruct them in the ways of God. This becomes our role as Christians: literally to become spiritual foster parents; to gather to ourselves hundreds and thousands of children whom we can tell about Jesus, whom we can show the truth, and whom the truth can set free. A generation that desperately needs Jesus.

In order to maximise our effectiveness in this great task we must learn to think differently. We must not be held back by the misconceptions of children's ministry models we have grown up with. We must begin to see large gatherings of children; congregations full of children eager to hear the good news of a God who died for them; children eager to praise and worship the king of the universe; children eager to express their love for the creator of humankind. If we are to see this happen we must learn some very important truths:

God likes teams: Ephesians talks of apostles, prophets, evangelists, teachers and pastors. Many people run their children's services with one woman or man looking after a dozen or so children in a certain age group. There is obviously a contradiction: God gave us teams but we only allow our children to be influenced by a single person. Within the scope of our children's ministry there should be those with a capacity for teaching, those with an affinity for pastoring, those who are evangelists. We must allow our children to experience the impact of all these gifts. And if we need to pull all our 'groups' or 'classes' together to do this, then that's what we must do.

Children watch television: *Sesame Street* is one hour long and fits approximately 45 different items within that time frame. *Live & Kicking*, the flagship of BBC Children's Television (certainly at the start of the 21st century), is built on short, sharp items. The format used is called 'magazine style'. It involves lots of different items all joined together in a fast-paced way. This is the way children process information at this moment in history. We must adopt our programmes to incorporate this technique.

There are golden rules: We think our battle is in the area of apologetics, in what we say. It's not – children are more interested, initially, in who you are than in what you say. If children don't like you, they will not listen to you. If you will not have fun with them, they will not listen to you. If you will not listen to them, they will not listen to you. They have very little respect for authority. But they will respect those who are genuine and those who love them.

There's more to life than the children's event: We must learn to expand our influence beyond that one or two hour slot we use each week. We need to visit the children at home. We need to be involved in their schools, we need to organise other activities, games sessions, football teams. Stretch your influence as far as possible.

Failing is not a problem: I am more and more convinced that we don't fail enough. The reason we don't fail enough is that we don't try enough new things. We play it very safe. We must never be afraid of experimenting, we must allow our programmes to evolve, and we must be as creative as the God we serve. What we will fear is the absence of creative, corrective and constructive responses to our failures, but we will never fear failure itself. Richard Branson, the famous entrepreneur, said: 'If we never make mistakes, we won't make anything.'

Advertising is important: It doesn't matter how good your communication is, how much the children like you, how dynamic your personality or how wonderful your programme, if no children come, it's all pointless. Visit their schools to give out leaflets. Put posters in shop windows, offer great prizes for those who come the first week. And if nobody comes, do it all again – and (this is vital), if lots of children do come, still do it all again. Keep promoting, keep inviting.

Ingredients are vital: Build your programme on a spiritual basis. Build it on prayer and praise and preaching. Make sure these are all kept at the forefront of all your activity.

Even Peter Pan grows up: Children will not stay children forever. Make sure you have a thriving youth congregation to move them into. If one doesn't exist, start one. And, of course, teenagers become adults – eventually – so learn to incorporate them into the main life of your church. They'll become your deacons and elders and even your senior ministers, so it's worth the investment.

We rarely have the privilege of working in the ideal situation, but we must work towards that ideal. We must teach the vast army of un-churched children who will come to us the importance of serving Jesus, the significance of a life that is totally dedicated to him, and the impact they can have on the world. But also, we must never lose sight of the ideal. These children will grow up. They will grow up to marry others with a like mind. So, when they have children they know they have the God-given responsibility to teach those children the ways of God.

If we can reach enough of these children, we can change our cities and nations and world. If we can touch a generation with the message of truth and hope, a message of a God of love, we can truly affect our world.

We rarely have the privilege of working in the ideal situation. But with all our hearts, with all our strength, with all our zeal, with all our passion, let's work towards that great ideal that once again our nation might be truly Christian.

What Makes a Good Curriculum?

This is a much debated subject. Lawrence O. Richards in his excellent book, *A Theology of Children's Ministry*, identifies the following areas as evidence of a good curriculum:

Theological considerations
- Are the materials based on the Scriptures as the major instructional source for Christian education?
- Do they provide a faithful record of, and a friendly commentary on, biblical events and teachings, rather than an interpretation of events and teachings that is actually or potentially negative?
- Do the materials speak with assurance of God's power and goodness in performing miracles, including the great miracles of Christ's virgin birth and his resurrection?
- Do they uphold the Bible's validity in helping people solve problems today?
- Do they emphasise the stable, dependable values that the Scriptures teach?
- Do the materials encourage the learners to commit themselves to Jesus Christ as their personal saviour?
- Do they make it clear that the learners' right relationship with God is a necessary precondition to their right relationships with other people?
- Do they help those learners who have given themselves to Christ to increase their faith and trust him?

Substance and organisation
- Do the materials state understandable and acceptable objectives?
- Do they contain specific data, main ideas and key concepts in balanced proportion and arrangement?
- Do they achieve a focus on main ideas and key concepts to which all other content clearly contributes?
- Are the materials appropriate to the learners' abilities, needs and interests?
- Do they cause learners to repeat important experiences and review important ideas?
- Do the materials increase in difficulty throughout the span of years they cover?

Features helpful in learning
- Do the materials provide a variety of ways to stimulate learning?
- Do they contain and suggest supplementary aids to learning?
- Do they make thrifty use of the time available for learning?

Features helpful in teaching
- Are inexperienced teachers able to use the materials without difficulty or confusion?
- Are teachers' guides or teachers' editions of the materials genuinely helpful, suggesting procedures that make teaching easier and more effective?
- Do they contain suggestions for teacher planning and growth and for ways of evaluating teaching and learning?

I have endeavoured to incorporate the majority of the above into this series. I am also aware of the background of modern children and therefore found it necessary to ensure a fast-paced magazine-style approach without diluting the very important theological aspects. The Fusion Curriculum aims to teach the word of God. Its subject matter is the Bible and will therefore meet needs in many environments.

However, I am very aware that the children God has given you are unique individuals. From time to time, you will need to seek God yourself (possibly using the structure contained within this series to help you – I have enclosed a blank programme in the appendix for this purpose) and develop a curriculum that meets the needs of your children at that specific moment. Each lesson contains two games and three illustrations. From time to time, it will help your personal development and the development of your staff to add an extra game or extra illustration of your own invention. The more you do this, the easier it will become.

THE TOPICS CHOSEN

The curriculum covers a wide range of doctrinal issues. But, it is intentional that the cross is the central point and we return to it again and again. It is envisioned that new children will be joining your project on a regular basis, therefore I have included multiple presentations of the gospel throughout the curriculum. Themes covered include the gospel, evangelism, the character and nature of God, the character of a Christian and various topics within the wider framework of Christian living.

Mission is included because I am committed to children understanding that God is very interested in us having a worldwide perspective and not just a localised one. I dare to believe that children from your projects may grow up and become world changers for Jesus.

A Good Curriculum Is Not Enough

What you have in your hands is the meat and the flesh of the curriculum. It needs a bone structure before you have something which is truly effective. The following guidelines (and they are only guidelines) will enable you to present the curriculum material to its maximum potential.

HALL SET-UP AND STRUCTURE

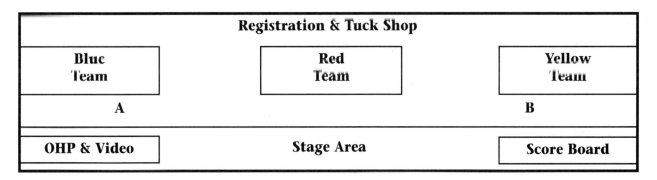

Registration & Tuck Shop		
Blue Team	**Red Team**	**Yellow Team**
A		B
OHP & Video	Stage Area	Score Board

Registration

It is important to have a full list of all the children who attend the club/project. It is best to send out a registration form beforehand containing:

1. Name and address
2. Date of Birth
3. Any medical conditions we should be aware of
4. A contact number for a parent/guardian

The registration forms then need compiling into a weekly attendance register for fire regulations and to allow you to see how the club/project is growing.

Tuck Shop

Whether we like it or not, big visions need big provision. Tuck shops allow you to make a small profit which can be pushed back into the project.

The Scoreboard

Instead of giving prizes weekly, which is incredibly draining on resources, the scoreboard works from week to week over the period of the term (usually 10–14 weeks). The team that wins at the end of the term will take the biggest prize, the other teams will take lesser prizes. (For example, at the end of the Christmas term give a large selection box to the winning team and a smaller selection box to the two other teams.) This is not to say that you shouldn't use an incentive from time to time to attract the children; giving a free jam doughnut to every child on a certain week may increase your attendance; and offering a video or two of their favourite pop groups for the people who bring the most friends may also benefit your attendance.

Why Three Teams?

Some children's groups work with two teams, one of boys and the other of girls. There are several disadvantages to this system: there is very rarely an equal mix of boys and girls; it leads to unnecessary tension between the teams, and it may perpetuate inappropriate sexual stereotypes.

If two teams are used there is a winning team and a losing team. Having three teams allows one team to win and the others to come joint second. It allows an element of healthy competitiveness without there needing to be a loser.

STAFFING

Registration

Three team members should be responsible for registration. This is where you meet the parents. This is the initial contact point. First impressions do last so put some of your best people here. The registration people will also need to be armed with information regarding trips, etc. This is your public relations department.

Team leaders

There should be a sprinkling of leaders in each team. Problems should not be dealt with from the front but sorted quickly from within the team. It will be a process of education for the staff as well as the children.

Scorekeeper

A competent and upbeat member of the team is needed who will periodically announce the scores.

Technical support

A person who can operate PA systems, videos, OHPs, etc. is invaluable. If done well this will help you greatly. If done badly this can destroy your programme.

Front people

Two front people will be responsible for the illustrations. Given two competent front people, you can introduce a third as a trainee. Training staff should be a continuous process and allows you to move or sow out into other children's works. The choice of the third person is very important: they may not be particularly gifted, but they must be humble, teachable and have the heart of a servant. Don't choose anyone without these qualifications.

Others

If you run crafts as part of your programme, you will need artistic people. A qualified first aider should not be overlooked. Members of the team will also need to be involved in the weekly visitation programme.

LITTLE THINGS MATTER

- Allow the children to bring in pictures of the leaders.
- Allow the children a talent slot in the programme.
- Form a diary committee that records your club's activities (keep it accessible).
- Cancel the programme from time to time for a barbecue or a video evening with popcorn.
- You must win the right to speak into the children's lives.
- Maintain a sense of fun in, and with, your team.

THEY WILL ONLY LISTEN TO YOU WHEN YOU HAVE WON THE RIGHT TO SPEAK

- Don't run the curriculum every week. Have an all games week with bouncy castles, snooker, basketball, computer games, etc. If practical have a longer session so this can take place before your teaching time. This will give you a chance to get to know the children. Have fun with the children in this time and they will listen to you much better in the curriculum weeks. We actually give an hour of our two and a half hour programme, to free play activities to balance the curriculum session. It allows us to spend time teaching and time building relationships.
- Visit them in their homes to let them know what's coming up the following week. Remember God is interested in the families not only the children.
- Send, or give out, information about future activities, and feedback on past activities. Do this on a regular basis.
- Build relationships with un-churched families, not just un-churched children.

The Programme From Beginning To End

Special Note: All the items within the programme need to be joined together quite rapidly. The usual length of a session is 90 minutes. The times given in brackets are approximations and represent the maximum time that should be taken on an item. Younger children may not cope with the full programme. Condense the programme and introduce a simple craft time if you are working with children under seven. 'Free play' of varying duration (up to 1 hour) can precede the programme.

WELCOME (3 minutes)

This is a chance to welcome the children, but also an opportunity to have fun with them. Remember, if you will not have fun with them, they will not listen to you. I prefer to lead the programme with two people at the front. This allows comical banter between them. Think differently! Have the two leaders enter dressed as Barney Rubble and Fred Flintstone to welcome the children. Be creative!

RULES (2 minutes)

If there are no clear rules then the children have no clues as to the behaviour you expect and cannot reasonably be reprimanded. Only two simples rules are necessary:

- Nobody leaves their seat. If someone needs to go to the toilet, they must put their hand up and ask permission from a leader.
- When the whistle blows, everyone stops speaking, sits down, faces the front and makes no sound. If you are uncomfortable with the use of a whistle, you can use a horn or a special word.

These two simple rules will keep everything controlled. Children feel safer and more secure in a disciplined atmosphere.

There must also be a method of enforcing the rules. We use the following twofold system:

- **Positive enforcement:** If a team is particularly good (e.g., they sit well, listen well, cheer the loudest, or win a game), they get to roll the dice. The score from the dice is added to their overall score. The team with the most points at the end of the term gets the biggest prizes, the other teams receive smaller prizes (e.g., at the end of the Easter term the members of the winning team receive Easter eggs, the others receive cream eggs).

- **Negative enforcement:** If a child talks after the whistle has gone or is not sitting and facing the front, their team instantly loses six points.

**REMEMBER IT'S YOUR ABILITY TO REPRODUCE LEADERS THAT
WILL MARK THE LONG TERM SUCCESS OF THE WORK**

PRAYER (5 minutes)

This can be divided into two sections:

- **Giving thanks:** Children who have prayed for something the week before (or several weeks before) and whose prayers have been answered should be asked to come and tell the others how God answered their prayer.

- **Bringing needs:** Some of the children will want to pray for certain things. Allow them to come and mention what they are praying for and ask God together to answer prayer.

PRAISE (7 minutes)

There are two slots for praise. Use this first slot for familiar songs with lots of actions. New songs can be introduced in the second section. Some children may not enjoy singing – give six points for the best team singing, suddenly you'll find they enjoy it a lot more!

GAME 1 (5 minutes)

Games differ from week to week. But the following points apply throughout:

- In order to play a game they must answer a question on the previous week's lesson.
- Choose one person from each team and then allow that person to choose the rest of the team.
- For games which mention point A and point B see the hall plan.

- Give points for the teams that cheer people the loudest.
- Play fast, lively music while the game runs.
- The first team to complete the game must sit down.

PRAISE (10 minutes)

This second praise slot is longer with several songs being used together. Encourage banners, streamers, dancing, etc. Allow some of the children to form a praise group that stands with a microphone to lead the others. I have included a list of CDs for children in the recommended resource appendix at the back.

FUN ITEM 1 (5 minutes)

We use several fun items to enhance the programme. For example:

Guess The Leader: We reveal an interesting fact about one of the leaders, e.g., 'This leader used to live in Spain.' Then four leaders are chosen who all try and convince the children that they used to live in Spain. The children then have to guess the leader who was telling the truth. A variation on this theme is to show a picture of the leader as a baby and the leaders all have to try and convince the children that they are the person in the picture.

Buy It or Bin It: This is a chance for music and video reviews. Ask the children to bring in the videos they watch and the music they listen to. It may not seem overtly Christian, but it is incredibly educational! Form a panel of three (one leader and two children) and allow them to view three videos/CDs for thirty seconds each. Then ask whether they would buy them or bin them, and why. Periodically introduce Christian music. This teaches the children critical thought which is very important for their development.

Who Wants To Be a Chocoholic: This item is based on the television game show *Who Wants To Be a Millionaire?* A child is chosen from the audience. They are asked questions in increasing degrees of difficulty. They are given four answers to the questions and have to choose the right one. For a right answer they gain more chocolate, for a wrong answer they lose it all. The trick is to know when to quit and take the chocolate. The children have two lifelines: they can ask the audience or a leader the answer to a question.

Aerobics Workout: A piece of music is played and the children copy the leader at the front performing their aerobic workout.

This slot can be used for all sorts of fun items such as puppet skits, etc. Use the time to have fun with the children. Be creative with your ideas.

GAME 2 (5 minutes)

Make sure the people who take part in Game 2 are different from those who played Game 1.

FUN ITEM 2 (5 minutes)

Other items may be added to the first section such as video clips of an outing, interviews with community members. Use your imagination.

BIBLE TEXT (3 minutes)

We display the memory verse on the OHP from the start of preaching time and refer to it frequently, but you may prefer to encourage the children to memorise the text. There are many ways to teach a Bible text. A few ideas are highlighted below but there are literally hundreds of possibilities. Be creative.

- Write the Bible text on balloons and burst the balloon as the verse is read.
- Make the verse into a jigsaw puzzle.

- Write the verse on an object which communicates its message, e.g., 'You are a light to my path' can be written on a lamp or a drawing of a bulb; 'The Lord is my shepherd' can be written on five cut out sheep.

Remember that memorisation of the verse is not as important as understanding. Being able to quote 'The Lord is my Shepherd' may win a prize, but understanding it will change their lives.

- All Scripture quotations are from the *Contemporary English Version*. New Testament © American Bible Society 1991, 1992, 1995. Used by permission. Anglicisations © British & Foreign Bible Society 1996.

Copies of each of the Bible verses are included in the OHP Appendix for you to photocopy onto acetate.

ANNOUNCEMENTS (2 minutes)

Summer camps, play schemes, colouring competitions, birthdays, special events, etc., all need mentioning here. If you are going to do birthdays, you must be consistent – don't do them one week and then miss for two weeks, as some children will miss out and feel hurt.

INTERVIEW (5 minutes)

Invite one of the leaders (or one of the children) to come and tell the group what Jesus has done for them; how he has helped them in work or school; how he cares for them; how they first made their decision to become a Christian. If the person is very nervous, interview them. If they are more confident, allow them to speak freely, taking notice of the timing allowed for this section.

WORSHIP (10 minutes)

A quieter time of worship where songs such as Ishmael's 'Father God' or Doug Horley's 'King of Love' can be introduced. Encourage the children who know the words to close their eyes and begin to think about King Jesus. Take your time here, it is important to introduce them to worship.

We instruct the children that praise is generally loud and lively, a time when we have fun singing to God. Worship is when we come closer to God, think about God more. Worship comes from our hearts and our minds. It involves all our emotions. The definitions of praise and worship may be much broader and more theological than this, but a bite-size theological portion is more easily swallowed by an eight year old.

PREACHING TIME

The rest of the programme falls under the heading 'preaching time'. This will include all Bible lessons, illustrations and the story.

Time for a very special announcement (3 minutes)

Inform the children that they are now moving into preaching time which is the most important thing that happens. Inform them that this section can change their lives. There are special rules:

When the whistle blows next, preaching time has begun. In preaching time:

- Nobody leaves to go to the toilet. In fact nobody moves
- Anyone talking loses six points straightaway without discussion

However, a leader will be walking around with tuck shop tokens or sweets and will place them in the hands of anyone who really deserves one:

- You must be excellent to receive one. Good is not enough, anyone can be good.
- You must keep facing the front. If you look at the leader (who we refer to as a quiet seat watcher) they will not give you a token/sweet.
- If you get a sweet/token and play with it (or try and open it), it will be taken away.

Blow the whistle (the whistle can be put away now, it will no longer be needed).

Bible Lesson (5 minutes)

There are various ideas to help with the presentation of the Bible Lesson:

- Dress some of the children up as characters in the story.
- Use videos. The recommended resource appendix will give you some ideas.
- If you are presenting the story in narrative form then tell the story as Hollywood would, don't just read the account.

Illustrations 1–3 (5 minutes each)

Illustrations can take many forms – object lessons, short drama sketches, puppet sketches, video clips, testimonies, etc. – basically anything that can be used to present the overall lesson.

Story (10 minutes)

The story is a modern parable which rolls all the themes presented so far, into one neat narrative package. Again various methods can be used to enhance the presentation:

- Use some of the children as characters in the story.
- Draw some of the characters on flash cards or acetates.
- Keep it dramatic, use your body and voice to maximise the presentation.

Prayer/Response (5 minutes)

Always ask for a response. Make an appeal. Ask the children who felt the lesson applied to them to stand. If it required forgiveness, pray a prayer of forgiveness together. Let the children respond by repeating the prayer after you. There must be a response.

Next Week (3 minutes)

Highlight next week's programme. Keep it exciting: 'Next week everyone who comes will get a cream egg', 'Next week we'll hear the concluding part of this exciting story', etc.

The Finishing Touch (2 minutes)

Give the children a picture which reinforces the day's lesson. Ask them to colour and return it. The best pictures will win prizes.

Ask a leader to dismiss the children a row at a time. Head for the door and say goodbye to the children, talk to some parents. Mix!

PREACHING

The material you have in front of you is designed to be preached.
Preached with fire and passion with gentleness and compassion,
proclamation that will sometimes by-pass the head
and speak directly into hearts.

The need of the day is children's workers who are full of the Holy Ghost
who will proclaim, in a relevant and contemporary manner,
the message of the cross and the principles of God's word.

DON'T JUST TELL CUTE STORIES – CHANGE LIVES!!!!

This is the part that can't be taught. The message either burns within you
or it doesn't. If it burns inside then lives will be changed.
If it doesn't then pray until it does.

Building Relationships With The Wider Family

We don't only have a responsibility to reach the children. In doing so we will almost certainly form some very positive relationships with parents who send their children to our programme but would not normally set foot in a church building. We must be sensitive to what God is doing at this point. There are many testimonies of children leading their parents to Christ. Here are some dos and don'ts:

DOS
- Organise social events such as barbecues, family fun days, children's entertainers, visits to sports centres, family day trips.
- Have open evenings where parents can come and watch your programme. Place these around Christmas, Easter, etc. and then use them as a springboard to invite parents to your special meetings for Christmas or Easter.

DON'TS
- become the confrontational evangelist looking for the instant response. You stand the chance of losing your link with both the parent and the child. Sometimes 'softly, softly catches the monkey!'
- only run events with a view to 'evangelism'. Sometimes it's good just to have fun (having fun is very evangelistic!).

The Curriculum In Various Contexts

THE EVANGELISTIC CHILDREN'S CLUB

The material was written with this context in mind. The format should be used as it appears, but feel free to add your own games and illustrations as you see fit. The stories at the end of each lesson may not suit everyone. Some people will prefer to add visual aids to them, some people will prefer not to use them at all and instead add an extra illustration. If it works for you then it is right for you. It is important that you don't try and wear Saul's armour!

THE HOLIDAY PLAY SCHEME

Deciding how much of the Christian message can be packaged into what is essentially a community project always requires sensitivity. I recommend that the format is followed as listed, but only one of the illustrations and the story is used.

THE BIBLE WEEK

Follow the guidelines for the evangelistic children's club but opt for a series that has five parts or can be shortened to five parts easily.

THE SCHOOL ASSEMBLY

The stories may be used as they are, or a single illustration expanded to form the fifteen-minute school assembly block.

THE CHURCH SUNDAY SCHOOL

The first section will need condensing, but the preaching time could be used in this context without any major amendments. It is important to work out how you want to format your Sunday school. We prefer our Sunday school programme (by which we mean the children's programme that runs while the preaching takes place on Sundays) to be informal and almost cell group in nature. Because of this, the programme must become much more interactive. Allow lots of questions and time for discussion on the illustrations and Bible lesson.

SUMMER CAMP

Within this context, I would maintain the format as it stands, but expand the illustrations and Bible lessons. I would not normally use the stories, instead bringing about opportunities for response from the illustrations.

Characterisations or Puppet Characters

From time to time we use characters to present the illustrations. Characters tend to overlap different series. Sometimes a character will only make one appearance in a particular series but will return in another series several weeks later. They are deliberately kept simple.

THERE ARE THREE REAL CHOICES

- A real person acts the part. If you have a church drama group, then this will be an easy option for you.
- Use puppets for the characters. This has the advantage of being more flexible and allows children to be the puppeteers if you feel you have suitable candidates.
- A combination of the above. This has generally been the route we have chosen.

The characteristics are what matters, you may change the names and appearance as you see fit. The characters used in this series are:

Toby Christian (formerly Toby Trouble)
Personality traits: Toby became a Christian recently. He is about thirteen years old and still carries a high degree of bad attitude.
Appearance: T-shirt, a baseball cap, jeans which are too short, etc.

Mr Geeky
Personality traits: His trademark is his ability to get things completely wrong and to misunderstand the simplest of concepts.
Appearance: Handkerchief on his head, an old coat, very thick glasses, brown trousers, etc.

PC Blob
Personality traits: He investigates, he searches for clues. He sometimes tries to arrest people!
Appearance: Policeman's hat, black trousers and a large number of balloons up his jumper.

Encounters With The King

A Series in Six Parts

Introduction

Title	Themes covered
1 The Disciples	Following Jesus
2 Nicodemus	Embarrasment
3 The Samaritan Woman	Worship, Jesus knows everything about us
4 A Woman Caught In Sin	Jesus takes what is bad and gives what is good
5 Lazarus	Jesus can do anything
6 The Man Born Blind	To experience is better than to know about

Series Overview

'The Word became a human being and lived here with us. We saw his true glory, the glory of the only Son of the Father. From him all the kindness and all the truth of God have come down to us' (John 1:14).

Each of the gospel writers has a different emphasis. Matthew is quick to point out that Jesus is the promised Jewish messiah of the Old Testament. Luke's themes are angels and healing and he focuses heavily on the birth narratives. Mark's Gospel is much shorter and far more direct.

John is interested in the signs and miracles that Jesus performed, particularly when they bring insight to Jesus' deity. John is also far more relational. The love of God consumes John and he draws particular attention to the way that love is expressed to those who Jesus meets. For this reason, we look primarily to John's Gospel when seeking to understand the effect of Jesus on others.

Jesus only lived, in bodily form, on this earth for thirty three years. His public ministry was only three years long. Yet no one has had a greater impact on the world than the Son of God who became man. This series looks at some of the people who met Jesus, what they learnt and how an encounter with the King changed them forever.

The life application stories for this series are based on the exciting adventures of Alexander the Great.

The Disciples

	Programme	Item
Section 1	Welcome	
	Rules	
	Prayer	
	Praise	
	Game 1	Table Tennis Tap
	Praise (x2)	
	Fun Item	
	Game 2	Wobble
	Fun Item	
	Bible Text	Matthew 4:19
	Announcements	
	Interview	
	Worship (x2)	
Section 2	Bible Lesson	The Disciples
Preaching	Illustration 1	The House Builder
Time	Illustration 2	Promises
	Illustration 3	The Balance
	Story	Who Will Follow Me? (Alexander The Great 1)
	Prayer	

Overview

A disciple is someone who follows. What does it mean to be a follower of Jesus? Is it a good or bad idea to follow him?

games

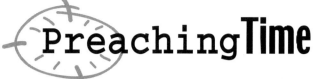

PreachingTime

Game 1

Table Tennis Tap

PREPARATION	One table tennis bat and one table tennis ball for each team.
PLAYERS	Five from each team.
SET-UP	The teams line up in relay formation at A with the person at the front holding the table tennis ball and the bat.
OBJECT	The children must run from A to B and back again whilst tapping the ball in the air. If the ball falls they must stop and pick the ball up. On their return to A they pass the bat and ball to the next member of their team, who repeats the process.
WINNING	First team to complete and have all its players sitting down.

Game 2

Wobble

PREPARATION	A paper cup and a table tennis ball per team.
PLAYERS	Five from each team.
SET-UP	Five players in relay formation at point A. The person at the front holds the cup upside down with the table tennis ball balanced on top.
OBJECT	The children run from A to B and back again, balancing the table tennis ball on the cup. They pass the cup and ball to the next player who repeats the run.
WINNING	First team back and sitting down.

 **BIBLE LESSON**

THE DISCIPLES

'Come with me! I will show you how to bring in people instead of fish.' (Matthew 4:19)

A disciple is someone who follows someone else. Jesus' disciples were people who followed Jesus.

The way Jesus recruited his first disciples was quite strange. He was walking along the shore of Lake Galilee when he saw two fishermen throwing their nets into the sea. One of the fishermen was Andrew and the other Peter. Jesus said to them, 'Come with me! I will show you how to bring in people instead of fish.'

As soon as Andrew and Peter heard these words they left their nets and followed Jesus. They became his disciples. Peter and Andrew were two of Jesus' first disciples. They had met Jesus before this, so they knew there was something very special about this man and they felt that being his disciples would be far more exciting than being fishermen. They didn't really know he was the Son of God. It wasn't until much later that they discovered he was King Jesus, the creator of the universe. They only knew a little about him but they still felt that following Jesus would be the most exciting decision they would ever make.

It wasn't always easy. Some people refused to believe them when they said that Jesus was the Son of God. Some people were very nasty to them. When Jesus was arrested and crucified things looked very bad for the disciples. But when Jesus rose from the dead they knew for certain that being his disciple was the greatest thing they could ever be.

King Jesus worked through Peter. Lots of people who Peter prayed for were healed. On one occasion his shadow alone caused people to be healed. Peter talked to thousands of people at once and told them about King Jesus and how he had died on the cross for them, so that the wrong things they'd done could be forgiven. Five thousand of them became Christians on that day alone. It wasn't always easy being Jesus' disciple, but Peter was glad he put down his nets and followed Jesus. Life was so exciting!

When Peter was an old man he was arrested for talking about King Jesus and telling others how much King Jesus loved them. He had been arrested many times before and he had spent a lot of time in prison just for telling people about Jesus but this time it was more serious. They beat him and then they ordered that he be crucified upside down. They nailed him to a wooden cross and left him hanging there until he died. But even then, if you had asked Peter, 'Are you glad you followed Jesus?' he would have replied, 'Yes, of course.' And, if you had said to him, 'Peter, if you hadn't followed Jesus that day, you wouldn't be on this cross now,' he would have said, 'I'm glad I followed Jesus. It was the most exciting life anyone could ever have, and now I'm going to be with King Jesus for ever in heaven.'

It's not easy to be a disciple. It's not easy to follow Jesus. But it's the most exciting way to live.

The House Builder

Objects needed: *Building bricks.*

Toby walks on and begins to build a house with the bricks. He places four of them on top of each other and stops.

LEADER: Toby! What are you doing?
TOBY: I'm building a house.

Toby looks around and sits down.

LEADER: Toby! Why have you stopped?
TOBY: I've run out of building bricks.
LEADER: Then why did you start something you couldn't finish?

Toby shrugs his shoulders and looks sad.

It's not a very good idea to start something you can't finish. Some people begin to build houses and then have to stop, leaving a pile of bricks in the middle of nowhere. Some people try to climb huge mountains but give up halfway. Some people start to run long races but never finish the race. There is nothing clever in starting things we cannot finish. If we decide to do something then we need to do it.

Jesus told Andrew and Peter to follow him. If they had given up after just a couple of days they

would not have been true disciples of Jesus. When we make a decision to follow Jesus it must be serious.

Promises

Who's ever had a friend make them a promise? Who's ever had a friend make them a promise that they didn't keep?

'I'll be your best friend forever, I promise! I'll keep the secret, I promise! We won't go to the park without you, I promise!'

Lots of people make promises. Lots of people make promises they don't keep. How do you feel when someone makes a promise to you and doesn't keep it? Sad? Hurt? Upset? Angry?

I wonder how many people have said to Jesus, 'I promise to follow you forever,' and then haven't. I wonder if Jesus feels sad and hurt? I think he probably does. If we say we will follow Jesus then that's what we need to be doing.

We need to be promise keepers and not promise breakers.

The Balance

Objects needed: *Long pole with hooks on.*
Signs saying:
'People may laugh.'
'People won't understand.'
'I'll go to heaven when I die.'
'It's exciting to live for Jesus.'
Several blank signs

Ask one of the leaders to stand centre stage holding the pole.

Many people are unsure about whether they should follow Jesus or not. Should I? Shouldn't I? We have to balance all the factors up before we can make a decision. Let me show you what I mean.

What are some of the reasons for following Jesus and for not following Jesus?

'If I follow him people may laugh at me.'

Hang the sign on the end of the pole. The leader should make the pole tilt in that direction.

'People won't understand.'

Place the sign on the next hook. The leader tilts the pole slightly more.

Repeat the procedure with the two positive signs to bring the pole back to the level.

So the pole is balanced again. Are there any more things we need to think about?

Write the children's ideas on the spare cards and hang them on the appropriate side, moving the pole in correlation with the positioning of the signs.

You see there are decisions which only we can make. But it needs thinking about.

● STORY – Who Will Follow Me? (Alexander The Great 1)

This is not the story of an ordinary man, this is the story of Alexander The Great.

'Who will follow me?' Alexander began. 'I am the new king.'

Alexander had been standing in the temple when his father's bodyguard had taken a knife and plunged it into his father's heart. The bodyguard tried to escape but was beheaded long before he reached the exit. The court was in stunned horror. No one knew what to do. Then Alexander issued his challenge, 'Who will follow me?'

He had grey eyes and thick blond hair. He was nineteen years old. He was asking men twenty years older to follow him. He was asking great generals, with great military experience, to follow him. Each of the men knew something of Alexander. They had heard the stories of his bravery. But he was only nineteen. How could he be king? How could he lead the Macedonian army, he was barely a man?

We are often faced with the question; 'Who will follow me?' Sometimes it's our friends, on other occasions it's our teachers or our parents. Who should we follow? In the end it is our decision and our decision only. We have to ask ourselves some very important questions:

- **Can I trust this person?**
- **Can I be trusted to keep following them? We shouldn't be disciples who turn back after a week or two.**

'Who will follow me?' roared Alexander.

Many of the people in that room made their decision. They decided that they would follow Alexander. They believed they could trust him.

All over our world right now thousands upon thousands of people are making that decision to follow Jesus. They know they can trust him.

Alexander led over 35,000 men from Greece. He marched with them for some ten years fighting and conquering as he went. He marched 11,000 miles, making the Alexandrian empire – named after him – the greatest and strongest power in the entire world.

Many of those men were unsure if they should march with him or not. They were unsure that day in the temple, but they took a chance and followed him. And if you had the opportunity to talk to those same men at the end of their lives, when they were very old, and asked them if they were glad they'd followed Alexander, they would all say, 'Yes.' They lived lives of great excitement and adventure, following one of the greatest leaders of world history.

We're going to be looking at some of Alexander's adventures over the next five weeks and see the incredible things he accomplished. But the bottom line is this: many people were unsure about following him, but those who did never regretted it.

Many people are unsure about Christianity. A Christian is a disciple or follower of Jesus. Many people are unsure about following Jesus. But, if they do, their lives will be very, very exciting.

2 Nicodemus

	Programme	Item
Section 1	**Welcome**	
	Rules	
	Prayer	
	Praise	
	Game 1	Knee To Bucket
	Praise (x2)	
	Fun Item (2)	
	Game 2	Pie Man
	Fun Item	
	Bible Text	Matthew 10:32
	Announcements	
	Interview	
	Worship (x2)	
Section 2	**Bible Lesson**	Nicodemus
Preaching	**Illustration 1**	Embarrassing Moments
Time	**Illustration 2**	Embarrassment Mime
	Illustration 3	The Girlfriend
	Story	The Watchman (Alexander The Great 2)
	Prayer	

 **Overview** Nicodemus came at night. He was embarrassed to meet the king of the universe. Many people seem to be embarrassed by Jesus.

games

PreachingTime

Game 1

Knee To Bucket

PREPARATION	Lots of table tennis balls. One bucket for each team at B.
PLAYERS	Five from each team.
SET-UP	The teams line up in relay formation at A with the person at the front holding a table tennis ball between their knees.
OBJECT	The children run from A to B where they drop the ball into the team's bucket without using their hands. They then return to A for the next player.
WINNING	The team with the most balls in the bucket after three minutes wins.

Game 2

Pie Man

PREPARATION	Lots of paper plates with shaving foam on them stacked at B. A leader from each of the teams also at B.
PLAYERS	Five from each team.
SET-UP	Five players in relay pattern at A.
OBJECT	The children run from A to B, place a shaving foam plate into the face of the leader and return to A for the next person to begin.
WINNING	The team which has placed most shaving foam pies in their leader's face after three minutes wins.

 **BIBLE LESSON** ## NICODEMUS

'If you tell others that you belong to me, I will tell my father in heaven that you are my followers.'
(Matthew 10:32)

There was a Pharisee – a Jewish leader – who wanted to know about Jesus. But he was embarrassed. He didn't want people to see him visiting Jesus so he came at night.

Many people are embarrassed about coming to Jesus. But the main reason is that they don't know who he is or what he's like. If they knew that he was the Son of God and the creator of the universe then they wouldn't be so embarrassed, they would be very proud to meet him.

Nicodemus didn't know him yet, so he was embarrassed. He crept out to talk to him at night. But Nicodemus was going to have an encounter with the King of the universe.

Nicodemus came to know Jesus. Later on, after Jesus had been killed on a cross but before he came back to life, Nicodemus went to the ruler of Jerusalem, a man called Pilate, the man who let Jesus be killed, and asked for permission to go and help prepare Jesus' body for burial. Even Jesus' disciples had run away because they were frightened of being killed by the Roman soldiers or the Pharisees. But Nicodemus was there. He knew who Jesus was now, so he wasn't embarrassed anymore. He was proud to know the King of the universe.

When we really know who Jesus is, we are proud to say we are Christians, we are not embarrassed any more.

Embarrassing Moments

Substitute your own embarrassing moment.

Who would like to tell me about their most embarrassing moment? Here's mine.

I had just finished eating my dinner at college and was walking towards the door when a friend of mine had this great idea. He thought it would be funny to run up behind me and rugby tackle me. Well that wouldn't have been too embarrassing. If it had worked, it might even have been funny.

He ran up and dived at my legs but missed and ended up grabbing just my trousers. He slid to the ground still holding my trousers. So there I stood in front of a packed college dining room in my underpants. My trousers were around my ankles and my friend was lying on the floor laughing so much he was crying. Needless to say everyone else in the room started to laugh as well. I was very, very embarrassed. I went bright red. It was one of the most embarrassing moments of my life.

I wonder what makes you embarrassed?

Embarrassment Mime

Objects needed: *An audio tape containing thirty seconds of hymn singing and thirty seconds of spy music (theme music from* The Saint *should work).*

The mime artist walks through the pretend door of the church and sits in his pretend pew. The hymn begins so he stands and sings with all his heart.

NARRATOR: It's easy to be a Christian in church.

The mime artist leaves his pew, walks to the church door, opens it and steps outside. As soon as he is outside the music changes to the spy music. Now the mime artist is hiding; ducking behind cars; pulling newspapers over his face to conceal himself.

NARRATOR: But sometimes the same people who are happy to be Christians – followers of Jesus – in church don't want anyone outside to know about it.

The music stops. The mime artist looks very embarrassed, shrugs his shoulders and leaves the stage.

NARRATOR: Jesus said, 'If you tell others that you belong to me, I will tell my father in heaven that you are my followers. But if you reject me, I will tell my father in heaven that you don't belong to me.'

The Girlfriend

Object needed: *Love heart.*

Is anyone in love?

I have a friend who's met this girl. She's really nice, but he's absolutely crazy about her. He talks about her all the time. Before I ever met her, I knew everything about her. He couldn't stop talking about her. We used to talk about football, but not anymore. All he talks about now is Matilda. That's her name. We used to talk about cars, but not any more. All he talks about now is Matilda.

The day before he asked her out he was unbearable. He kept walking up and down the room, practising his lines: 'Matilda, will you go out with me?' 'Matilda, will you go on a date with me?' Matilda, I love you.'

When he eventually got around to asking her it took him ages. But she said 'yes'. He came straight round to my house to tell me. He banged on the door until I opened it and told me all about it. He was so happy.

When you're excited about someone, you tell everyone. He was really excited about Matilda, far more excited than some people are about Jesus. All Matilda ever did was kiss my friend. Jesus died on a cross for him so that all the wrong things he had ever done could be forgiven.

I don't know why it is, but he wants to tell everyone about Matilda. He almost seems embarrassed about Jesus.

● STORY – The Watchman (Alexander The Great 2)

It was the night before an important battle and Alexander's armies were in need of a rest. The Persians were camped nearby and there was a sense of great unease in the camp. Alexander knew that his men were very vulnerable as they slept. There was nothing to stop the Persians creeping into the camp, wiping out hundreds of Alexander's soldiers and maybe killing Alexander himself.

To protect the army Alexander came up with the idea of using watchmen. He made the 35,000 soldiers sleep in a large circle and every five hundred metres around the circumference of the circle he set a watchman. The watchman's job was very simple: he was to keep watch and if he saw the enemy approaching he was to blow his trumpet.

The soldiers hated taking their turn as watchman. It would mean a long night of standing and watching out into the darkness. One of the soldiers on this particular night really hated it. He had marched all day long and hadn't slept very well last night. And now here he was in the cold night, waiting and watching. His eyelids were very heavy. He would love to be asleep but he knew that instead he needed to stand and watch.

When 10 p.m. came, the camp was quiet except for one or two soldiers chatting. The soldier felt very tired but kept watch.

By 11 p.m. he was feeling sleepy, but he leaned against a nearby tree and kept watching.

At midnight the camp was totally silent apart from the sound of snoring in the distance. The soldier felt very, very tired. He sat down, still leaning against that tree.

At 2 a.m. the soldier's eyes began to close. He pushed them open again, but he was so tired. It was getting cold now. He reached into his bag and wrapped a blanket around himself.

By 3 a.m. his eyes were nearly closed.

By 4 a.m. he was fast asleep, wrapped in the blanket and leaning against the tree.

At 5 a.m. he felt a hand grab his throat. He felt himself leaving the ground and being slammed against the tree with his legs dangling in the air. He was sure that when he opened his eyes he would look into the face of one of the Persians and was sure that any moment now a dagger would be pushed into his chest. He began to open his eyes slowly and the sight which met his eyes was far more frightening than any Persian. There, gazing up at him, holding him with one enormous arm, fingers clenching his throat, was Alexander The Great.

Alexander looked at the soldier, his eyes burning with anger, his fingers able to squeeze the life out of the man with ease. 'What is your name soldier?' Alexander demanded.

Through his tight throat the soldier croaked, 'Alexander, sir. My name is Alexander.'

'What?'

'Alexander, sir. My mother named me after you.'

Alexander looked at the soldier, then released him. The soldier fell in a heap on the ground. Alexander looked down at him and with venom in his voice said, 'Soldier, either change the way you behave or change your name.'

Lots of people call themselves Christians. It means 'followers of Christ'. Sometimes I think Jesus says to some of those people, 'Either change the way you behave or stop calling yourselves Christians.' Some people call themselves Christians but continue to swear and fight and steal. Jesus says, 'Either change the way you behave or stop calling yourselves Christians.' We are either Christians or we are not. If we are, we must act like Christians.

3 The Samaritan Woman

	Programme	Item
Section 1	Welcome	
	Rules	
	Prayer	
	Praise	
	Game 1	Squirt!
	Praise (x2)	
	Fun Item (2)	
	Game 2	Hockey Dribble
	Fun Item	
	Bible Text	John 4:14
	Announcements	
	Interview	
	Worship (x2)	
Section 2	Bible Lesson	The Samaritan Woman
Preaching	Illustration 1	Giving And Taking
Time	Illustration 2	Things Which Just Don't Last!
	Illustration 3	Overflow
	Story	The Beards (Alexander The Great 3)
	Prayer	

Overview The Samaritan woman meets Jesus at the well. The woman thinks he wants to take something. In fact, he wants to give her living water!

games

Preaching Time

Game 1

Squirt!

PREPARATION	Three lengths of hose pipe each about one metre long and a T-joint to join them at the centre. Pour some water into the pipes and hold up the ends so the water doesn't leak.
PLAYERS	Three players from each team.
SET-UP	The three players line up with the front member of the team holding the hose pipe on their side in their hands.
OBJECT	When the game begins, the front players blow through the pipe. They keep blowing until the water squirts out of one of the pipes. The team whose pipe squirts out first loses that player who is replaced by the next player in the team.
WINNING	When all the players on one team are out, the team with the most players left wins. If it is equal, then it is a draw.

Game 2

Hockey Dribble

PREPARATION	A hockey stick and a ball for each team.
PLAYERS	Five from each team.
SET-UP	The teams line up in relay pattern at point A.
OBJECT	The players run from A to B and back again, dribbling the ball with the hockey stick. When they reach B they pass the ball and stick to the next player.
WINNING	The first team back and sitting down wins.

BIBLE LESSON **THE SAMARITAN WOMAN**

'The water I give is like a flowing fountain that gives everlasting life.' (John 4:14)

Jesus was on his way to Galilee. He decided to go through Samaria on the way. Although Jesus was the Son of God, he had been born a Jew. The Jews didn't like the Samaritans and the Samaritans didn't like the Jews.

Jesus and his disciples came to a well and sat down beside it. He sent his disciples on to a nearby town to buy some food.

As Jesus was sitting by the well, a Samaritan woman walked up to get some water. Now Jews were not supposed to speak to Samaritans, but this was no ordinary Jew. Jesus loved all people, no matter where they came from. He loves all people whether they're English or German, Irish or African. He loves everyone.

Jesus asked the woman, 'Could you get me some water?'

The woman was surprised. She didn't want Jesus to talk to her. She had been married many times and now lived with someone who was not her husband. Perhaps she expected Jesus to condemn her, to criticise her. But Jesus did none of these things. He was just kind to her.

She was shocked at Jesus' request. 'How can you ask me for water? I am a Samaritan and you are a Jew.'

He replied, 'You don't know who I am. If you did, you would ask for the river that gives life.'

Jesus wasn't just talking about ordinary life. He was talking about everlasting life – being able to live forever.

That woman had so many wrong ideas about Jesus:

She thought he only liked people from certain places and only liked good people. Jesus loves everyone, no matter what they've done.

She thought he only wanted to take things away. But Jesus only comes to take the bad things away and to give us good things. He takes away the junk, the garbage, the rubbish, the stuff the Bible calls sin and instead he gives us everlasting life – we get to live forever. She thought he'd come to take something from her. He'd actually come to give her everlasting life.

This woman was about to have an encounter

with the King of the universe. She would never be the same again.

Giving And Taking

A person playing the part of God (dress him in white) stands on a chair with a big stick, waving it frantically.

A small boy walks past.

GOD: Give me that Mars bar. Don't you know it's bad for you?

Another boy walks past.

GOD: Give me that money, I want it now.

A girl walks past.

GOD: Stop smiling, you are not to have fun.

God continues to wave the stick ominously.

NARRATOR: People actually think God is like this. He stands on a cloud taking things from us, telling us what to do. But, God isn't really like this.

The person playing God gets off the chair, shrugs his or her shoulders and walks off.

NARRATOR: God only takes the bad things in our lives. And in return for taking away all the bad things, he actually gives us many good things. He fills our hearts with joy and promises us everlasting life if we ask him to forgive the wrong things that we've done.

Things Which Just Don't Last

Objects needed: Snicker bar

As you talk, begin to eat the Snicker bar.

Some things last forever. Some things don't. This Snicker bar is not going to last forever. It probably won't last until the end of today. The sort of things God wants to give us will last forever. They are not like Snicker bars. God wants to give us everlasting life. That means we will live forever with him.

Overflow

Objects needed: *Two transparent jugs of water, cooking oil, tray*

Fill one of the jugs with water and display it at the front on the tray, on a table.

This is like we were when we were born: clean and pure.

Begin to pour the oil into the jug of water saying,

Slowly our lives get all messed up with junk and garbage, the stuff the Bible calls sin. The sin increases and increases.

Allow the mix of water and oil to settle as you say,

We try and keep the bad things we do a secret but eventually they come to the surface and everyone can see them.

Now begin to pour in the water from the other jug very gently until the oil overflows into the tray.

But gently God pours his love into our lives – if we allow him – and the bad stuff slowly is dealt with. It's called sanctification, but that's too long a word so we'll call it God cleaning us up.

God wants to take all the junk out and leave us as clean and as pure as when we first came to know him.

● STORY – The Beards (Alexander The Great 3)

Alexander made his men do some strange things but what he had asked them to do before one battle with the Persians must have seemed the strangest thing yet.

He ordered them all to shave off their beards. The men were very confused. Why should they shave off their beards? Some of them had spent many years growing them. They thought they looked quite good. Some of the men had long beards, some had goatee beards and some had beards which looked more like haystacks than beards. Why should they shave them off?

Some of the bad things we do, we like doing. So why should we stop when King Jesus says so? Why should we give things up? Does God really know best?

Did Alexander know best? Well, yes. He knew that sometimes the Persians would grab the beards of their enemies, pull on them and, holding them tight, cut off their heads. Losing their beards was a small price to pay for gaining their lives. Giving up those bad things in our lives is a very small price to pay for gaining everlasting life.

So, Alexander's men had to make a decision. They could keep their beards and lose the battle or lose their beards and win the battle. Alexander's men made the right decision. They won the battle as a result.

We too have to make some decisions. We can ask Jesus to forgive the wrong things we've done and ask him to take the bad things away and gain everlasting life or we can refuse to ask Jesus. What decision will we make? More to the point, what decision will you make?

4 A Woman Caught In Sin

	Programme	Item
Section 1	**Welcome**	
	Rules	
	Prayer	
	Praise	
	Game 1	Hula Hoop Hugs
	Praise (x2)	
	Fun Item	
	Game 2	Hopping, Hopping, Hopping
	Fun Item	
	Bible Text	Romans 8:1
	Announcements	
	Interview	
	Worship (x2)	
Section 2	**Bible Lesson**	The Woman Caught In The Act Of Sin
Preaching	**Illustration 1**	Planks And Splinters
Time	**Illustration 2**	Geeky Meets Geeky
	Illustration 3	Silence In Court
	Story	Memnon (Alexander The Great 4)
	Prayer	

 **verview** A woman had been caught in sin and thrown before Jesus. 'Judge her Jesus!' came the cries of the crowd. But he refused to criticise and judge others.

games

PreachingTime

Game 1

Hula Hoop Hugs

PREPARATION	Three hula hoops are needed.
PLAYERS	Three players from each team.
SET-UP	The teams line up at A with the front member of each team holding the hula hoop.
OBJECT	The first person gets inside the hoop and runs from A to B and back again. The next player joins them inside the hoop and they repeat the process. Then the third person joins them.
WINNING	First team back and sitting down wins.

Game 2

Hopping, Hopping, Hopping (for under sevens)

PREPARATION	None.
PLAYERS	Five from each team (all under sevens).
SET-UP	The teams line up in relay pattern at point A.
OBJECT	The teams hop in relay formation from A to B and back again.
WINNING	First team back and sitting down wins.

BIBLE LESSON | **THE WOMAN CAUGHT IN THE ACT OF SIN**

'If you belong to Jesus Christ you won't be punished.'
(Romans 8:1)

One day Jesus was at the temple when a commotion erupted outside. The Pharisees (the religious rulers in Jerusalem) burst into the temple and threw a young woman to the ground. She was crying and clearly very upset.

They said, 'We've caught this woman doing wrong things. She was sinning. What shall we do to her? Our law says we should throw stones at her until she's dead. What do you say?'

They were trying to trap Jesus. Instead of answering their question, he knelt down and began writing in the sand.

The Bible says that we have all done things wrong. It calls them sin. The Bible then goes on to say that the result of sin – of doing things wrong – is death.

'What shall we do?' they demanded.

Jesus looked at the men and said, 'If any one of you has never done anything wrong, then let him throw the first stone.'

The Pharisees looked at each other. They didn't know what to do. They began to walk away, feeling embarrassed. They knew that they had all done things wrong.

When all the men had left, Jesus looked at the woman. She was still very upset. 'Where are the men who accused you?' he asked.

'They have all gone,' she replied.

'Well, if not one of them accuses you, then neither do I. Now go and don't sin any more.'

We have all done things wrong and we all deserve to be punished for our sins, but Jesus doesn't want to punish us. The punishment for doing things wrong is death, but Jesus wants to give us the gift of everlasting life. People may condemn us, but Jesus loves us.

Planks And Splinters

Objects needed: *Plank of wood.*

Man walks on with a plank of wood held over his eye. He sees the leader trying to get something out of his eye.

MAN: Ah! Ah! Ah! Look at you. You've got a splinter in your eye. It looks really silly.

The man walks around with the plank (the leader has to duck several times to avoid it), then walks towards the children.

MAN: Look! *Pointing to the leader.* He's got a splinter in his eye.

LEADER: Amazing, isn't it? He can see the splinter in my eye, but he can't see the plank in his.

The man continues to walk around with the plank in his eye.

LEADER: This may all seem very silly, but some of us are at least as bad as this. We see the faults in everyone else and never see our own faults. We have all got faults. Some people have big noses; some have big tummies. Some people would see these as faults. It's wrong to try and point out everyone else's faults.

MAN: *Still pointing at the leader.* Ah! Look at that splinter.

LEADER: That's why Jesus said, 'Before you try and take the splinter out of someone else's eye, take the plank out of your own.'

MAN: Oh!

Man walks off looking sad.

Geeky Meets Geeky

Mr Geeky (see notes on characterisations in the introduction – this particular illustration could work very well with puppets) walks on and looks around. Ten seconds later another person dressed as Mr Geeky walks on – we'll call him Geeky 2. Geeky looks at him and begins to laugh.

GEEKY: Look at those glasses. You look really stupid. You look so geeky.

GEEKY 2: Look at that thing on your head. You look ridiculous. You look more geeky than me.

GEEKY: Look at those trousers. You geek!

GEEKY 2: Look at that jacket. You are the most geeky person I've ever seen.

The leader breaks in as they continue their argument in mime. We think this is hysterical. They are equally bad and yet each finds fault in the other. But we too have faults and only see the faults of others. Jesus doesn't like it when we argue like this. He wants us to follow his example. When he saw the woman who had done something wrong, he didn't criticise her, he was kind to her.

Silence In Court

Object needed: *Toy hammer.*

A leader (the judge) and a boy or girl mime the parts as the narrative unfolds.

The judge took his position behind the desk. He banged the gavel *(toy hammer)* and shouted, 'Order in court – bring in the defendant.'

A small boy/girl walked in and stood before the judge. The judge began to reel off a long list of bad things he/she had done. The boy/girl hung his/her head low. He/she knew he/she was guilty. There was nothing he/she could do.

He/she simply stood and waited for the punishment to be announced.

The judge read out the punishment. 'The result of doing wrong things is death.'

What could the boy/girl do? He/she was clearly guilty, he/she deserved to be punished.

Then an amazing thing happened. The judge walked forward and took the boy/girl's place. He was punished instead.

The judge's name was King Jesus and that was exactly what happened. We had all done things wrong, but Jesus took our punishment. Not only did he not condemn us, he actually died on that cross. He took our punishment so that all the bad things we've done could be forgiven if we ask.

Jesus doesn't condemn, he wants to forgive.

● STORY – Memnon (Alexander The Great 4)

While Alexander the Great was a young man in Macedon he had a friend. His name was Memnon. They grew up together, learned to fight together, learned to hunt together and on many occasions marched to battle on the same side. But Alexander and Memnon had an argument and Memnon left Macedonia to join the Persians, Alexander's greatest enemies.

Alexander's army had defeated many armies on their way through Asia and now they were about to fight yet another Persian army. But this would be an unusual fight. This Persian army was led by none other than Memnon, Alexander's old friend. Alexander had already faced him in battle once, but Memnon had escaped with his army by sea to the Greek island of Cos. Now they were ready to face each other again.

The two friends faced each other on the battlefield. Alexander's were skilled soldiers with lots of experience of battle. They were ready for this challenge. Memnon felt unsure about fighting Alexander, but it was too late to back off now.

The armies charged. They fought. Swords clashed. Shields were hammered and knocked to the ground. Many men were killed as the battle continued. The hours went by, but it was clear that Alexander's awesome army would win the day. Most of the Persians turned and fled from the battlefield, leaving only Memnon and a handful of men who were loyal to him to fight on. It wasn't long before Memnon and his men were trapped inside a circle of Alexander's men.

'Kill them!' came the chant from Alexander's soldiers. 'They betrayed you, Alexander. Kill them!'

What was Alexander to do? Memnon had once been his friend. But Memnon had clearly betrayed and hurt him.

God has a similar choice with us. We have all done wrong things. Whether we know it or not, these things hurt God. What should God do? We deserve to be punished.

Memnon deserved to be punished, but Alexander didn't want to punish him. He let his old friend go.

God actually does something even greater. He not only doesn't want to punish us, he says, 'If you belong to Jesus Christ, you won't be punished.' But he also goes further and offers to forgive all the wrong things we've done, if we ask him.

God doesn't want to condemn or criticise or punish us and neither should we condemn or criticise or want to punish each other.

Lazarus

	Programme	Item
Section 1	Welcome	
	Rules	
	Prayer	
	Praise	
	Game 1	Mummies
	Praise (x2)	
	Fun Item 2	
	Game 2	Feed Me! Feed Me!
	Fun Item	
	Bible Text	Genesis 18:14
	Announcements	
	Interview	
	Worship (x2)	
Section 2	Bible Lesson	Lazarus
Preaching	Illustration 1	Everywhere
Time	Illustration 2	Everything
	Illustration 3	Bigger Than Anything
	Story	Persia Can't Be Taken (Alexander The Great 5)
	Prayer	

Overview A God who can create an entire universe simply by speaking can do absolutely anything. Before Jesus comes into our lives part of us is dead. Our spirits are dead. God brings them back to life.

games

PreachingTime

Game 1

Mummies

PREPARATION	Three toilet rolls for each team.
PLAYERS	Three players and a leader from each team.
SET-UP	The leader stands on a chair with the three players around them (each equipped with a toilet roll).
OBJECT	To cover as much of the leader as possible in the time allowed.
WINNING	The team with the most mummified leader after three minutes wins.

Game 2

Feed Me! Feed Me!

PREPARATION	A baby bottle of blackcurrant juice, a bowl of water and an antiseptic wipe for each team.
PLAYERS	Five players and a leader from each team.
SET-UP	The players line up in relay pattern at point A. The leaders sit at B with the bottles, bowls and cloths.
OBJECT	The first person from each team runs from A to B. At B they must sit on a stool and be fed for ten seconds. They then return to tag the next player at A. The bottles will need washing between runs, hence the bowls of water and cloths.
WINNING	The team that drinks the most juice in three minutes wins.

BIBLE LESSON

LAZARUS

'I am the Lord! There is nothing too difficult for me.' (Genesis 18:14)

He had a strange name – Lazarus. But his name didn't matter now because he had been dead for the last four days. They had buried him in the usual way: they had wrapped him in bandages, placed him in a cave and put a rock against the entrance.

His sisters were very sad. They were sure that, if Jesus had been around, he would have prayed for Lazarus and Lazarus would have got better.

They knew that Jesus was very powerful and that he could do wonderful things, but they didn't really know how powerful. They didn't fully understand how much power King Jesus and those who serve King Jesus really have. But they were about to find out. Lazarus had been dead for four days, but he was about to have an encounter with the King.

One of the sisters, Martha, was waiting for Jesus. When he arrived, she said, 'Oh Jesus, if you'd been here my brother would not have died.'

You see, she knew Jesus was powerful, but she didn't know how powerful.

Then Jesus met Lazarus' other sister, Mary. She was crying. Others also wept for the death of Lazarus. 'Take me to where he is buried,' Jesus asked.

They took him to the entrance to Lazarus' grave. Jesus asked for the rock to be taken away, and then with a loud voice he prayed and commanded Lazarus to come out of the grave.

Lazarus had been dead for four days, but at the sound of Jesus' voice Lazarus came out.

Sometimes we know that King Jesus is very powerful, but we forget how powerful.

But it's not just Jesus who does amazing things. The Bible says those who follow King Jesus will also do amazing things. They will pray for sick people and see them made well and do even greater things. Don't forget how powerful King Jesus is.

Everywhere

Right now I'm here. *(Point to your feet.)* In a couple of seconds I'll be over there. *(Now walk to the place you have just indicated.)*

You see, now I'm here. And now I'm going back where I came from. *(Walk back.)*

I'm either there or here. I can't be in both places at once. Nobody can be in two places at once. Actually that's not true. Someone can! God can.

The Bible teaches us that God fills all time and space. What on earth does that mean? The posh word for it is 'omnipresence'. It basically means that God is everywhere. He fills this room; he fills this city; he fills this country; he fills this continent; he fills this world; he fills this galaxy; he fills this… You get the idea. There is no place God isn't.

But God is even more incredible than that. Not only is he everywhere that we can think of, he's everywhere that has ever been and everywhere that ever will be. If you could travel back to the Battle of Hastings in 1066, you'd discover that God is there as well. But God is not just in Hastings in 1066, he is everywhere in 1066.

It gets even more complicated. God is everywhere in 1066 and everywhere right now and everywhere in the year 2199 and everywhere in any date that you can think of. As I said, God fills all time and space! King Jesus is God. Isn't God amazing?

Everything

Objects needed: *Mastermind chair, Trivial Pursuit questions.*

Welcome to Mastermind. In the seat today we have *(any leader)*. They will be answering a range of general knowledge questions.

Work your way through fifteen Trivial Pursuit questions. The leader needs to get some wrong for this to work.

They did quite well. Not many people could get them all right.

Wouldn't it be amazing if you knew everything? You could appear on any game show in the world and get every question right. You'd win the lottery every week because you'd know all the numbers that would come up. You'd know who the Prime Minister was two hundred years ago. And – this is where it gets interesting – if you knew everything, you'd know who the Prime Minister will be in two hundred years' time.

A lot of people know some things, a few people know lots of things, but nobody knows everything except, of course, God. God knows absolutely everything about absolutely everything. He knows everything about the things that have already happened and everything about what will happen. King Jesus is God. Isn't God amazing?

Bigger Than Anything

Object needed: *Flash paper*.*

Watch this. *(Light a fairly large piece of flash paper and throw it in the air.)* Impressive or what! I'll show you it again.

It looks good. But really it's just a couple of chemicals that burn very quickly on a piece of paper. I've watched some magicians who have been very impressive. I watched a man called David Copperfield trick people into thinking the Statue of Liberty had disappeared. But they were all just tricks.

But what if you could speak one word like, 'Light!' and instantly there was light? Not a trick, but real light appearing from nowhere. And what if you said, 'Jupiter', and instantly the planet Jupiter appeared? That's what God did. He created the universe with just a word. We

---

* Flash paper is available relatively cheaply from Mr Paul Morley, 91 Green Street, Middleton, Manchester M24 2TB (telephone: 01706 649921; e-mail: www.tricksfortruth.com or paul@morley54.freeserve.co.uk).

shouldn't really be surprised that he brought Lazarus back to life.

God can do anything. King Jesus is God. Isn't God amazing?

● STORY – Persia Can't Be Taken (Alexander The Great 5)

Darius was the commander of the Persian armies. He was the emperor of Persia and a formidable warrior. He could not believe that anyone would be so stupid as to attack him. He felt that Persia was the greatest nation in all the world and had the best army. He would put an end to Alexander and his men once and for all.

Darius left Issus with 70,000 trained soldiers and marched around the back of Alexander's army to surprise them. He lined up his troops on the north bank of the Pinarus River and prepared to crush Alexander once and for all.

Alexander was caught off guard. His men were tired and it was already late in the afternoon. Alexander's men were afraid. They were vastly outnumbered and feared Darius greatly so they urged Alexander to wait until the morning and let them rest, but Alexander refused. He assembled his 35,000 men and prepared to fight.

The Persians watched as Alexander rode up and down the lines of soldiers, encouraging his men and giving them instructions. The Persians expected Alexander to run away but they were wrong. He roused his men. And they were ready to fight. The Persians had never met a leader like Alexander and they began to fear him.

Then Alexander did the unthinkable. He gave the command to attack and led his men straight towards Darius. They knocked down the soldiers in the way and kept advancing on the emperor himself. Darius was afraid and turned to flee. Without their leader, the Persians were lost and fled in all directions. Darius only barely escaped with his life.

Darius did not believe Alexander was strong enough to defeat him. He was wrong. He knew Alexander was a great leader but he didn't find out, until it was too late, how great he really was.

We know God is great. We know King Jesus can heal the sick. But this King Jesus also raised Lazarus to life. Nothing is impossible for God. And nothing is impossible for those who serve King Jesus.

The Man Born Blind

	Programme	Item
Section 1	**Welcome**	
	Rules	
	Prayer	
	Praise	
	Game 1	Water Jets
	Praise (x2)	
	Fun Item (2)	
	Game 2	Choo! Choo! Trains
	Fun Item	
	Bible Text	Psalm 34:8
	Announcements	
	Interview	
	Worship (x2)	
Section 2	**Bible Lesson**	The Man Born Blind
Preaching	**Illustration 1**	Apple
Time	**Illustration 2**	Ice, Baby!
	Illustration 3	Opinions And Realities
	Story	I Was There (Alexander The Great 6)
	Prayer	

Jesus had healed the man born blind and now a great argument had erupted. Some said it wasn't the same man; some said he was never blind. The man himself ended the discussion by saying, 'I am that man, I was blind but now I see.' Lots of people had theories, but this man had an experience.

 **games**

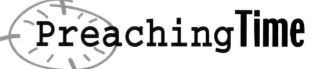 Preaching**Time**

 Game 1

Water Jets

PREPARATION	A washing up liquid bottle full of water and a bucket for each team.
PLAYERS	Six players from each team.
SET-UP	Five players line up at A with the front member of the team holding the bottle. The sixth person stands at B holding the bucket.
OBJECT	The first person runs from A to a point about five metres before B. They then have five seconds to squirt as much water into the bucket as possible. A leader needs to monitor the time. The player then returns to A and passes the bottle to the next player.
WINNING	The team with the fullest bucket after five minutes wins.

 Game 2

Choo! Choo! Trains

PREPARATION	None.
PLAYERS	Five from each team.
SET-UP	The players line up in relay pattern at point A.
OBJECT	The first person runs from A to B and back. The second holds on to the waist of the first and together they run to B and back, then the third player joins them, and so on.
WINNING	The first team back and sitting down wins.

 **BIBLE LESSON** ## THE MAN BORN BLIND

'Discover for yourself that God is kind.' (Psalm 34:8)

A certain man had been born blind. He had never seen a sunrise; he had never seen a summer's day; he had never even seen the faces of his mother and father. But today all that would change. He was about to have an encounter with the King of the universe.

Jesus saw the man and walked up to him. He knelt in front of the man, made some mud and smeared the mud onto the man's eyes. 'Now go,' Jesus said, 'and wash yourself in Siloam Pool.'

The man did what Jesus told him and, as soon as he washed, he could see. He could see clouds and trees; he could see colours; he could see people and animals.

However, as we know, the Pharisees didn't like Jesus very much. They were afraid that, if people found out that Jesus had healed somebody who'd been born blind, he would become far too popular. They started telling people that the man who could now see was not the same man who had been blind. But the people knew it was the same man. The Pharisees then called the man's parents and tried to convince them to say that the man had never been blind. But how could they? He had been blind.

Many arguments broke out. Until eventually the man himself said, 'Listen to me, I was blind but now I see.'

Everyone else had an idea, a theory, a thought of what might have happened, but the man himself knew exactly what had happened. We may have many ideas about what Jesus is truly like but, until we actually have our own encounter with the King, we will never discover what King Jesus is really like.

The blind man had an encounter with Jesus and nothing would ever be the same again. It's time for you to have your own personal encounter with Jesus.

Apple

Objects needed: *Two apples.*

I'm sure this apple is going to be delicious. It makes my mouth water just thinking about it. It's so green, so lovely, so – words just fail me – I can't fully describe how lovely this apple is going to taste. *(Bite into the apple.)*

Wow! This apple is amazing! It tastes absolutely delicious. I wish I could really tell you how good this apple tastes.

We've spent a lot of time trying to tell you how great Jesus is, and how much we want you to ask him to forgive the wrong things you've done and to live for him. But all the words and stories aren't really enough. It's difficult to describe to you how wonderful living for Jesus really is.

I guess there is a way to show you how great this apple tastes. I need a volunteer who will come and taste this apple. *(Pull out the second apple and allow the volunteer to bite into it.)*

Now we both know how great these apples taste. The only way you'll really know how great these apples taste is to bite into one. It's only when you experience the apple that you know how good it is.

It's the same with Jesus. I can talk as long as I like but I'll never really convince you until you have your own encounter with King Jesus.

Ice, Baby!

Object needed: *Ice cube.*

I know some people who are missionaries. They went to Mongolia to tell people about Jesus. Now Mongolia is a very cold place. It's so cold in winter that you don't need a freezer to keep your meat frozen, you can simply hang it out of the window and it will freeze solid. It really is cold.

My friends wanted to take their dog with them. They had to leave him in quarantine for some time but eventually they were allowed to bring him into the country.

His name was Clyde and he was a funny dog. When it snowed, he spent time running around trying to catch the snowflakes. He couldn't understand why they just disappeared when he caught them.

They didn't keep Clyde on a lead. Even though he was a crazy dog, he always walked just a few metres behind the missionaries.

Clyde was very inquisitive. He liked to sniff everything; he liked to investigate everything. So he couldn't understand why my friends wouldn't let him investigate the puddles he saw along the road. Every time he tried to visit one of the puddles, he was called away. 'Don't go near them, they're too cold. That's ice,' he was told. But even though he'd been told, he still wanted to investigate for himself.

Some of us are like that. It's not altogether a bad thing. Wanting to experience lots of new things can be good as long as the things we're trying to investigate are good for us. Some of you will never believe me when I tell you that asking Jesus to forgive your sins, the wrong things you've done, and becoming a Christian will be the greatest thing you'll ever do. But when you try it, you'll know it's true.

Clyde walked over to what he thought was a puddle. He had to experience it for himself. He leaned over and tried to drink from the puddle. But Mongolia is freezing cold. When he discovered that the puddle wasn't runny like water but cold and hard, he tried to lick it. He got a nasty surprise when he tried to step back. The ice was so cold his tongue had stuck to it. He was trapped. When my friends turned round there was poor Clyde, crying like a baby, stuck to the puddle. They had to pull him off, leaving some of the top layer of his tongue behind.

His tongue hurt a lot but he learned that what my friends had told him was true. Some people have to experience it before they believe it.

Opinions And Realities

Object needed: *Piece of paper cut into the shape of a triangle.*

There is a massive difference between what is true and what is someone's opinion. Let me explain: When we do 'Buy It or Bin It', it's all about opinions. Some of you will like the song and some of you won't. Nobody is right or wrong. It's your opinion. If I asked you, do you like my T-shirt? some of you would say, 'Yes,' and some of you would say, 'No.' It is just a matter of opinion, not of right or wrong.

If I asked you what shape this piece of paper is, that would be a totally different thing. Now there is a right and a wrong answer. It is a triangle. If you said it was a triangle, you would be right. If you said it was a square or a circle or any other shape, you would be wrong. This is not about your opinion. You are either right or wrong.

When we talk about Jesus it's exactly the same. You could have all sorts of theories about who he is, but unless you said he was the Son of God and the King of the universe you would be wrong. You can have lots of opinions about how to get to heaven. But unless you said that it was by asking Jesus to forgive the wrong things you've done and living for him you would be wrong.

Unless you have had an encounter with the King of the universe, King Jesus, you cannot go to heaven.

● STORY – I Was There (Alexander The Great 6)

Alexander never returned to his home country of Macedonia. When he was in his early thirties he died. But before he died he had successfully marched his armies over a third of the known world (that was in the days before trains and aeroplanes and cars). He had established himself as Alexander The Great, the greatest military mind of the time. He had defeated armies that others said could never be defeated. He had conquered kingdoms that people said would never fall. Alexander had become a legend.

In the market place in Macedon people loved to come and talk and discuss all sorts of things. It was several years after Alexander The Great had died and many theories were flying around as to what he had actually done. There were many opinions.

'He could never have conquered so many people,' one man began.

'It's all been exaggerated, he could never have killed so many Persians,' another added.

'He probably wasn't such a great leader,' a third commented.

They talked for some time, unaware that a man stood nearby listening to their conversation.

Lots of people have lots of different theories and ideas, don't they? Not all of them are right.

'He couldn't have done half the things that people say!' looked like being the final comment.

The man who had been watching, walked into the group which now numbered about twenty. 'It's all true and more,' he stated boldly.

The astonished crowd just looked at him. Then a tall man at the back of the group called out, 'We don't believe it's so.' He wasn't going to give up on the argument so quickly.

'All that is said and has been written about Alexander is only part of the story. He did even greater things,' the man replied.

'How can you be so sure?' the tall man asked.

'Because I was there! I was in the royal palace right at the start, when Alexander announced that he was king and challenged us to follow him. I followed him through many battles, over thousands of kilometres of ground. Once I felt his hand round my throat because I fell asleep on watch in the middle of the night. I experienced it. I was there. I was there with him when he marched across Persia, when we defeated Darius, when he let Memnon go, when he conquered Egypt and established the port of Alexandria. I was there when he took Iraq and Iran. I was there.'

No one could argue with the man. He had been there. He had experienced it with his own eyes.

No one can argue with a person who has had an experience. Christians are people who have had an experience, who have asked the King of the universe to forgive their sins and have given their lives to him. They've had an encounter with the King: King Jesus.

This is the end of the series on people who had encounters with King Jesus, but it isn't really the end. Millions of people

have an encounter with Jesus every year. Millions of people find out that he really is the King of the universe. As we leave this series now, which of you are ready for an encounter with the King?

Mountain Climbing

A Series in Four Parts

Introduction

Title	Themes covered
1 Mount Moriah	A place of testing
2 Mount Sinai	A place of rules
3 Mount Carmel	A place of power
4 Mount Moriah	A place of ultimate sacrifice

 Series Overview

Mountains in the Bible are often significant. There is usually something significant in the people of Israel arriving at a mountain, or a man or woman of God going up a mountain. Over the next four weeks we will be looking at three different mountains. We will look at Mount Moriah twice but, in historical terms, there will be approximately 6,000 years between the two visits.

The series will look at four different men and their experiences on these mountains. The life story will look at three animals related to mountains, starting with a family of eagles.

As a whole the series will show that God uses people he has tested, whom he can trust and who are prepared to do anything for God. It climaxes by showing us that the whole thing is possible only because of the Son of God who was tested, was shown to be blameless and would do anything for the Father even if it meant laying down his life.

You will need to construct a chart. At the start, all areas will have question marks. As the series progresses, the relevant words can be inserted.

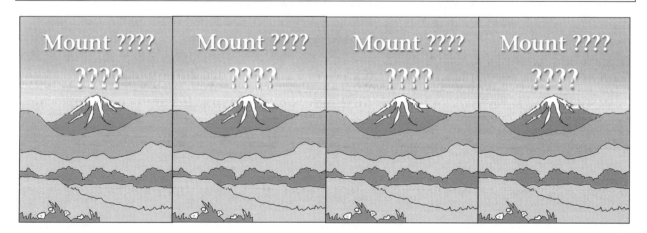

Mount Moriah

	Programme	Item
Section 1	Welcome	
	Rules	
	Prayer	
	Praise	
	Game 1	Obstacles
	Praise (x2)	
	Fun Item 1	
	Game 2	Obstacle Trusting
	Fun Item 2	
	Bible Text	1 Corinthians 4:2
	Announcements	
	Interview	
	Worship (x2)	
Section 2	Bible Lesson	Abraham And Isaac
Preaching	Illustration 1	Light Bulb
Time	Illustration 2	'L' Plates
	Illustration 3	Questions
	Story	The Eagles
	Prayer	

Overview Most of the things we buy in the shops go through rigorous checks first. The more important the object, the more tests it has to undergo. When God wants to use a person in his Kingdom, he tests that person first. God wants to know that we are really committed to him and that he can trust us. The more he wants us to do, the more he tests us. Abraham would be the father of a nation. His test would be difficult.

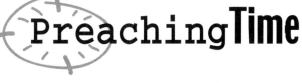

Game 1

Obstacles

PREPARATION	Arrange a small obstacle course using chairs and other items which are at hand. They should be positioned so that the children can go over some, under others, etc.
PLAYERS	Six players from each team.
SET-UP	Players line up in relay formation at A.
OBJECT	To complete the obstacle race first.
WINNING	The first team to complete and sit down wins.

Game 2

Obstacle Trusting

PREPARATION	Use the obstacle course above.
PLAYERS	Two players from each team.
SET-UP	One of the players from each team is blindfolded.
OBJECT	The blindfolded person must complete the obstacles by listening to the voice of the other player only.
WINNING	The first team back and sitting down wins.

BIBLE LESSON ABRAHAM IS TESTED

'…our first duty is to be faithful to the one we work for.'
(1 Corinthians 4:2)

God had to test Abraham before he could do the amazing things with Abraham that he wanted to do. God wanted Abraham to become the father of an entire nation. It was a big responsibility. God had to test him first to see if he could be trusted.

God said to Abraham, 'Go and get Isaac your only son, the one you dearly love! Take him to a mountain called Moriah and there I want you to sacrifice him on an altar.'

Abraham was horrified. God wanted him to kill his only son! But he was ready to do anything for God, so he loaded the firewood onto a donkey, collected his son and set off for Mount Moriah. It took him three days to get there. As they travelled, Isaac kept asking his father what they were going to sacrifice. Abraham only replied, 'God will provide.'

Eventually they climbed the mountain and Abraham prepared the wood. Then he took Isaac in his arms and lifted him onto the top of the altar he had made. He raised the knife above his head ready to kill his only son. He was about to bring his arm down when an angel appeared in front of him and commanded, 'Stop! God now knows that you can be trusted. You did exactly what he wanted even though it would mean losing your son. Now God will trust you with anything.'

God had tested Abraham. Abraham passed the test and was ready to be used by God.

Our first mountain. Mount Moriah… The place of testing. Before God will use us, he must test us. Are you ready to be tested?

Mount Moriah TESTING | Mount ???? ???? | Mount ???? ???? | Mount ???? ????

Light Bulb

Object needed: *A light bulb.*

Most things that we use have been tested. Before you buy a Playstation or Nintendo 64 you can be sure that it has been tested at the factory. It's been tested so that when you switch it on and put in your latest computer game, you can be sure that it will work. If the machine doesn't work properly in the factory it isn't sent to the shop to be sold. If it doesn't pass the test, then it can't be used.

This is a light bulb. The same thing happened to this light bulb. It was tested. Before it could leave the factory it had to pass the test.

God wants to use us. God wants to do amazing things with our lives, if we'll let him. But before God will use us, he must test us. If we pass the test, God uses us. If we fail the test, we have to wait until God tests us again.

Before we pass the first mountain, Mount Moriah, we must pass the test.

Driver

Object needed: *L-plates.*

Mr Geeky rushes on driving a cardboard car with L-plates. He screeches round a corner and knocks down the narrator. He then rushes off into the distance. The narrator stands up and brushes himself down.

That was Mr Geeky. He's a bit crazy!

In this country, before you can drive a car you have to pass a test. If you don't pass the test then you are not allowed to drive the car. The driving examiner doesn't think you are safe to drive by yourself until you have passed the test. Cars are very powerful and people can be killed if you don't drive them properly. Before you can drive, you must prove that you can be trusted to drive sensibly.

God works the same way. When we do things for God, he gives us the things needed to make sure the job is done. Some of the things God puts into our lives – we call them gifts from God – are very powerful. If God can't trust us, he will not give us jobs to do for him and he will not equip us with his gifts.

Before we can pass the first mountain we must prove that we can be trusted. That's the first test.

Questions

Object needed: *A copy of this table on acetate and placed on the OHP.*

You've probably seen lots of questionnaires in magazines. They try and work out things like, are you cool or are you not, and other things like that. This one is to work out whether you can be trusted.

	A	**B**
Someone calls you a name you don't like. Do you?	Lose your temper and punch them	Ignore it
You try and tell people about God. They laugh. Do you?	Never talk to them about God again	Smile, but try again later
You fail a test in school. Do you?	Give in and never try again.	Work hard to pass the test next time
Your friends are saying some pretty bad things about the new person in school. Do you?	Join your friends and say nasty things about the new person.	Tell them to be a bit nicer. They wouldn't like to be talked about like that.

If you answered mainly A to the questions, you're not yet ready to be used by God. If you answered mainly B, then maybe God can trust you. Maybe you'll pass the tests he gives you.

If you want to be used by God, you must prove that you can be trusted. That's the first test. That's the first mountain.

● STORY – Eddie The Eagle

'Jump! Go on jump!'

Eddie looked over the side of the cliff. His nest was halfway up a huge mountain. It was a long way down, a very long way down. Even for an eagle this was a long way down.

Eddie's mother shouted again: 'Jump! Eddie, go on jump!'

Eddie didn't really want to jump. He'd seen the huge eagles soaring above him day after day, but he didn't think he'd ever be able to fly like that. His feathers had only just started to appear. When he came out of his egg just three months ago he was covered in fluffy down.

'Eddie! You have to jump!'

Eddie looked at his mum. He'd only known her for a few months. Of course she'd sat on his egg for weeks, waiting for him to hatch, but he didn't really know about that. Then at last he popped out of his egg, his mum took one look at him and called him 'Eddie'.

Even though he'd only known his mum for a few months, Eddie loved her dearly. She brought him food several times a day, even though some of that food consisted of very wiggly worms that were very difficult to eat. She protected him under her wings when it poured with rain and kept him close when the wind had been cold. Eddie loved his mum very much and he knew he could trust her.

Sometimes we too find it difficult to do the things God wants. But we need not worry. Even though the things God asks us to do may be difficult, God can be trusted always to help us.

'Jump, Eddie! Jump!'

Eddie leaned towards the edge of the cliff and jumped. He flapped his wings as hard as he could but nothing seemed to happen. He spiralled down and down. The ground came closer and closer. He could see the rocks getting closer; he could see the sea water splashing onto those jagged rocks. Three months old and he was going to die. Four metres, three metres, two metres. He was about to go splat!

How could he have been so wrong? He was sure he could trust his mother. She loved him dearly. He was convinced she would always take care of him.

Sometimes we too may think that God has let us down, but God can always be trusted.

Eddie was only a couple of centimetres from the ground when he heard a mighty swoosh! And then the ground was moving away from him. He was going upwards, not downwards any longer. His mother didn't let him die. She had flown down at the last minute and rescued him from the rocks. Now together they were soaring upwards again, getting higher and higher. Then, without warning, Eddie felt himself being dropped again.

'What's going on?' Eddie shouted. 'I can't fly. You'd better come and rescue me.' But down and down he went again.

God tests us again and again until we pass the test!

Again Eddie got within a few centimetres of the ground when his mother swooped and pulled him back into the air. He was feeling a bit sick of falling down and getting carried back up but, sure enough, when they were very high up, his mother dropped him again.

'What is going on?' Eddie yelled. 'I'm getting sick!'

He opened his wings to get ready for his mum to catch him and the most extraordinary thing happened. He began to fly. He began to ride on the currents of wind. He began to climb higher and higher. He loved it. It was amazing. He climbed higher and higher. He could fly.

God wants us to do amazing things for him. But we must pass the tests God gives us. We must be trusted, be able to trust God and do what God asks.

Eddie the eagle could fly. He passed his first test.

2 Mount Sinai

	Programme	Item
Section 1	Welcome	
	Rules	
	Prayer	
	Praise	
	Game 1	Mountain Makers
	Praise (x2)	
	Fun Item 1	
	Game 2	Mountain Makers – The People Factor
	Game 3	In The Jelly
	Fun Item 2	
	Bible Text	1 Timothy 1:8
	Announcements	
	Interview	
	Worship (x2)	
Section 2 Preaching Time	Bible Lesson	Moses At Mount Sinai
	Illustration 1	The Racer
	Illustration 2	The Football Rule Book
	Illustration 3	Chaos Or Order
	Story	Lily The Mountain Lioness
	Prayer	

 **Overview** We live at a time in church history when the grace of God is preached regularly. We preach passionately against the idea of God waving a big stick and punishing our every mistake.

games

Game 1

Mountain Makers

PREPARATION	A variety of items such as boxes, chairs, hockey sticks, etc. All the items are placed at B.
PLAYERS	Six players from each team.
SET-UP	The players line up in relay formation at A.
OBJECT	The players take turns running from A to B, collecting an item from B and returning to A. The items at A need to be built into the highest mountain/structure possible.
WINNING	The team to build the biggest structure in two minutes wins.

Game 2

Mountain Makers – The People Factor

PREPARATION	None.
PLAYERS	Seven players from each team and a leader from each team to supervise them closely.
SET-UP	The players stand at A.
OBJECT	The teams have to get as high as possible. They can form themselves into pyramids, stand on each others shoulders or do anything else as long as they get as high as possible without hurting themselves or others.
WINNING	The highest team after one minute of effort wins.

Note: This game needs careful supervision and plenty of cushions or mats to land on. If you feel uncomfortable about using it, the following is a less risky alternative!

Game 3

In The jelly

PREPARATION	A prepared jelly per team with five Jelly Babies in each and a set of plastic cutlery per player.
PLAYERS	Five from each team.
SET-UP	Five players in standard relay pattern at point A. Each player has a set of cutlery. The jellies are placed at B.
OBJECT	The players run from A to B, find a Jelly Baby using a knife and fork and return to A.
WINNING	First team back and sitting down wins – if all the Jelly Babies are gone!

PreachingTime

 **BIBLE LESSON** ### MOSES AT MOUNT SINAI

'... We know that the law is good if it is used in the right way.' (1 Timothy 1:8)

Mount Sinai was covered with smoke because the Lord had come down in flaming fire. Smoke poured out of the mountain just like a furnace and the whole mountain shook. The sound of trumpets filled the air. Moses spoke and God answered him with thunder.

The Lord came down to the top of the mountain and Moses met him there. God gave Moses a list of rules or what the Bible calls commandments. At Mount Sinai, God gave us rules. Despite what many people think, you can't become a Christian and do what you want. God's commandments given on Mount Sinai came written on two stone tablets. They said:

Present them to the children on two pieces of card in this format:

✖ Do not worship any God except me.
✖ Do not make idols that look like anything in the sky or on the earth or in the sea under the earth.
✖ Do not misuse my name.

✖ Keep one day a week for a day of rest.
✖ Respect your mother and father.
✖ Do not murder.
✖ Keep your family together.
✖ Do not steal.
✖ Do not tell lies.
✖ Do not envy what others have.

God does give us rules to live by. We can't just behave as we want. The second mountain is:

The Racer

Object needed: *The car from last week's second illustration.*

Shundi Calagaseeta rushes on, driving a cardboard car with L-plates. He screeches around a corner and knocks down a policeman standing at the front. He then rushes off into the distance. The policeman stands up and brushes himself down.

POLICEMAN: Oy! What do you think you're doing? Come here!!

Shundi drives across knocking the Policeman down again. He stops. The Policeman stands up and the dialogue begins.

POLICEMAN: What on earth do you think you're playing at?

SHUNDI: I was just going for a little ride in my car, officer.

POLICEMAN: But you were going far too fast.

SHUNDI: The law doesn't apply to me officer. I'm a Christian.

POLICEMAN: What?

SHUNDI: I'm a Christian! I don't have to do what the law says.

POLICEMAN: I think you're a bit mixed up. The law applies to everyone.

SHUNDI: Oh! Fair enough! But there's no point in keeping it, is there? What's the point of driving slowly?

POLICEMAN: You really don't know anything, do you? The law keeps us safe. It protects us.

SHUNDI: I don't think so! I think it's just there to spoil my fun.

POLICEMAN: No, let's think about this. If you drive too fast and on the wrong side of the road, people are going to get killed. That's why we have a law.

SHUNDI: So you don't have a law to spoil my fun?

POLICEMAN: No! The speed limit is there to keep you safe. We have rules because they keep us safe. They protect us. God gave us rules not to spoil our fun, but to protect us.

SHUNDI: Oh! I see. Fair enough. I'll just be off then.

POLICEMAN:	Not so fast, I need to give you something.
SHUNDI:	What? I like getting things.
POLICEMAN:	This is a speeding ticket. You owe us £50. Oh, by the way, if you break God's law, the penalty is much more than a £50 fine.

Shundi drives off slowly looking sad.

POLICEMAN:	The next mountain is Sinai. It's the place of the law. You have to learn to obey God's rules to go any further.

The Football Rule Book

Objects needed: *A book (with the words 'football rule book' written on the cover) and a football.*

A person stands on the stage dribbling the ball and performing various tricks – a talented football player on your staff would help. As he performs more volleys and headers someone rushes on, grabs the ball and runs into the distance pretending to play rugby.

FOOTBALLER:	What are you doing? You can't do that!
RUGBY PLAYER:	Why not?
FOOTBALLER:	Because it's against the rules.
RUGBY PLAYER:	No it's not. You pick up the ball and you try to score a try.
FOOTBALLER:	No you don't. Not in this game. Look! *(Hands the rugby player the football rule book.)*
RUGBY PLAYER:	*(Reads and hands it back.)* Well, I guess you're right. Quite a soft game though!
FOOTBALLER:	When we play a game we must play by the rules of that game, or the game is no fun. When we become Christians we are making a commitment to play by the rules that God sets: not rules to hurt or harm us, rules to protect us. This is the rule book for football. It shows me how to play the game properly. *(Holds up a Bible.)* This is my Bible. It is

my rule book for life. It tells me how God wants me to live. If I don't live according to this book, I'll never pass the second mountain.

Chaos Or Order

Object needed: *The list of rules you use in the club/children's organisation.*

This is the list of rules we run our group with. We use really simple rules such as:

> **NOBODY SPEAKS DURING PREACHING TIME UNLESS THEY ARE ANSWERING A QUESTION**

Now this rule doesn't exist to spoil fun, it's there to give you more fun. You can't play a game while everyone's shouting because no one will hear the rules. You can't explain about God while people are talking because you won't be able to hear. We have rules to make things better, not worse.

Your mums and dads give you rules. They tell you to be in at certain times. Some parents tell you to be in before dark. They don't make these rules to spoil your fun but to keep you safe.

Some people work in factories. They have lots of rules, not to spoil people's fun but to stop them getting hurt. Rules protect us.

God gave us rules to help and protect us, but until we agree to live by those rules, we can't pass mountain two: Mount Sinai.

● STORY – Lily The Mountain Lioness

'Listen to me Lily. You can go anywhere you want and do anything you want. Most animals will run away from you, some will play with you, but all will respect you. You are a mountain lioness. You are very fierce.'

Lily listened. She liked the fact that she was the toughest animal on this part of the mountain. Well, one of the toughest. Her mum, who was giving the talk, was tougher and her cousins, who shared the pride with her, were also very fierce. Then, of course, there was Carro. He was the head of the pride and Lily didn't know anyone who was even half as scary as him. He didn't talk to her much even though he was her father. He just stood on a large rock looking over the pride. He was in charge.

Lily's mum continued, 'Play in the woods, chase the squirrels, frighten the rabbits, jump over the stream, climb the trees, do whatever you want, but don't wander onto the open fields. The hunters set their traps there and will happily trap you and send you off to some zoo where you'll be caged up for the rest of your life. Don't go onto the open fields.'

Lily listened patiently. She loved her mum very much, but she did go on sometimes. She was a bit of a nag. But Lily smiled politely and nodded. She heard the same talk every morning. She knew it word for word: 'Don't go onto the open fields.'

Today it was sunny! It usually was. Lily wandered out, looking for something to do. She wandered over to the squirrels. 'Let's see if I can catch one of those,' she thought to herself.

Lily raced after the squirrels, but they all dodged her very quickly and ran up some trees. She tried climbing up after them, but she couldn't get high enough. Lily soon gave up. 'Maybe I'll go and catch a rabbit for my lunch.'

But, even though she looked around for almost an hour, not a single rabbit came out of their holes. She tried climbing some more trees, she jumped over the stream a couple of times, she frightened away some vultures who were looking for a snack and eventually she lay in the sun. But she still wanted something a little bit more interesting to do.

She lay sunbathing for some time until a butterfly came and landed on her nose. She snapped at the butterfly but the butterfly flew a few metres away and stopped on a flower. Lily jumped towards the butterfly, but again the butterfly easily avoided her jaws and moved to another flower a bit further away.

'At last,' Lily thought, 'a decent challenge.' She leapt towards the butterfly again, and again the butterfly flew off. This time the butterfly kept flying and Lily ran behind, swinging her tail in fun and trying desperately to catch the butterfly.

The game went on for some time, with Lily pouncing and snapping her mouth and the butterfly dodging and gracefully flying. Eventually Lily came to the edge of the open fields and stopped dead. She looked onto the fields. She couldn't see anything or anyone, just wide open fields. There, in the middle of the field, the butterfly still flew, almost teasing Lily into following.

Lily hesitated at the edge of the field. She knew the rule: 'Don't go into the open fields.'

Remember rules are not there to spoil our fun. They are there to protect us.

But she saw the butterfly and couldn't resist it. She ran into the field and straight at the butterfly. She took one final leap at the butterfly and sailed through the air towards it. She opened her mouth, snapped it closed, but missed the butterfly. She prepared herself to land. She put her front paws down. But, as she touched the ground, the ground gave way. She fell and fell and then landed with a heavy bump. Where was she? She looked around. She was in a trap. A hunters' trap.

When we break the rules, we end up in trouble.

Lily felt very sad as she sat there. Soon afterwards the hunters came and were overjoyed at their catch. They hauled Lily out of the hole and, try as she might to escape, they pushed her into a cage.

Several weeks went past. Lily was kept in a wooden box. She was eventually let out. She made her way out slowly and looked around. She was inside a cage. It was quite a large cage with trees and things inside, but it was still a cage. Outside the cage lots of people stared at her. Some made strange sounds. She growled, but they just laughed. They knew she couldn't get to them. Lily was in a zoo and trapped.

Rules don't trap us, they keep us free. When we break the rules, we end up trapped.

If we want to do amazing things for God, we must learn to live by the rules.

③ Mount Carmel

	Programme	Item
Section 1	**Welcome**	
	Rules	
	Prayer	
	Praise	
	Game 1	Tug-of-war Mountain
	Praise (x2)	
	Fun Item 1	
	Game 2	Name That Mountain
	Fun Item 2	
	Bible Text	Zechariah 4:6
	Announcements	
	Interview	
	Worship (x2)	
Section 2	**Bible Lesson**	Elijah on Mount Carmel
Preaching	**Illustration 1**	Revival Story (The Past)
Time	**Illustration 2**	The Wind And The Sun
	Illustration 3	Revival Story (Present Day)
	Story	Billy the Goat
	Prayer	

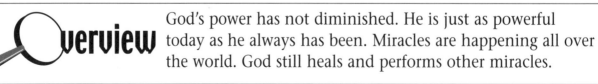

Overview God's power has not diminished. He is just as powerful today as he always has been. Miracles are happening all over the world. God still heals and performs other miracles.

Game 1

Tug-of-war Mountain

PREPARATION	A box is constructed for each team. If there are two teams, the boxes should face each other. If there are three teams, the boxes should be placed at the three corners of a triangle. The boxes are made by marking out squares of masking tape. A rope is needed. A second rope will need to be tied at the centre of the first rope if there are more than two teams.
PLAYERS	Six players from each team.
SET-UP	Players line up in their boxes.
OBJECT	The boxes are the teams' 'mountains'. The object is to pull the other teams off their 'mountains'.
WINNING	The team that stays inside their box wins.

Game 2

Name That Mountain

PREPARATION	Ten A4 sheets with the name of a mountain on each. Ten A4 sheets with the name of a river on each.
PLAYERS	Six players from each team.
SET-UP	The players stand at A. The twenty sheets are mixed up and stuck to the wall at B.
OBJECT	The players run from A to B where they pick out what they believe to be the name of a mountain. Then they return to A with that sheet and the next person runs.
WINNING	The team with the most mountains wins.

BIBLE LESSON

ELIJAH AT MOUNT CARMEL

'God said "Don't depend on your own power or strength, but on My Spirit."'
(Zechariah 4:6)

Elijah was a prophet of God. He had been hiding in various places for a couple of years because the wicked King Ahab and his even wickeder wife Jezebel wanted to kill him. They wanted to kill him because he was a prophet of God and they prayed to someone called Baal, who wasn't a god at all but part of the Devil's army.

Eventually God told Elijah to go to Ahab and tell him it was time to find out who was really in charge – God or Baal. God told Elijah to go to Mount Carmel for the big contest and to tell Ahab to bring his 450 priests of Baal with him.

Elijah was afraid. He knew that people would think him mad. He knew that Ahab and Jezebel would be there to kill him. But he also knew what was ultimately important: that doing what God wanted was more important than what people said. And he knew that God had more power than the Devil.

There was to be a competition. Elijah would compete with the priests of Baal to discover whether God or Baal was in charge. He asked for two bulls to be brought up and placed in front of the groups. Firewood was assembled around the two dead bulls and the people waited. Then Elijah said, 'If Baal is in charge, let him send fire to consume the bull.'

The priests of Baal prayed all day long, crying out to Baal, but nothing happened.

Elijah began to make fun of them. 'Are you sure Baal is powerful?' he mocked. 'Maybe he's on holiday, maybe he's asleep or maybe he's on the toilet!!'

Eventually the priests of Baal gave up.

'Now it's my turn,' said Elijah, 'but first cover the bull with water. Let's make this a little more difficult.'

The priests of Baal didn't think that God was very powerful. But they were in for a big surprise. If we have proved that we can be trusted and we live the way God wants us to live, then the next mountain we come to is Mount Carmel, the place of power.

Elijah prayed and fire fell. The bull was consumed. God was victorious. God always has been and always will be more powerful than the Devil. And God wants to use us powerfully just like he used Elijah.

God gives us power to be used mightily for him. We are more powerful than we think.

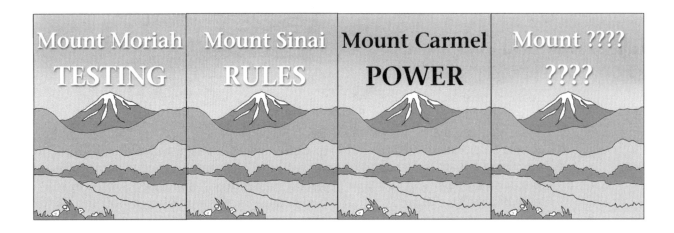

Revival Story (The Past)

Object needed: *None.*

Early in the 1900s, a man named Steven Jeffreys travelled from Wales to various parts of Great Britain to tell people about Jesus and how he wanted to take away their sins. Jeffreys also prayed for sick people wherever he went, because he knew that God could heal the sick.

When he came to the North of England he made his way to a place called Bishop Auckland and put up posters telling people that he was holding meetings. One night a young girl came to his meeting. She was led in by some people because she was blind. Not only was she blind, but she had no eyeballs at all. She only had sockets. That night Steven Jeffreys felt God tell him to pray for the girl. He did what God asked.

Note that. He just did what God asked. He wasn't going to heal the girl, he was just going to do what God said.

Steven prayed for the girl. He placed his thumbs in the empty eye sockets and asked Jesus to give the girl eyes. As he prayed, his thumbs were pushed out as two bright blue eyes grew in the sockets.

God can do these things. He did it then and he can do it now.

The Wind And The Sun

People needed: *Three actors, one of whom wears a coat.*

Aesop's Fables is a collection of stories written many, many years ago. One of the stories involves a competition between the sun and the wind. Here's what happened:

WIND: Hello, Sun. Are you still shining on the earth?

SUN: Yes, that's what I do.

WIND: Well, I hope you enjoy yourself. But doesn't it make you sad knowing that you're not as powerful as me? I am the most powerful of all. I blow and I sweep things away, and I knock buildings over. I am so powerful.

SUN: Is that true? Well, how about a competition?

WIND: *blowing and howling* This will be fun. I'll show you who's the most powerful.

SUN: See that man down there. The one with the big raincoat. Well, let's see who can make him take his coat off first. You can start.

WIND: Well, this is going to be so easy. Here we go. *The wind blows and howls, but it just makes the man pull his coat on even tighter.*

This is impossible. If I can't do it, it can't be done.

SUN: We'll see about that. Now it's my go. *The sun shines down on the man, getting hotter and hotter. Eventually the man takes his coat off.* I think I win.

WIND: That's not fair. *Blows away*

We try and do things like the wind sometimes. We work very hard to try and make things happen ourselves, but if we learn to ask God to help us and learn to do what God tells us, if we learn to ask God to make us strong then we will do much more.

Revival Story (Present Day)

Object needed: *None.*

In the 1980s a large youth meeting was organised in Birmingham. Twelve thousand people went to the meeting. One of the people who turned up wasn't particularly young. She was a woman named Jean Neil. She couldn't walk so she came in a wheelchair. Doctors said she would never be able to walk.

The speaker was a German named Reinhardt Bonnke. As he was speaking, he felt God tell him to go and pray for the woman. He did so and the woman stood up. She didn't only stand up, she actually found she could walk.

The doctors said it was a miracle. Just because a man listened to what God said, a miracle happened.

If you listen to God, you too can pray for the sick and see them healed.

● STORY – Billy The Goat

Billy the Goat lived near the top of the mountain, just below the snow-capped peaks. He was an angry sort of goat, always rushing about, always head-butting things, always knocking things over. If he wasn't chewing grass, he was charging at rocks.

He was usually quite angry, but there were days when Billy was particularly angry. Those were the days when the boys from the village climbed to the top of the mountain to tease him and call him names. Sometimes they would steal his food and run away. That made him really angry. But whenever he saw them and chased after them, they would run away down the mountain, through the gate halfway down and close it before Billy reached it. He would charge at the gate as hard as he could. He would push and push at the gate, ramming and charging and butting, but the gate wouldn't open. The boys would stand on the other side and laugh and giggle and make fun of Billy's goatee beard.

Billy would eventually give up and storm off back to the top of the mountain in a major huff. He would be angrier than ever. Then he would pass Squirrel. Squirrel would make him even angrier by saying, 'I know how you can get through the gate. It's really quite easy.'

But Billy wouldn't listen. He would grunt, 'If I can't get through, you have absolutely no chance. Now go and eat some nuts or something.'

He'd make his way back to the very top of the mountain and practise ramming some rocks. He imagined he was charging those boys. But he knew that he would never get the chance while that gate stayed there.

The boys usually came every Saturday, but now that the summer holidays had arrived, the boys were coming every single day. Billy was angrier than ever. Every day they would come and tease him; every day he would charge down the mountain; every day he would get stopped by the gate; and every day the boys would laugh and call him names. As if that wasn't enough, every day Squirrel would say, 'You can get past the gate you know.'

Billy hated school holidays. The boys had been teasing him every single day for a whole month. He hated what was happening, but he refused to listen to Squirrel.

We too sometimes refuse to listen. We refuse to listen to God. God tells us that we can do much more for him if we ask him to help us, but sometimes we are just too stubborn.

Eventually, after another week had gone past, Billy snapped at Squirrel, 'So how do I get past the gate?'

Squirrel smiled. 'Interested now are you?'

Billy demanded, 'Tell me, if you know. Tell me now!'

Squirrel remained calm. 'I think you are missing a word.'

Billy thought and then said, 'OK! Please tell me. Please!'

Squirrel nodded. He spoke quietly. 'The gate opens inwards. You need to pull and not push.'

Billy couldn't believe it. It was so simple. Why hadn't he seen it?

When God begins to help us, we can do amazing things. We can pray for people and see them healed; we can see people coming to know Jesus themselves. We can do all sorts of amazing things, if we just ask God to help us and give us his power.

Billy couldn't wait for the next day. The boys came up as usual; they teased him as usual; and they ran back down the mountain as usual. But today they were surprised to see that Billy didn't charge the gate after they had gone through. They stopped and stared. Their mouths dropped open as Billy calmly used his strong horns to pull the gate open.

The boys ran as quickly as they could, but it wasn't quick enough. Billy rammed into them again and again. When they eventually got home they were covered in bruises and decided never to go up the mountain again.

Billy walked back up the mountain triumphant. He held his head high and strutted forward. When he passed Squirrel he stopped. He turned slowly and said, 'Thank you!'

Then he continued his journey to the top of the mountain.

We need to learn to do things in God's strength, not in ours.

Back To Mount Moriah

	Programme	Item
Section 1	Welcome	
	Rules	
	Prayer	
	Praise	
	Game 1	Touch The Summit
	Praise (x2)	
	Fun Item 1	
	Game 2	Snowy Cap
	Fun Item 2	
	Bible Text	1 John 5:12
	Announcements	
	Interview	
	Worship (x2)	
Section 2	Bible Lesson	The Whole Thing Comes Full Circle
Preaching	Illustration 1	The Past Part
Time	Illustration 2	Present
	Illustration 3	Future
	Story	Jesus of Nazareth
	Prayer	

Overview Mount Moriah, where Abraham went to sacrifice Isaac, has amazing prophetic significance. Historians tell us that it is probably where Jesus died 6,000 years later, making it possible for us to live.

games

Game 1

Touch The Summit

PREPARATION	A picture of a snow-covered mountain placed about three metres above the ground at B. (Suitable posters can often be obtained from travel agents.)
PLAYERS	Six players from each team.
SET-UP	Four players line up at A and two players stand at B.
OBJECT	A player runs from A to B. The two players at B must lift them up to touch the top of the mountain picture. After touching the summit, the player returns to A and the next player sets off.
WINNING	The first team that completes the race and sits down wins.

Game 2

Snowy Cap

PREPARATION	A baseball cap per team and a large number of rolled up newspaper balls.
PLAYERS	Six players from each team.
SET-UP	One player stands on a chair at B with the baseball cap in his hand. The others stand at A with the newspaper snowballs.
OBJECT	A player runs from A to a point two metres in front of B. They take one of the snowballs and throw it towards the cap. The person at B must try to catch the snowball in the cap. Then the runner returns to A and the next person runs.
WINNING	The team with the most snowballs in their hat after three minutes wins.

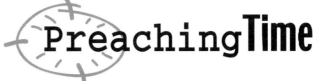

Preaching Time

BIBLE LESSON | ## THE WHOLE THING COMES FULL CIRCLE

'He who has Jesus has life!'
(1 John 5:12)

For this dramatic presentation you will need a narrator, three people on seats, a server and Shundi.

The three people stand in front of their seats pretending to come to the end of a song. As the drama begins they finish their mime singing and sit down. The seats are arranged stage left, the narrator stands stage right.

SERVER: It's time for breaking of bread *(use the term your church is familiar with)*.

The server walks past the three people and hands them pieces of bread. He repeats this with a cup of wine (Ribena!). As this goes on the narrator reads from 1 Corinthians 11:23–32. When the reading comes to an end, the three people on chairs bow their heads and Shundi arrives in his car. Shundi should have his own soundtrack by now that is played whenever he arrives.

SHUNDI: What's all this about dude?
NARRATOR: It's called the breaking of bread service. You must have one of these in your church.
SHUNDI: Of course! Still don't know what it's about though!
NARRATOR: It helps us remember what Jesus did for us. I'll explain it all to you, but first I need to fill in my last mountain.
SHUNDI: But we have already had that mountain. That's where Abraham was tested. He was going to sacrifice Isaac but God stopped him and provided the sacrifice.
NARRATOR: Well remembered! This is the same mountain, but it's now 6,000 years later and the Son of God, King Jesus, gives his life so that we can have real life. This special service helps us remember what Jesus has done for us. The red stuff (some people use Ribena, some people use

wine) helps us remember his blood that ran from his wounds and the bread reminds us of his body. I'll explain it, there are three parts:

The Past Part

Objects needed: *A poster bearing the word 'Past', Ribena in a cup, bread.*

The Bible tells us that, on the night he was betrayed, Jesus took some bread, broke it into pieces and said, 'Take this bread and, when you eat it, remember the way I died. Remember I died so that all the wrong things you did could be forgiven.'

And then he took some wine, drank it and said, 'When you drink this wine, remember the blood that I shed for you.'

We do this to help us remember what Jesus did for us. We do it so that we never forget what Jesus did.

Present

Object needed: *A poster bearing the word 'Present'.*

But there is a special part to the breaking of bread which is for right now. It tells us that when we eat the bread and drink the wine we must make sure there is no sin in our lives. We do that by asking Jesus to forgive all the wrong things we have done. But if we eat the bread and drink the wine without asking his forgiveness, we are failing to show respect for what Jesus has done.

The Bible goes further. It says that some people have actually become sick and others have even died because they haven't respected what God has done for them.

Future

Object needed: *A poster bearing the word 'Future'.*

Now Jesus didn't tell us we were to do these things forever. He actually told us to do these things until he comes back! This may surprise some of you but it is true. Jesus said that, though he died and rose again and ascended back to heaven, he would also come back one day. That's exciting.

It's exciting if you are a Christian. It's not so exciting if you're not, because it means that when Jesus returns you will not be ready. And, if you are not ready, you will not be going to heaven.

● STORY – Jesus of Nazareth

Show an extract of the video *Jesus of Nazareth* from the Last Supper to the end of the Crucifixion. There are various videos of the Gospels, but I think this is the most visually effective. Available from: Jesus Video Project, Fairgate House, Kings Road, Tyseley, Birmingham B11 2AA. Tel: 0121 765 4404.

The Shepherd Boy Who Became King

A Series in Six Parts

Introduction

Title	Themes covered
1 The Shepherd Boy	Forgiveness, belonging, family, our hearts
2 The Worshipper	Worship, moods, setting free
3 The Giant Slayer	Problems, overcoming
4 The Friend	Friendship, peer pressure
5 The Outlaw	Doing the right thing
6 The King	Destiny, potential

 **Overview** When you ask Christians to name their all-time favourite Bible characters, David usually appears close to the top of the list. If you ask children to list their favourite Bible stories, the story of David and Goliath is likely to feature strongly.

The next six weeks will focus our attention on one of God's heroes. The shepherd boy who became one of the greatest kings the world has ever seen – a warrior king, brave, fearless, just, honest, righteous and very, very human.

David came from nowhere. His birth is a mystery. He testifies to having been conceived in iniquity. His brothers weren't too fond of him. His father put him on the hillside to hide him from the prophet Samuel. He certainly had a different mother from his brothers. Maybe, just maybe, the greatest king who ever lived came from the same sort of background as some of the children you minister to – children from broken homes, of unclear parentage, etc. Yet God's only interest in their past is to heal them of any hurts, giving them an opportunity to see more clearly their glorious future in King Jesus.

The Shepherd Boy

	Programme	Item
Section 1	Welcome	
	Rules	
	Prayer	
	Praise	
	Game 1	Water World
	Praise (x2)	
	Fun Item (2)	
	Game 2	Towers
	Fun Item	
	Bible Text	Psalm 27:10
	Announcements	
	Interview	
	Worship (x2)	
Section 2	Bible Lesson	Samuel Chooses David
Preaching	Illustration 1	The Spiral
Time	Illustration 2	The Home Drama
	Illustration 3	Bitter Lemon
	Story	Little Jay
	Prayer	

The eyes of the Lord search the face of the earth looking for those who in their hurt and pain don't become bitter but instead turn to him. This lesson touches on very sensitive issues. Be gentle. There are issues in this lesson that need to be addressed – that's why it is included.

games

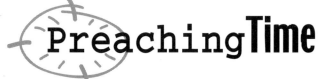

PreachingTime

Game 1

Water World

PREPARATION	An empty bucket, a large bucket full of water and a paper cup for each team. It may be wise to have a few spare cups to hand.
PLAYERS	Five children and a leader from each team.
SET-UP	The teams line up at A with a cup and a bucket of water. The leaders sit at B with an empty bucket on their heads.
OBJECT	The children run in relay to fill the bucket of their leader using their paper cup.
WINNING	The team with the most water in the bucket after three minutes wins.

Game 2

Towers

PREPARATION	Lots of paper cups per team.
PLAYERS	Five from each team.
SET-UP	Four players from each team line up at A with the cups. The fifth player stands at B.
OBJECT	The children run in relay to bring cups one at a time from A to the player at B, who must build the biggest tower.
WINNING	The team with the tallest tower after three minutes wins, not the team with the most cups.

BIBLE LESSON SAMUEL CHOOSES DAVID

'Even if my mother and father should desert me, you will take care of me.'
(Psalm 27:10)

Choose several children to act out the parts as you come to them. The character you choose for David now can be the same throughout this series.

Samuel was a prophet. **A prophet is someone who hears what God is saying and tells others.** The nation of Israel already had a king. His name was Saul. The people had liked Saul because he was taller and stronger than the rest. When he first became king he was a good king and did everything God wanted him to do. Later on he stopped listening to God and became a bad king. God rejected Saul and decided to choose another king.

God said to Samuel, 'Don't be sad for Saul any longer. I have chosen a new king – one of Jesse's sons. He will be a great king. Go and pour the special oil on him.'

When a person was to be king he had special oil poured on him.

Samuel did as God had asked and went to the house of Jesse. Jesse brought all his sons and lined them up in front of Samuel. Samuel came to Jesse's oldest son, saw his great strength and was sure he was the new king. But God said, 'No!' Samuel came to the second son, saw how handsome he was and was sure he would be king. But God said, 'No!' Samuel looked at all Jesse's sons. Each time he was sure this one would be king, but God said no to them all.

Then Samuel asked Jesse, 'Do you have any more sons?'

Jesse looked very uncomfortable. You see, Jesse did have one more son, but Jesse was embarrassed by him. David was his name. He'd been sent up into the hills to look after the sheep, not because he was the youngest, but because Jesse was embarrassed: Jesse's brothers were David's stepbrothers; Jesse's wife was probably not David's mother. Jesse was embarrassed by this son from a different woman and his brothers didn't like him at all. They were cruel to him. So there he sat on the hillside with the sheep. But this was the boy God had chosen to be king.

But, ask yourselves this: why did God choose David? It wasn't because his father was embarrassed by him: lots of people have fathers who have been unkind to them. It wasn't because his brothers were cruel to him: lots of people have arguments with their stepbrothers and sisters. It was because of the way David reacted.

Some people would have become angry and bitter, but not David. He sat on the hillside and said this to God, 'Even if my mother and father should desert me, you will take care of me.'

He never got angry or upset or bitter. He forgave his brothers for being mean to him. He forgave his father. His heart was not full of anger. So God chose him to be great.

God still looks over the entire world at the hearts of every boy and girl. He looks for those who, in their hurt and pain, don't get angry inside but instead turn to King Jesus and say, 'Even if my mother and father should desert me, you will take care of me.' It's very exciting to know that there is a God who loves people this much.

The Spiral

Object needed: *Spiral (large piece of paper cut into a spiral shape by cutting concentrically from the outside towards the centre. Attach string to the centre point. It should hang down like a helix).*

Ask for a volunteer to hold the spiral by the string, so that it spirals down.

The point at the very top of the spiral represents the best that any person can possibly be. The point at the bottom represents the worst that any person can possibly be. Most of us are near the top. We're mostly good, but every now and then we do something which is a little bit bad.

Everything we do, no matter how small or how great, will either make us better or worse. If we do something which makes us worse, we go down the spiral and, if we do something which makes us better, we go up the spiral. For example,

if you went out today and got in a fight with someone, would that make you better or worse? Which way would that make you go on the spiral: up or down? But, if you were to colour a picture, taking your time and doing it very carefully, would that make you better or worse? Which way would that make you go on the spiral: up or down?

Use further examples if you feel it necessary to establish the principle.

So everything we do has a result. It makes us better or worse. We go up or down.

Ask the person holding the spiral to sit down near you. You will need them for the next illustration.

The Home Drama

Object needed: *A heavy weight with 'unforgiveness' written on it.*

Ask for volunteers to mime the parts of dad, mum and baby.

Mum and dad like each other a lot and after being married five years they had a baby. When baby *(person's name)* was first born mum and dad loved him/her a lot. They would take him/her shopping and to the zoo, to the beach and to the fun fair. they loved him/her so much. They also loved each other a lot.

But when *(baby's name)* was seven, mum and dad began arguing a lot. *(The parents mime an argument.)*

And when *(baby's name)* was nine, dad came to him/her one day and said, '*(baby's name)*, I can't take any more. I'm leaving. Please forgive me.' And dad walked off leaving mum and baby by themselves. *(Get dad to go and stand at the side for a while.)*

Now *(baby's name)* had a choice. One reaction would take him down and the other would take him up. He could forgive his dad or not.

Dad had said 'I'm sorry,' but *(baby's name)* just couldn't forgive him. As soon as we decide not to forgive someone, we automatically pick up this heavy weight called 'unforgiveness'. *(Produce the heavy weight with the word 'unforgiveness' on and give it to [baby's name] to hold.)*

Although most people can't see this thing called unforgiveness because it's inside, you can usually tell it's there. A person with unforgiveness is usually grumpy and moody and horrible. Everywhere *(baby's name)* goes from now on he/she will carry this big heavy weight called unforgiveness with them. It's not going away. *(Ask the volunteer with the spiral to come and hold it up.)* Which way would *(baby's name)* be going on the spiral: up or down?

Now this is the big question. How does *(baby's name)* get rid of unforgiveness?

He/she phones up their dad and says this, 'Dad, I want you to know that, when you walked out and left mum and I, you made me feel really sad. But I want you to know that I forgive you.' As soon as *(baby's name)* says that and means it, the weight of unforgiveness is gone. *(Throw the weight to one side.)* All the bitterness begins to go and *(baby's name)* is free.

You see, unforgiveness makes us worse and takes us down. Forgiveness makes us better and takes us up. In fact, there's a statement in the Bible that says, 'If we can't forgive those who hurt us, God the Father will not forgive us.'

Bitter Lemon

Object needed: *Bitter lemon juice.*

Ask for a volunteer who likes sweet drinks like Coke. Give them a drink of the bitter lemon and ask them to describe how it tastes. They'll say things like horrible, bitter, sour, etc. Then explain:

And that's what it's like inside us when we refuse to forgive people and we carry around lots of hurts. We become bitter and sour inside.

King David could have become like this. His brothers didn't like him. His father was embarrassed by him and put him on the hills to look after sheep. But God chose him, not because he'd been rejected (lots of people get rejected), not because he felt nobody liked him (lots of people feel like that), but because, in his hurt and pain, he turned to God and decided not to get bitter but to trust God to help him.

● STORY – Little Jay

The wind was blowing hard. Flash! Boom! Lightning and thunder. The rain kept falling. More lightning and thunder. The wind kept blowing. Little Jay was wet through. It was very dark. The wind made strange sounds through the trees. His red T-shirt was so wet it stuck to his skin. His trainers were making squelching sounds and his jeans had become so tight it was getting very difficult to walk.

Flash! What was that? Jay was sure he'd seen something move.

He'd heard that there were wolves in this part of the forest: big wolves with razor-sharp teeth. And he was sure that he could see eyes in the darkness: big green, glowing eyes. He was very wet, very cold, very lost and very scared. And the eyes seemed to be getting closer.

Little Jay didn't have any friends. He had arrived in the forest only the week before and didn't know anybody. He was a fox. He was five years old. Mr and Mrs Fox had adopted him. Little Jay never knew his dad and when he was only two his mum decided she didn't want him any more, so she had sent him to an orphanage. He had spent a lot of time crying and a lot of time hoping his mum would come and collect him, but this didn't happen. He stayed in the orphanage for three whole years until Mr and Mrs Fox came and asked if they could adopt him.

'Nobody wants me!' he would say to himself. 'My mother didn't want me, I haven't got any friends and now I'm living in a strange house with Mr and Mrs Fox.'

Have you ever felt like that? Felt that nobody wanted you or cared for you? Most people have at one time or another.

Mr and Mrs Fox had one other child. His name was Rusty. Rusty was a little bit older than Jay and didn't really know if he was happy having another fox in his house. It meant that he would have to share his bedroom. 'Well!' he said to himself, 'I'll share my bedroom, but I'm not sharing my toys.'

It was raining outside. Jay didn't have any toys of his own and he was bored. He looked out of the window at the rain falling and the trees flowing. 'I know,' he thought, 'I'll play with some of Rusty's toys while he's not around. It'll be OK.'

And that's when Rusty walked in and found Jay playing with his train set. Rusty got very angry and shouted at Jay, 'You leave my train set alone! It's not yours. It's mine. You don't even belong here. You're only here because no one else wanted you.'

Jay ran out of the room crying. He ran around the corner so fast that even when he saw Mrs Fox in front of him he couldn't stop and knocked her over.

'Jay! Watch where you're going!' she shouted. And then, 'Jay, stop! What's wrong?'

Jay ran to the front door still crying, he slammed the door and ran out into the rain. He kept on running deeper and deeper into the forest. And that's where he was now! Deep in the middle of the forest and lost.

He was sure something was walking towards him. Flash! More lightning. But, this time, he caught a glimpse of a creature. It was very big, with large teeth and big eyes. It was a wolf and it was getting closer. Jay was now very frightened! He didn't know much about God. He knew that Mr and Mrs Fox went to church a lot, but he'd only been once. Still, he was so frightened that he began to pray. 'God help me!'

Flash! Another flash of lightning. The wolf was only metres away. Jay was sure that he was going to get eaten. Just then some lights appeared nearby. The wolf came closer. The lights glinted off his sharp teeth.

The Devil is just like that wolf. He is the enemy of God. He hates God and he hates us. He wants nothing better than to mess us up and destroy our lives and, when we're feeling sad, he likes nothing more than to make us feel even worse.

The wolf came closer. But what was that? A torch, then another, then there seemed to be lots of them. People were calling his name, 'Little Jay! Where are you?'

'All those people looking for me. I didn't think anyone would come. I didn't think anyone wanted me,' thought Little Jay.

The wolf looked up and saw he was outnumbered. He snarled at Little Jay before he turned and ran back into the deeper forest.

Jesus loves us very much. He said, 'I am the light of the world.' When the Devil sees the light he has to run away. Jesus has come looking for us tonight. He knows that sometimes we have felt lonely and hurt and upset, but he wants to be our friend. He wants us to come to him. He wants us to feel loved and cared for.

'I'm here!' Jay shouted.

There must have been over twenty people and they'd all come looking for him. Mr Fox was the first to arrive. He rushed to Jay and said: 'Thank God you're alive.'

Rusty came soon after. He said, 'I'm sorry. I thought my mum and dad would stop loving me when you came and would love you instead. But now I know that they love us both. I'm special because I was born into the family, but you're really special. Mum and dad actually chose you.'

'What, chose me?' he asked.

'Yes, they chose you!'

The Bible says, 'We didn't choose God, but he chose us.' Can you believe that the creator of the entire universe chose us?

Jay began to cry, not with sad tears, but with tears of happiness. He'd never felt wanted before. He never felt he belonged before. They took Jay home and, after a warm bath and some milk, he went to bed in his new home, with his new brother and new mum and dad.

The next morning Jay was up first. He was so excited he ran around his new forest neighbours to tell them his news. He went to the rabbit and said, 'Hey, my mum and dad, Mr and Mrs Fox, chose me.'

He passed a badger and said, 'Hey, badger. My mum and dad chose me.'

He met another fox and said, 'Hey, Bushy Fox. My mum and dad chose me.' He was so excited. He felt he belonged.

You can leave this place today knowing that you belong, that you are cared for and that you are loved by King Jesus. If you want to do that, you need to pray with me right now.

2 The Worshipper

	Programme	Item
Section 1	**Welcome**	
	Rules	
	Prayer	
	Praise	
	Game 1	Chubby Bunnies
	Praise (x2)	
	Fun Item (2)	
	Game 2	Deep Sea Divers
	Fun Item	
	Bible Text	Psalm 27:4
	Announcements	
	Interview	
	Worship (x2)	
Section 2	**Bible Lesson**	Saul Asks David To Come
Preaching	**Illustration 1**	The Smurfs
Time	**Illustration 2**	More Than Songs
	Illustration 3	Surrender
	Story	The Perfect Day
	Prayer	

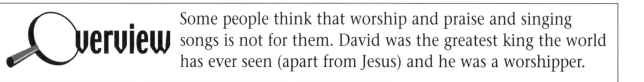

Overview Some people think that worship and praise and singing songs is not for them. David was the greatest king the world has ever seen (apart from Jesus) and he was a worshipper.

games

PreachingTime

Game 1

Chubby Bunnies

PREPARATION	Lots of marshmallows.
PLAYERS	Two people from each team.
SET-UP	Sit all the players at the front.
OBJECT	Each player places a marshmallow in their mouth. They must then say 'chubby bunnies'. If they say it clearly, continue to the next player. The marshmallows must stay in their mouths. They must not swallow. All the players who say the phrase get another marshmallow.
WINNING	The last player who can say 'chubby bunnies' wins.

Game 2

Deep Sea Divers

PREPARATION	A bowl of water containing six coins for each team.
PLAYERS	Six from each team.
SET-UP	The players line up at A. The bowls are placed at B.
OBJECT	The first person runs to the bowl, removes a coin and returns. The next player repeats the process and so on until all the coins have been collected.
WINNING	The first team back and sitting down win.

BIBLE LESSON

SAUL ASKS DAVID TO COME

'I only ask one thing Lord: Let me live in your house every day of my life to see how wonderful you are and to pray in your temple.' (Psalm 27:4)

Choose several children to act out the parts as you come to them.

Saul didn't know what was happening to him. From time to time he would feel upset and very, very sad. The only thing that ever seemed to help was music – especially music sung to God – special music called praise or worship.

David was a worshipper. He would sit on the hillside and sing his songs of praise and worship to God. Worship means that we don't just sing the words from our minds, but we really mean what we sing from our hearts.

Saul asked David to come to the royal palace. Every time Saul felt deeply sad he would call for David to come and play. Saul knew that praise sets our spirits free. He knew what the Bible said: that in God's presence is fullness or great joy.

When David became king he remembered that he felt happiest in God's presence and so he wrote: 'I only ask one thing Lord: Let me live in your house every day of my life to see how wonderful you are and to pray in your temple.'

He was king. He could have anything he wanted: gold or massive houses or anything he could think of. But all he wanted was to be in God's presence.

It makes me think that, if a king could have anything but still chooses God's presence and worship, maybe it's worth having.

The Smurfs

Object needed: *A Smurf (or the video featuring the scene mentioned below).*

When I was little I used to watch a cartoon. It was a brilliant cartoon featuring papa Smurf, Smurfette and a whole host of other Smurfs and, of course, a baddy called Gargamell. Some of you may have seen it, it's still on now.

I remember this really good one. Some of the Smurfs had been out exploring the woods when Gargamell spotted and captured them. They were all tied up to this tree. The Smurfs are really tiny creatures and Gargamell was going to feed them to his cat. They really thought they were in trouble. Then one of the Smurfs had a brilliant idea. They started to sing songs and all the chains that were holding them to the tree came loose and fell off. I thought it was brilliant. But I was very little. And, of course, it was only a cartoon. It wasn't real.

Things like that just don't happen. Or do they? I was reading in my Bible – and the Bible is full of true stories – about Paul and his friend Silas. They had been out on the streets of Philippi telling people about King Jesus. The authorities didn't like this much and so they were beaten up and locked in prison. But, despite being hurt and in pain, they still managed to sing praises to God. They began to sing, their chains came off and the prison doors flew open.

Praise and worship does something amazing, it causes our spirits to be set free. That part of us that lives forever gets excited and joyful when we praise King Jesus.

More Than Songs

Object needed: *A basketball.*

We must remember something very important. Most people think that worship is only singing songs to King Jesus. Worship is much more.

When we are kind to someone then that is worship. When we help somebody that is worship. In fact, whenever we do something that makes King Jesus happy then that is worship. When I play basketball it can be worship, if I play with the right attitude and don't lose my temper. Actually, I think King Jesus quite likes basketball – I think he's a Chicago Bulls fan. *(You may wish to substitute your favourite sport and team.)*

Surrender

Object needed: *None.*

So how do you worship? We've already said that worship can be anything that makes King Jesus happy. But there are special songs we can sing and special actions we can do as well. These are some of the things we can do when we worship:

- We can sing songs from a book or a screen to King Jesus.
- We can sing our own songs, songs we make up ourselves, which tell Jesus how much we love him.
- Some people sing in different languages to King Jesus.
- Some people lift their hands. This means, 'I surrender to you Jesus.'
- Some people clap their hands.
- Some people just sit or stand quietly and listen.

There are lots of different ways of worshipping. As long as what we do comes from our hearts, it's just fine.

● STORY – The Perfect Day

Rusty the fox woke early in the morning. It was Sunday and every Sunday Rusty would sit with his brothers and listen to his dad reading from the Bible – his dad had always told him that Sunday was a special day for worship. Later they all prayed together and then they would eat breakfast and only then did Rusty go out to play. This Sunday was no different, he had listened to his dad reading one of his favourite parts of the Bible, eaten a bowl of Weetabix and two pieces of toast covered in marmalade, drank his milk and now he was on his way to call for his friend Bushy.

Bushy had been reading his Bible with his family, but was more than ready to come out to play when Rusty arrived. They had a brilliant day; the sun was shining brightly, the hedges were perfect this time of year for jumping over, the stream was perfect for splashing through and getting sips of refreshing water when they had run too far.

Bushy was having a fantastic time. He was rolling and running, leaping and spinning, this was a great summer's day. Rusty was also having an amazing time, but every now and then he would stop and remember his father's words:

'Sunday is supposed to be a special time for worship.'

Rusty wasn't sure he should be enjoying himself so much.

Bushy noticed that even though Rusty seemed to be having fun, every now and then he would stop and look almost sad.

They played for the rest of the morning until the sun was high in the sky and the two foxes knew it was time to sit in the shade for a while and rest – they knew it wasn't very wise to play in the hottest part of day when you had a thick fox's coat. As they sat they talked. Bushy told Rusty about his new school teacher and Rusty told Bushy that his mum was going to have more cubs. They talked about many things, but eventually Bushy asked Rusty the question that he had been meaning to ask all morning:

'Rusty, what do you keep thinking about? Why do you stop playing and keep thinking?'

Rusty looked embarrassed, he didn't mean to have shown his feelings to Bushy. But he tried to explain:

'I was feeling bad. My father told me that this was a special day for worship and instead of worshipping, I am out here having fun.'

Bushy laughed. He was only a year older than Rusty, but sometimes he was much more sensible. He tried his best to explain:

'When you were reading your Bible this morning, Rusty, what were you doing?'

Rusty knew this one:

'It was part of my worship to Jesus, of course.'

Bushy continued: 'And when you prayed?'

'Worship, of course,' Rusty exclaimed.

'Now what about when we were chasing that squirrel and laughing hysterically as we ran?' Bushy asked.

Rusty looked embarrassed, 'That was me having fun.'

Bushy smiled and then said: 'Rusty, that was also worship. Worship is something we do that brings pleasure to Jesus. When we live our lives right, then we bring pleasure to Jesus. Worship doesn't mean being serious. It means bringing pleasure to Jesus. We can worship Jesus by praying and playing and sometimes just sitting still and looking at the amazing world that he created.'

Rusty thought, and then he smiled. The two animals sat still and listened to the birds sing as the warm breeze moved the grass slowly. They sat for a while and... And worshipped.

Then suddenly Rusty jumped up, tagged Bushy on the shoulder, shouted: 'You're it.' And ran off into the field.

'What are you doing?' Bushy shouted after him.

'I'm worshipping!' came the answer from a now disappearing Rusty.

Bushy jumped up and ran after him into the perfect day.

The Giant Slayer

	Programme	Item
Section 1	**Welcome**	
	Rules	
	Prayer	
	Praise	
	Game 1	Table Tennis Toss
	Praise (x2)	
	Fun Item (2)	
	Game 2	Cucumber Relay
	Fun Item	
	Bible Text	Proverbs 29:25
	Announcements	
	Interview	
	Worship (x2)	
Section 2	**Bible Lesson**	David and Goliath
Preaching	**Illustration 1**	Giants
Time	**Illustration 2**	Failures
	Illustration 3	Family
	Story	Rusty And The Angel
	Prayer	

Goliath was a warrior. David was a shepherd. But David knew a secret – he who fights for the Lord fights with the Lord on his side and there is no problem that can't be overcome.

 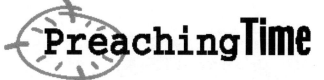

Game 1

Table Tennis Toss

PREPARATION	Lots of table tennis balls and a bucket for each team.
PLAYERS	Four from each team.
SET-UP	The buckets are set up at B and marked according to the teams. Mark a line on the floor two metres in front of B. The players start in relay formation at A.
OBJECT	When the game begins players from each team run with a table tennis ball to the line and toss their ball into their bucket. If it lands in someone else's bucket, the other team picks up an extra point. The player then returns to A and the next player repeats the process.
WINNING	The team with the most balls after three minutes wins.

Game 2

Cucumber Relay

PREPARATION	A cucumber for each team.
PLAYERS	Six from each team.
SET-UP	The players line up in relay formation at A.
OBJECT	A simple relay race between A and B with a cucumber instead of a baton.
WINNING	The first team back and sitting down wins.

Preaching Time

 **BIBLE LESSON** ## DAVID AND GOLIATH

'Don't fall into the trap of being a coward – trust the Lord, and you will be safe.' (Proverbs 29:25)

Choose several children to act out the parts as you come to them.

David had only gone to the battlefield to take some sandwiches to his brothers. The sight that greeted him was quite amazing.

In the middle of the battlefield stood a giant, shouting 'Who will fight me? If your champion defeats me, all my people will become your slaves. If I defeat your champion, then you will become my slaves. Who will fight me?'

David stood and watched. Nobody from Israel stepped forward. Was no one going to fight the giant? Sure, he was a problem, a big problem, a giant problem. But David knew that God always helped him to face his problems and solve them. God would help him now.

David asked Saul if he could fight the giant. At first Saul thought it was a joke and began to laugh. When he realised David was serious, he didn't know what to do. Eventually he gave in and let David face the giant, whose name was Goliath.

David chose five stones and marched out to face Goliath. Other men and women would have backed away. Many people never face their problems. Even when they know God will help them, they never face their problems. David did, and that was another reason why David would one day be the great king God wanted him to be.

The giant laughed when he saw David approaching. He called him names. But David knew that God was with him, so he put a stone in his sling and threw it at Goliath. Goliath was knocked to the ground. David then took Goliath's sword and used it to chop off his head. With God's help David overcame his problem.

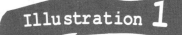

Giants

Objects needed: *Large sheet of white paper or OHP, acetate and OHP pens.*

Giants can come in different shapes and sizes. They don't have to be huge men like the one who attacked David. Giants are things or people that seem enormous or overpowering. Let me give you some examples.

When I was in school this boy used to pick on me sometimes. I was littler and thinner then. He was a giant to me, someone I was afraid of and thought of as huge. When I was younger, I was afraid of the dark – so being afraid of the dark was a giant to me. Things we are afraid of often seem like giants. When I was in school I sometimes found it hard to tell my friends I was a Christian. That was a giant to me, something I was afraid of.

Let's see how many giants – things we are afraid of – we can list. I will start us off with 'Bullies' and 'The dark'.

Write these up and prompt the children until you compile a list. It will probably include things like spiders and snakes.

We must learn something important. David defeated the giant Goliath in God's name. And with the help of King Jesus we can defeat all our giants. If bullies pick on us, we need to pray and ask for help. We need to know that God will keep us safe in the dark. If we ask King Jesus he will help us overcome our giants.

Failures

Object needed: *A Disney character.*

Listen to some of these stories about real people:

Walt Disney
Walt went to three hundred banks before he got the financial backing for Disney World. Nobody believed it would work.

Thomas Edison
- In 1847 he was born.
- He was in school for only one year. The teachers said he was too stupid to learn.
- In 1878 he was in trouble, nobody believed he could invent a light bulb. He said he could.
- In 1879 he was a hero – he'd done it!

Abraham Lincoln
- 1809 He was born in a cold log cabin.
- 1831 He failed in business.
- 1832 He was defeated in his attempt to become a local councillor.
- 1833 He failed in business again. He became a councillor, but his wife died.
- 1836 He had to leave his job because he was so ill.
- 1838 He attempted to get elected to the government, but was defeated.
- 1840 He was defeated again when standing for government.
- 1846 He was elected to government.
- 1848 Defeated again.
- 1855 Defeated in his attempt to join central government; defeated in campaign for vice-president.
- 1858 Defeated again when he tried to join central government.
- 1860 He became the President of the United States of America.

What all these people have in common is this: They overcame their giants and kept on trying. If you want your life to be incredible, you need to overcome some giants and always keep on trying.

Illustration 3

Family

Object needed: *Photograph of younger brother/sister.*

This is my sister. She's a bit younger than me. When we were in school she was always getting into trouble. She'd call people names and upset people. She didn't care because she knew that, if someone was nasty to her, she'd just call her big brother – me – and I'd sort it all out. It was OK for her, but I never had a big brother to sort it out when I was in trouble – I wish I had.

I have learnt something special since I became a Christian though. I still don't have a big brother, but I do have a Father who owns the entire universe. When people mess with me, I just tell King Jesus about it and he helps me. I now have a helper who is king of the entire universe.

● STORY – Rusty & The Angel

Rusty had gone to church every week since he was born. He'd listened to the man at the front explain why we should tell others about Jesus. He'd listened hard and when the man said, 'Even our closest friends or our mothers and fathers will not be going to heaven and cannot be God's friends if they don't know Jesus and haven't asked him to forgive their sins,' Rusty knew that he had to tell his schoolfriends all about King Jesus as soon as possible. He couldn't put it off any longer. If he didn't tell them and something sad happened and one of them died, he would feel terrible that they couldn't go to heaven, just because he hadn't said anything. Rusty made up his mind, the following day he would tell them.

He woke up early on Monday morning and got ready for school. He was so nervous, he had butterflies in his stomach and couldn't eat his food. Mrs Fox thought he might be ill.

Little Jay asked what was wrong, but Rusty wouldn't say. All the way to school they walked and Rusty never said a word to Little Jay. He just got himself ready to tell everyone about King Jesus.

He sat through his morning classes. Mrs Squirrel was talking about mathematics but he wasn't listening. He was concentrating on what he would say at break. He was going to stand on the climbing frame and tell them all about Jesus. He was scared.

Break eventually came. Rusty climbed to the top of the climbing frame and called everyone to gather round. They came, laughing and joking and wondering what Rusty was up to. They all looked up.

'I've got something to say,' he began. 'I need to tell you about somebody really special.'

His knees were shaking, his voice was quivering and then his knees shook so much he tumbled off the climbing frame. Bang!

When he looked up everyone was laughing at him. There was no way he could carry on now. He went to the nurse's room and got a plaster. That afternoon he went home very disappointed, wishing he'd said something. Later that night he tried to think about how he was going to tell them and what he could say.

The following day he was ready, he waited until break, then stood on the same climbing frame and began.

'I've got to tell you something really important. It's about King Jesus.'

The animals stood there looking. Someone shouted, 'Are you going to fall off again?'

Rusty's voice became very dry. He tried to speak but his tongue was sticking to the roof of his mouth. He tried to tell them how much Jesus loved them but all that came out was, 'I... I just... I... I.' He was too nervous to speak. They all began to walk away.

That night he lay awake looking at his ceiling. He was very concerned. He wanted so much to tell his friends about Jesus but he was too nervous. What was he going to do? He began to cry.

Just then a bright light entered his bedroom. It shone everywhere. Rusty had never seen such a blinding piercing light before. It was an angel, robed in white. He stood seven feet tall and had a gleaming sword at his side. He said, 'Rusty. I want you to know that when you stand up on that climbing frame tomorrow I'm going to be there with you. Don't be afraid. Just say what must be said.'

The light disappeared. Rusty wasn't sure what he'd seen. He was still shaking. 'An angel came to visit me?' he wondered.

The next day he was fearless. He couldn't wait for break. He stood on the climbing frame and began, 'I need to tell you what King Jesus has done for you. We have all done things wrong. These things are called sin...'

All the animals came around and listened.

Rusty kept on speaking fearlessly. He had an angel with a big sword watching over him.

God's word tells us that we all have angels watching over us. More than that, King Jesus himself told us that he would never leave us or forsake us, he would always be with us. Whatever we do, whatever tough situation we face, King Jesus will be there.

We don't need to be afraid of anything or anyone – except King Jesus, of course – God is with us. We may never see an angel but King Jesus has promised that they are there looking after us. Even better than that, King Jesus himself said that he would always be with us even until the end of time. And King Jesus is even more powerful than an angel.

4 The Friend

Programme	Item
Section 1	
Welcome	
Rules	
Prayer	
Praise	
Game 1	Apple Dunking
Praise (x2)	
Fun Item (2)	
Game 2	Choco Find
Fun Item	
Bible Text	Proverbs 13:20
Announcements	
Interview	
Worship (x2)	
Section 2 **Bible Lesson**	David And Jonathan
Preaching Illustration 1	Bananas
Time Illustration 2	Pulling Up
Illustration 3	Good Friends, Bad Friends
Story	Bushy And Rusty
Prayer	

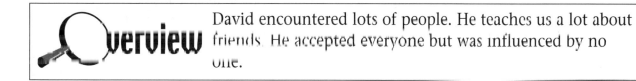

Overview David encountered lots of people. He teaches us a lot about friends. He accepted everyone but was influenced by no one.

games

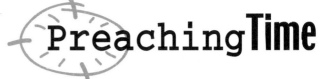

PreachingTime

Game 1

Apple Dunking

PREPARATION	Bowls of water each containing three apples are placed at B for each team.
PLAYERS	Three from each team.
SET-UP	The teams start at A in relay formation.
OBJECT	The players in turn run from A to B, collect an apple using only their mouths and return to A.
WINNING	The first team back and sitting down wins.

Game 2

Choco Find

PREPARATION	Several chocolate bars.
PLAYERS	One player (blindfolded) and one to help from each team.
SET-UP	The players start at A. Hide the chocolate bars around the room.
OBJECT	The helper tries to direct the blindfolded player to the chocolate bars using the words 'left', 'right', 'up', 'down'. Everyone else is allowed to call out, this will add confusion.
WINNING	The team with the most chocolate bars after three minutes wins.

BIBLE LESSON **DAVID & JONATHAN**

'You hurt yourself by going around with fools.' (Proverbs 13:20b)

Choose several children to act out the parts as you come to them.

David knew how to choose his friends well. One of his closest friends was Jonathan, the son of Saul. Jonathan was a very good friend indeed.

There came a time when Saul became very jealous of David. The people began to sing a song that said, 'Saul may have killed thousands of enemies but David has killed tens of thousands.' Saul was so jealous he wanted to kill David, but Jonathan warned him. He was a good friend.

Even when times were tough for David, Jonathan stayed his friend. Do you have friends like Jonathan or do you have the sort of friends who get you into trouble or even leave you when times are difficult for you? God wants you to have good friends.

David was forced to escape from the palace and become an outlaw, hiding in the hills. But Jonathan was always his friend.

Illustration 1

Bananas

Objects needed: *Bananas.*

Choose one person from each team to stand at the front (make sure they like bananas). Blindfold the three volunteers. Ask the three teams to cheer for them. Tell them that, no matter what happens, they must keep cheering for their person.

Give each of the volunteers a banana and tell them that when you shout 'Go' they are to eat the banana as fast as they can with one hand kept behind their backs. When they finish, they are to rip the blindfold off.

Shout 'Go!'

Now quickly remove the blindfolds of the two end people and return them to their seats, leaving the

middle person to race against himself while the rest laugh a lot, but keep cheering for the three people.

(It works best if you stand at the side as soon as the fun starts. When the victim eventually rips off his blindfold, he is left standing alone looking a bit lost.)

You see, if we do things just because our friends are doing them or even because we think our friends are doing them, we can look very silly indeed.

Ask the volunteer to return to his seat, thanking him for being such a good sport. You've dented his ego so make sure you re-inflate it.

NB: Because this lesson needs the children to shout it may be advisable, just as a one off, to use this illustration just before the first game by way of introduction to the topic.

Pulling Up

Object needed: *A chair.*

Stand on the chair and ask for a volunteer, one who is much smaller and weaker than you.

Some people think it doesn't matter what friends they have. It doesn't matter how bad they are because they can always pull them up to their level. But there is a problem with that idea.

Ask the volunteer to take your hand and try and pull them up to the chair. It's really difficult to try and pull people up.

Ask the volunteer to try and pull you down. It's much easier to pull someone down.

Don't think you can always pull your friends up. I've known a lot of young people mess up because they thought they could pull their friends up. They couldn't!

Good Friends, Bad Friends

Ask the children to shout out things which make friends bad and things which make friends good, write them up on a piece of paper like this:

Bad Friends	Good Friends
> Steal	> Are Kind To You
> Tell Lies	> Help You

If you have friends who fall mainly on the bad side, maybe they're not your friends after all.

● STORY – Bushy And Rusty

This is a story about two young foxes. The first was called Rusty. I know that's a strange name but, when he was born, his mum and dad looked at him and decided he was the same colour as a rusty old car, so they called him Rusty! The second was called Bushy. That name seems even stranger than Rusty. When he was born his mum and dad looked at his tail and decided that it looked as if a large bush had been stuck on his back, so they named him Bushy.

Bushy and Rusty were incredibly good friends. Each day they would meet together after breakfast and go into the meadow to play their favourite games. They would play chasing each other's tails until they were both very dizzy and then lie on the ground to catch their breath. Or they would chase the butterflies through the meadow. They could never catch the butterflies because butterflies fly too fast, but they liked to run after them just the same.

Rusty was a little bit older than Bushy so, when it came time for the foxes to start school, Rusty started first. Rusty didn't like school much because he didn't have any friends there. He tried playing with the squirrels but that wasn't much fun, and he tried playing with the rabbits but they only wanted to dig holes and bounce about.

Rusty was very sad. Near Rusty and Bushy's homes was a stream that flowed through the woods. Every evening Rusty would meet his friend Bushy at the side of the stream and they'd talk about what kind of day it had been. Rusty would tell Bushy how lonely he was and how much he hated school. Bushy tried to cheer Rusty up but he could see that his friend was really sad.

One day while Rusty was walking around the school playground, feeling very sad and lonely, someone walked up to him and said, 'Hey Rusty, I'd like to be your friend.' Well, you would think that Rusty would be happy, but the person who was asking was a naughty weasel whose name was Walter. Walter was probably the naughtiest animal in the entire school. He would always talk in class, fight in the playground and never do what he was told. But Rusty was so lonely and wanted a friend in school so badly that he became Walter Weasel's friend.

After school that day Rusty told Bushy about his new friend. Bushy wasn't happy at all. 'Walter will get you in trouble,' he told Rusty. But Rusty didn't listen. He was just glad that he'd found a friend in school.

'Hey, Rusty,' said Walter as they were walking home from school the next day. 'Let's go and throw some stones through Farmer Brown's windows.'

'We can't do that,' replied Rusty. 'That would be wrong.'

'Are you scared?' asked Walter with a wicked grin on his face.

'I'm not scared of anything,' replied Rusty who was scared. He just didn't want to show it.

So Walter and Rusty walked up to the front of Farmer Brown's house and threw stones at the windows as hard as they could. Smash!!! A window shattered into thousands of little pieces.

'Quick! Run!' shouted Walter. The two animals ran away as fast as they could before Farmer Brown had a chance to come out with his gun.

That night Rusty told Bushy what had happened. Bushy was absolutely furious. 'I told you that Walter would get you in trouble but you wouldn't listen.'

The following day Walter and Rusty were again on their way home from school when Walter said, 'Hey Rusty, it's your turn to throw the stone through the window today.'

'I can't do that,' replied Rusty. 'I'm sure it would be wrong.'

'Not scared are you?' Walter asked with the usual wicked grin on his face.

'I'm not scared of anything,' came Rusty's quick reply.

'Then do it!' retorted Walter.

Rusty was more than a little bit scared, he was very scared. But he didn't want Walter to know that, so quietly he tip-toed to the gate, picked up a stone and…Smash! It went straight through the twins' bedroom window. Farmer

Brown ran out of his house as fast as he could, but too late. Walter and Rusty had gone.

That night, Bushy couldn't believe what Rusty had done. 'I told you Walter would get you into trouble, but you didn't listen. Now look what's happening.' Bushy was so mad he was shouting at Rusty.

But Rusty didn't want to listen. 'I don't care,' he replied. 'Anyway, Walter Weasel's my best friend now and I don't want to see you anymore.'

Bushy was very upset by what Rusty was saying. But there was nothing more he could say, so he walked away with his head held low.

Two weeks later Rusty and Walter were walking home from school together when Walter turned to Rusty and said, 'Let's do something different. Let's sneak out tonight and steal some chickens from Farmer Brown's hen house.' Rusty didn't really want to do it, but he didn't want to lose his friend.

That night Walter and Rusty made their way to Farmer Brown's hen house and when they arrived Walter said, 'OK Rusty. I'll keep guard while you sneak in and steal a chicken.' Rusty was really frightened.

The chickens started clucking and crowing and making all sorts of noises. All the lights went on in the house and Farmer Brown came out as fast as he could with his gun in his hand. But too late. Walter and Rusty had gone.

Several days passed before Walter turned to Rusty and said, 'Let's do it again. Let's sneak out tonight and steal some more chickens from Farmer Brown's hen house.' Rusty didn't want to do it, but it was too late. He felt trapped.

That night Walter and Rusty made their way to Farmer Brown's hen house. When they arrived Rusty crept up to the hen house, opened the door, grabbed a chicken and ran out.

The chickens went wild. They started clucking and crowing and making all sorts of noises. All the lights went on in the house and Farmer Brown came out as fast as he could with his gun in his hand. But too late. Walter and Rusty had gone.

Two days later Walter turned to Rusty and said, 'Let's do it one last time. Let's go and steal one more chicken from Farmer Brown's hen house. Then we'll have more chickens than him.'

That night Walter and Rusty once again made their way to Farmer Brown's hen house. When they arrived, Walter took his usual place on guard outside and Rusty crept into the hen house. But Farmer Brown was not as stupid as Walter and Rusty thought. This time he was hidden behind a tree with his gun in hand. As

Rusty crept up Farmer Brown lifted his gun and aimed it at the hen house door.

Walter saw the gun when it moved and ran away as fast as he could. Rusty was left all alone in the hen house with Farmer Brown waiting outside ready to shoot whoever came out.

Bushy was sitting by the stream all by himself. Whoosh! Walter ran past Bushy as fast as his little weasel legs would carry him. 'Walter, where's Rusty?' Bushy shouted. But Walter wasn't going to stop, he just kept running. Bushy knew that Rusty must be in trouble and headed towards Farmer Brown's house as fast as he could.

Meanwhile, Rusty was still in the hen house. 'Is everything OK, Walter?' he called very nervously. No reply came. Walter was miles away by now. 'Walter, are you there?' But no answer came. He began to push the hen house door open with his nose. Farmer Brown got ready to shoot. Rusty pushed the door open and looked up. His eyes became the size of saucers as he looked straight up into Farmer Brown's gun.

Just as Farmer Brown pulled the trigger,

Bushy jumped over the fence and straight into Farmer Brown. Bang! The gun went off but missed Rusty by centimetres.

'Quick! Run!' shouted Bushy.

As the smoke began to clear Farmer Brown picked himself up off the ground and tried to work out what had happened.

Rusty and Bushy ran towards the woods as fast as they could. Bang! Farmer Brown fired again but only managed to hit a nearby tree. Bang! He tried a third shot.

Too late. The foxes had got away. When Bushy and Rusty eventually stopped, they were exhausted. Rusty was shaking like a leaf but he turned to Bushy and said, 'I'm sorry. I thought Walter was my friend, but he just got me into trouble and then left me. You are my real friend, Bushy, because you came to help me when I needed you.'

And if you have friends that get you into trouble, then maybe they're not real friends after all.

5 The Outlaw

	Programme	Item
Section 1	Welcome	
	Rules	
	Prayer	
	Praise	
	Game 1	Hats
	Praise (x2)	
	Fun Item (2)	
	Game 2	Frisbee
	Fun Item	
	Bible Text	Philippians 4:8
	Announcements	
	Interview	
	Worship (x2)	
Section 2 Preaching Time	Bible Lesson	Saul Hunts David
	Illustration 1	Snowball
	Illustration 2	Tyre
	Illustration 3	Dust On The Computer
	Story	Syd Snake
	Prayer	

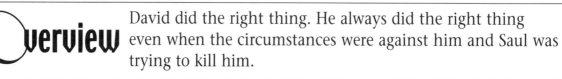

Overview David did the right thing. He always did the right thing even when the circumstances were against him and Saul was trying to kill him.

games

PreachingTime

Game 1

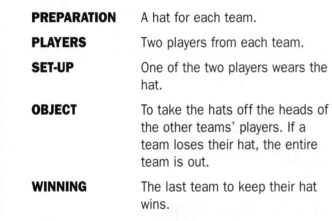

Hats

PREPARATION	A hat for each team.
PLAYERS	Two players from each team.
SET-UP	One of the two players wears the hat.
OBJECT	To take the hats off the heads of the other teams' players. If a team loses their hat, the entire team is out.
WINNING	The last team to keep their hat wins.

Game 2

Frisbee

PREPARATION	You need six frisbees.
PLAYERS	Six from each team: one catcher and five throwers.
SET-UP	Five throwers at A, one catcher at B.
OBJECT	Each team takes a turn, each thrower throws in turn.
WINNING	The team that catches the most.

BIBLE LESSON ## SAUL HUNTS DAVID

'Finally, my friends keep your minds on whatever is true, pure, right, holy, friendly and proper.' (Philippians 4:8)

David was forced to live as an outlaw. Saul was searching for him everywhere.

On one occasion Saul and his army of 3,000 men set up camp in the desert as they searched for David. In the middle of the night David crept into the middle of the camp and into Saul's tent. Saul was fast asleep and so was the man who should have been guarding him.

What was David to do? He was in the tent of the man who had been hunting him for months and had tried to kill him on many occasions.

What would you do? The man is trying to kill you, surely it's OK to kill him?

But David had learnt something very important. Even if others did wrong things to him, he would still do the right thing. Murder was wrong even if the other person was trying to kill him. David had learnt always to do the right thing.

David took Saul's spear to prove that he had been there and left. In the morning he would return Saul's spear and embarrass the man who was supposed to guard the king.

David always did the right thing. Do we always do the right thing? Or, when things are against us or we don't feel like doing the right thing, do we do wrong things?

God could make David great because he always did the right thing.

Snowball

Object needed: *Snowball (if possible!). Alternatively several balls of white paper of varying size.*

It really is amazing how small things can grow very quickly into large things. I used to try a little experiment when it snowed. I would take a little snowball to the top of a hill and begin to roll the snowball down. By the time it reached the bottom it was huge. It started off small and got big! Small things do that, they start off small and end up huge. When we tell a lie it may be a little lie, but then we have to tell another lie to cover the first.

David always did the right thing. Even when it meant trouble for him.

Tyre

Object needed: *A tyre.*

I know a boy who played with one of these. He would roll it about and sit on it and bounce it. His parents told him it wasn't a toy and that he should leave it alone. He ignored them. He would roll it at people on bikes and try to knock them off; he would roll it at cats and watch them run away; he would roll it down hills to see how far it would go. He was told not to play about with it, because when it starts rolling it's very hard to control. He didn't listen.

One day he rolled it down a steep road to see how far it would go. It started to get faster. Suddenly he realised that it was out of control. What was he going to do? There was a house at the bottom of the road. What was he going to do?

The tyre got faster and faster and was heading straight for the house. It hit the kerb and bounced into the air but it didn't stop. It flew through the front door of the house, knocking it off its hinges and finally came to rest in the hallway.

Sometimes we start things we can't control. Some people mess about with drugs or cigarettes. They know that they can't control it. It will control them and eventually end up in tragedy.

The only way to make sure that we don't get caught up in things we can't control is to make sure that we don't mess with things like that in the first place. We must only concentrate on and play with things which are pure and right and true; the sort of things David thought about; the sort of things David did; the things which would make him a great king.

Illustration 3

Dust On The Computer

Object needed: *Piece of dust (just pretend).*

On my finger I have something so small you can't see it. But it can cause a huge amount of damage. It's just a piece of dust. When this gets into certain things it causes chaos. When it finds its way into big computer rooms, it causes computers to crash. But it's only a tiny piece of dust. It really is amazing how such a small piece of dust can cause so many problems. Sin is much the same. It seems small and insignificant but just a small sin will stop you spending forever with King Jesus; just a small sin will stop you going to heaven.

Dust and sin are both very small and both must be got rid of. You use a duster to clear away dust. It's much harder to clear away sin. King Jesus died on a cross so that the wrong things you've done could be forgiven. That's what it took so that your sins could be forgiven. But you still have to ask Jesus to forgive those sins and take them away before they are gone.

● STORY – Syd Snake

Syd lived in the same forest as Bushy and Rusty and the other animals. But they tended not to mix too often because Syd was very naughty. Syd didn't mean to be naughty, he just was.

Syd liked eggs; he liked eggs very, very much. He would do anything to get eggs. But Syd liked his eggs warm and the only way to get warm eggs was to steal them from under the hens.

One day Syd was hungry. He really wanted an egg. He slithered over to the farmyard and looked around. Henrietta Hen was just laying an egg. He waited until the egg had been laid, then slithered over and stole it. He swallowed the egg with one great gulp and slithered away.

When he reached the farmyard gate he tried to slither underneath. Unfortunately the egg got stuck, trapping Syd. He pulled very hard once. He pulled very hard twice. Eventually the egg broke and the warm runny yolk ran down into Syd's tummy. It was delicious.

But when you start to do things wrong, it's very hard to stop. So the very next night Syd wanted another egg. He slithered over to Farmer Brown's farmyard and waited until Henrietta laid another egg. The same thing happened: he swallowed it, slithered back to the gate, got stuck, pulled until the egg broke and then, with a great big smile on his face, slithered home.

Farmer Brown was a bit concerned. Every morning he went to Henrietta, his best hen, to get an egg for breakfast but now there were no eggs. He asked Henrietta where the eggs had gone but she just clucked and he didn't understand.

Syd couldn't stop now. We are the same.

Once we start doing wrong things, we keep on doing them. That's why David had learnt always to do the right thing.

Syd kept on slithering over to the farmyard, stealing the eggs, breaking them under the gate and slithering home until one very sad day Farmer Brown set a trap. He couldn't work out where his eggs were going, so he took an egg from another hen, hard-boiled it, put it under Henrietta and waited.

Eventually Syd showed up. He slithered over as usual and stole the egg. He couldn't wait to get to the gate and break the egg in his tummy. He slid under the gate and heard the egg crack. But nothing broke. He pulled and pulled and pulled but nothing happened. He was stuck.

Farmer Brown crept up behind with his axe and… bang! He chopped Syd in two and the egg fell out.

All because Syd started doing things wrong: he stole just one egg and ended up being chopped in two.

Once we start to do things wrong, it's very hard to stop! That's why David learnt always to do the right thing.

6 The King

	Programme	Item
Section 1	Welcome	
	Rules	
	Prayer	
	Praise	
	Game 1	Link
	Praise (x2)	
	Fun Item (2)	
	Game 2	Dribble
	Fun Item	
	Bible Text	Philippians 4:13
	Announcements	
	Interview	
	Worship (x2)	
Section 2	Bible Lesson	David Becomes King
Preaching	Illustration 1	Flea In a Jar
Time	Illustration 2	Elephant
	Illustration 3	Pike
	Story	Bushy, Captain Of The School Football Team
	Prayer	

Overview David became a great king because he learnt some important lessons on the way and never forgot those lessons. He knew that with God's help he could become anything he wanted.

games

PreachingTime

Game 1

Link

PREPARATION	None needed.
PLAYERS	Six from each team.
SET-UP	The teams line up in relay formation at A.
OBJECT	The first player runs from A to B and back, then takes the hand of the next player. Holding hands both of them run from A to B and back. This is repeated until the entire team linked together runs from A to B and back. If the link breaks, the team is disqualified.
WINNING	The first team back and sitting down wins.

Game 2

Dribble

PREPARATION	A balloon for each team (plus a couple of spares).
PLAYERS	Six from each team.
SET-UP	The teams line up in relay formation at A.
OBJECT	The first person dribbles the balloon from A to B and back, passing it to the next person who repeats the process.
WINNING	The first team back and sitting down wins.

 **BIBLE LESSON** **DAVID BECOMES KING**

'Christ gives me the strength to face anything.'
(Philippians 4:13)

Choose some of the children to act out the parts of the story as you come to them.

Eventually Saul died and David became king. He had learnt many things on the journey:

1. He was a shepherd	and he learnt	how to forgive
2. He was with Saul	and he learnt	how worship sets you free
3. He faced Goliath	and he learnt	how to face his problems with God's help
4. He was with Jonathan	and he learnt	how to choose his friends well
5. He was an outlaw	and he learnt	always do the right thing

Today he becomes king and learns the final lesson of our series.

As soon as the Philistines heard that David had become king they sent a huge army to kill him. David had just become king, but because God had been teaching him on the way he knew what to do. He fell onto his knees and asked God for help.

God said to David: 'Get off your knees and prepare your army. Today you will totally defeat the Philistines with my help.'

And that's exactly what happened. David defeated the Philistines and learnt his final lesson:

6. He was king	and he learnt	how to do anything with God's help

We need to learn that final lesson as well. With God's help we can do anything, be anything, change anything.

Flea In a Jar

Object needed: *Jar.*

When people train fleas for flea circuses they do something special. They place the flea in a jar and put the lid on. The flea tries to jump out and bangs its head again and again and again. Eventually the flea learns only to jump as high as the lid. When the lid is removed the flea still only jumps to that level. The flea can do much better but because he's been taught that he can only jump that high he believes it.

Some people will tell you that you can only do certain things with your life. But because you're servants of King Jesus, you can do anything you want. If you really want to, you can do it. There's nothing you can't do for God. God took a poor shepherd boy and made him one of the greatest kings the world has ever seen.

Elephant

Animal trainers do a similar sort of thing with elephants. Obviously they don't put them in jars, but they do tie their leg to a big stick when they're just baby elephants. The baby elephant tries to pull its leg free but can't. The elephant grows up and could easily pull free but, because it remembers that as a little baby it couldn't do it, it never tries.

There may be things which you want to do for God that you can't do now. Don't give up! As you grow up and learn more and more about God, you'll find new things that you can do. You can do anything you want. If you want to be a missionary, then you can do that. If you want to start churches, you can do that. If you want to be a famous lawyer or doctor or vet or computer programmer, you can do it as long as you continue to serve King Jesus.

God took a poor shepherd boy and made him one of the greatest kings the world has ever seen.

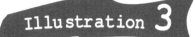

Pike

Once a fish called a pike was placed into a huge lake. The pike lived on one side of the lake. On the other lived some tiny fish that the pike wanted to eat. Between the two was a fence. The pike tried many times to get to the fish but always hurt himself on the fence. Eventually he gave up.

When the owners of the lake saw that he had given up, they took away the fence. Now the pike could swim across the lake and eat the fish any time he wanted. But he never tried. He was afraid of being hurt on the fence. If he had tried, he would have got through. He never tried.

Some of you will never be what God really wants you to be because you give up, you stop trying, you are frightened that maybe it will hurt. If you want to be above average, if you want to be particularly special, if you want your life to count, then you need to try and try and try.

● STORY – Bushy, Captain Of The School Football Team

Bushy had wanted to be the captain of the school football team for such a long time, but he was positive that he had no chance of being picked this year. Rusty was playing in the team and Rusty was brilliant. Walter Weasel had shown up and, even though he was incredibly naughty, he also happened to be a brilliant football player. Henrietta Hen was playing too and she could kick the ball harder than any of them. Bushy was sure he had no chance of being picked. Farmer Brown was the coach. He had watched the team play together and was sure they would win the league that year. But it would be very difficult to pick a captain. They were all so good.

At the end of the second training session, the week before their first match, he announced, 'I can't make up my mind who should be captain, so I'll decide at the end of the month.'

The month went by. The first proper game went very well: Henrietta scored three times, Walter scored twice and Rusty scored five times. Bushy hadn't scored but he had played his best. They won the game 10–2.

Henrietta didn't come to training the

following Wednesday nor the week after. When the coach asked her why, she simply said, 'I'm so good, I don't need to train.'

She had the wrong attitude: she was just too proud. The only thing that'll stop us being everything God wants us to be is having the wrong attitude.

A week later Walter didn't turn up for a match. When the coach asked why, he found that Walter had gone shopping with his girlfriend instead. There it is again: the wrong attitude. Walter wasn't committed to the team. He had the wrong attitude.

The following week there was a massive argument. The coach asked Rusty to play in defence and Rusty got very upset. He only wanted to play up front where he could score goals, so he wouldn't play. Once again, the wrong attitude.

At the end of the month the coach told the team he had decided on a new captain. The new captain was to be... Yes, you guessed it, Bushy Fox.

The coach decided the same way that God decides, not by choosing the best but by choosing the one with the best attitude. The one who was faithful and committed.

God chose David to be king because his heart was right, because he learnt how to forgive, because he knew how to worship, because he knew how to get through his problems, because he always did the right thing and because he knew that he could do anything and become anything with God's help. With God's help even a shepherd boy could become king.

Three Very Foolish Ideas

A Series in Three Parts

Introduction

Title	Themes covered
1 You Can Hide From God	God is everywhere
2 When In Trouble, Don't Ask For Help	God wants to forgive
3 God Wants To Punish People	God loves people

Series Overview

Jonah was a very interesting man: called of God; clearly a prophet; entrusted with the mission of bringing God's word to a staggering number of people (it took three days to walk through Nineveh, it was clearly a very big city). Yet he seems to have lacked a clear understanding of the character and nature of God. He thought he could run away from God and he saw his own comforts (the plant providing shade) as more important than all the people of Nineveh, who he thought deserved nothing but judgement.

He did have the sense to call out to God when he was in the belly of the great fish, but it probably didn't take a massive intellect to realise that going to Nineveh and fulfilling God's will was preferable to drowning or decomposing slowly in the stomach juices of a fish.

Our aim is to show the children the three mistakes illustrated negatively and positively by Jonah's life. The principles are further reinforced through stories involving the adventures of a cod called Kevin.

1 You Can Hide From God

	Programme	Item
Section 1	**Welcome**	
	Rules	
	Prayer	
	Praise	
	Game 1	Destroyers
	Praise (x2)	
	Fun Item (2)	
	Game 2	Balloon Nose
	Fun Item	
	Bible Text	Psalm 139:8
	Announcements	
	Interview	
	Worship (x2)	
Section 2	**Bible Lesson**	Jonah 1
Preaching	**Illustration 1**	Binoculars
Time	**Illustration 2**	A View From Above
	Illustration 3	Hide-and-Seek
	Story	Kevin The Cod Goes 'Shopping'
	Prayer	

 Overview God sees everything you do all the time, wherever you are, whatever you do.

games

Preaching Time

Game 1

Destroyers

PREPARATION	Three carpet tiles, or three sheets of newspaper per team.
PLAYERS	Two per team, one leading.
SET-UP	Each of the teams start at a different position in the hall with their carpet tiles.
OBJECT	The teams and leaders move around the room by standing on the carpet tiles. They can pick up the tiles behind them and stand on other team's tiles, but they mustn't touch the ground. They must avoid the leaders who are trying to tag them. If they are tagged they are out – deemed to be destroyed.
WINNING	The team that's left at the end wins.

Game 2

Balloon Nose

PREPARATION	A balloon for each team (plus a couple of spares).
PLAYERS	Six from each team.
SET-UP	The teams line up in relay formation at A.
OBJECT	Balancing the balloon on their nose the first person moves from A to B and back, passing the balloon to the next person who repeats the process.
WINNING	The first team back and sitting down wins.

BIBLE LESSON JONAH 1

"If I were to climb to the highest heavens you would be there and if I were to dig down to the world of the dead you would also be there.'
(Psalm 139:8)

Jonah was never particularly happy at any time of day, but first thing in the morning he was particularly miserable. This morning was even worse than usual. He was asleep in his bed when someone shouted his name. He woke up and looked around, but nobody was there. He hated practical jokes and, if he found out who was playing tricks on him, he would be very angry indeed.

But the voice came again and again. Who was it? He looked around. Nobody was there. He was getting cross. 'Who's there?' he shouted.

A voice came back. 'It's me, Jonah. It's God.'

Jonah was a bit surprised but, after all, he was a prophet (someone God spoke to) so he shouldn't have been too surprised. 'What do you want, God?' he asked.

God explained to Jonah that a lot of wicked people in a city called Nineveh needed to hear all about God. He told Jonah to go to Nineveh and tell them. But Jonah didn't want to go to Nineveh so he tried to trick God. Can you believe that? Can you believe that anyone would try and trick God? He really was foolish.

Jonah told God that he would go. He went to the docks to find a suitable ship, but when he got there, instead of getting on a ship for Nineveh, he got on a ship to Tarshish – completely the opposite direction.

Jonah thought he could hide from God – foolish Jonah – God is everywhere and sees everything. As Jonah's ship reached the middle of the ocean a great storm blew up and the ship looked as if it would sink. The sailors on the ship would surely have drowned if they hadn't realised that God had caused the storm to show Jonah that he couldn't run away. The sailors were very frightened. They didn't know what to do, but Jonah told them, 'Throw me overboard. It is the only way to stop the storm.'

Reluctantly the sailors did what Jonah asked. They threw him into the sea. Instantly the storm

stopped. It is impossible to run away from God. God is everywhere.

Jonah began to sink deeper and deeper. Until… What had happened? Something had swallowed him. Jonah was inside a great fish. What would become of him?

Binoculars

Objects needed: *Binoculars, telescope and periscope (at least one of the three).*

These are very interesting things. They all do something special.

The binoculars help me see people or objects a long way off. Some people use these to go bird spotting.

This is a telescope. Some people use these to look at the stars in the skies. They help you to see things that are far away.

This is a periscope. Submarines use these. They help you to see above the water and they also let you see around corners, if you position them right.

We need these things because we can't see very far without them. God doesn't need binoculars, telescopes or periscopes. He can see everything all the time.

A View From Above

Objects needed: *A chair and a stepladder*

(Lie on the floor.) It's very difficult to see anything from down here; just lots of smelly feet.

(Stand up.) This is better; at least I can see some of you now.

(Stand on the chair.) This is better still. I can see the very tops of your heads and I can clearly see the children at the back.

(Stand on the stepladder.) This is the best. I can see everything.

The higher I get, the more I can see. The Bible says that God is above all things. I guess that's one of the reasons why he can see everything.

Hide-and-Seek

Has anyone ever played hide-and-seek? I used to play it with my sister. It wasn't much fun because she always cheated. She would peep and see where I was. It's foolish to try and play hide-and-seek with someone who can see you all the time.

We know that God can see us all the time and yet we try and play hide-and-seek with him. We behave nicely and kindly when we're here because we think God can see us here. But when we get outside I don't think we really believe God can see us. But he can.

We swear at people, thinking God can't see us. But you can't hide from God. We steal things from shops, thinking God can't see us. But you can't hide from God. We're nasty and mean to each other, thinking God can't see us. But you can't hide from God. Don't be foolish, don't think you can hide from God. You can't play hide-and-seek with God. It's foolish to play hide-and-seek with someone who can see you all the time.

● STORY – Kevin The Cod Goes 'Shopping'

Kevin the Cod was not a very nice fish. He was always doing wrong things and thinking he could get away with it. And this seemed to be the case. He would walk down to the local shopping centre and go shopping. But it wasn't proper shopping. He would steal things: he would walk into the sweet shop, put Mars bars in his pocket and walk out; he would walk into the clothes shop, stuff socks up his T-shirt and walk out; he would walk into the music shop and walk out with a pile of CDs.

He never thought he would get caught. He had some close shaves but he never really thought he would get caught. Once he went into the toy shop and began to steal tennis balls until his pockets were full! But a security guard saw him and swam towards him at high speed. Kevin saw him coming and swam as fast as he could out of the shopping centre closely pursued by the security guard.

As the guard got closer he dropped the balls behind him and continued to swim. Eventually he made it to his home. The security guard came around the corner just as Kevin swam through his front door.

The security guard knocked on the door. Kevin had swum straight upstairs to his bedroom but Kevin's mother opened the door. The security guard explained what had happened. His mum called Kevin downstairs and there he stood in front of the security guard. But Kevin denied it all. 'I've been in my room all morning. I've not been out,' he stammered.

The security guard had no proof because Kevin had thrown away all the balls. Kevin's mother wouldn't believe the security guard so he shrugged his shoulders and swam back to the toy shop.

Kevin smiled. He went back upstairs. He really didn't think that he would ever get caught. The following week Kevin swam back to the shopping centre. He went back to the sweet shop and stole some Mars bars. He went to the music shop and stole some CDs. He went to the toy shop and stole a water-pistol. There was no sign of the security guard. He went to the clothes shop and stole some shorts. No one was going to catch him. He swam home. There was still no sign of the security guard.

At four o'clock that afternoon someone knocked on the door. It was the security guard. He asked for Kevin's mum. Kevin smiled. 'He'll never catch me,' he thought.

The guard began to tell Kevin's mum about the things Kevin had stolen. Kevin just smiled. 'He'll never catch me,' he thought. Kevin said, 'But I've been in all day. It wasn't me.'

Kevin was sure he wouldn't get caught. 'Nobody ever sees what I do,' he thought. 'I'm too good for them.'

We get like that sometimes. We think we can hide from God. We think we can get away with everything. It's not true. We can't hide from God. And Kevin was wrong too...

The security guard smiled and pulled out a videocassette. He walked over to the video machine and put the cassette in. The tape began to play. It showed Kevin in the sweet shop, the music shop, the clothes shop and finally in the toy shop. The video showed it all. Kevin was grounded for a month and had to pay for everything he had stolen. He was foolish to think he could steal things and never get caught.

When In trouble, Don't Ask For Help

	Programme	Item
Section 1	Welcome	
	Rules	
	Prayer	
	Praise	
	Game 1	Three-legged Race
	Praise (x2)	
	Fun Item (2)	
	Game 2	Black Sack Race
	Fun Item	
	Bible Text	Jonah 2:2
	Announcements	
	Interview	
	Worship (x2)	
Section 2	Bible Lesson	Jonah 2
Preaching	Illustration 1	Toby Is Grounded
Time	Illustration 2	Desert Choices
	Story	Kevin The Cod In Trouble
	Prayer	

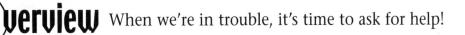

Overview When we're in trouble, it's time to ask for help!

games

PreachingTime

Game 1

Three-legged Race

PREPARATION	A piece of cord for each team.
PLAYERS	Six players from each team and three leaders.
SET-UP	The teams line up in pairs at A with a leader to tie and untie the cord. Tie the first pair together by their ankles.
OBJECT	The first pair runs from A to B and back. Their leader unties the string and ties the next pair who repeat the process.
WINNING	The first team to get all six people home and sitting down wins.

BIBLE LESSON | **JONAH 2**

'When I was in trouble I prayed to you and you listened to me.' (Jonah 2:2)

Jonah was in the stomach of a huge fish surrounded by rotting fish that it had eaten. The smell was unbearable. Was he to die?

Jonah may have been foolish in trying to run away from God, but he wasn't so foolish as to just lie in the belly of this great fish until he died. He began to pray. 'God forgive me for trying to run away from you. I need your help now. Please help.' Jonah was in deep trouble. But he knew that God was able to help. He continued to pray.

God heard Jonah's prayers and told the great fish to swim towards Nineveh. Several days later Jonah was catapulted out of the belly of the fish onto the coast near Nineveh.

He had cried to God for help and God had helped him.

Game 2

Black Sack Race

PREPARATION	A Black Sack for each team (keep some spares in case of rips).
PLAYERS	Four from each team.
SET-UP	The teams line up in relay formation at A with the first person standing in the sack.
OBJECT	The person in the sack hops from A to B and back again and tags the next person, who gets into the sack and repeats the process.
WINNING	The first team with all its people back and sitting down wins.

Illustration 1

Toby is Grounded

A disgruntled looking Toby walks onto the platform and sits down.

LEADER: Toby, you look miserable. What's up?
TOBY: I'm grounded.
LEADER: You're what?
TOBY: Grounded! They said I was naughty and grounded me. They said if I didn't say sorry for what I'd done then I'd be grounded for the rest of the week.
LEADER: So what have you done?
TOBY: Well, nothing really. I was playing football in the living room, and I kicked for goal and smashed this vase. So, they've grounded me until I apologise.
LEADER: Toby. You need to apologise.
TOBY: No chance! I'm not saying sorry to them.
LEADER: If you don't, you'll stay grounded.

TOBY: Then I'll stay grounded.
LEADER: That's foolish. If you say sorry, you'll
          be allowed out. But you're not willing
          to ask for forgiveness.
TOBY: That's right!

Desert Choices

Object needed: *A newspaper.*

An Australian newspaper once contained a very sad story indeed. It read something like this:

A family was driving through the Australian outback (a very dry desert area in Australia which stretched for hundreds of miles) when their car ran out of petrol. A car drove past, but they were so sure a petrol station was nearby that they didn't ask for help.

They were in trouble but they didn't ask for help: a sure sign that they're going to end up in more trouble. Let's read on.

All three of them started walking – dad, mum and their young son. Nobody wanted to wait in the car. They came to a junction in the road. One way went left, the other way went right. Which way should they go? They decided to go left. After walking for about fifteen miles the son became too tired to walk on. He insisted on sitting down and asked his mum and dad to find some petrol and pick him up on the way back. Mum and dad kept walking. Ten miles later mum had to sit down as well. Dad kept going. Ten miles later, with the Australian sun beating down on him, he fell to the ground with sunstroke and died. Mum, who was further back, also died and so did the son.

The really sad part of the story is that, if they'd asked for help from the people in the car which drove past, the driver would have told them that there was a petrol station only two miles after the junction on the right.

It's foolish not to ask for help when you're in trouble.

● STORY – Kevin The Cod In Trouble

Kevin the Cod was probably the most inquisitive fish you could ever meet. He was always asking questions. Why is the water blue? Why do crabs have claws? And why do sharks like eating cod? He was always asking questions. He would drive his mother crazy with question after question.

Today was no different. They sat on the sofa together and Kevin started. 'Mum, how's Cousin Cody? Is she OK?'

'Yes Kevin, she's fine,' his mother would reply.

'And how about Aunt Janet?'

'Yes, she's fine as well.'

'Uncle Arnold?'

'Yes, he's fine.'

'Mum, why has Uncle Arnold only got half a tail? What happened to him, mum?'

Well, this was a subject that Kevin's mum didn't like to talk about. Kevin asked and asked until eventually she gave in and began to tell him the story.

When Uncle Arnold was young he was always getting into trouble and one day he went out to try and find something to eat. Eventually he saw some juicy plants in the distance and he couldn't resist them. He swam towards them as fast as he could. But he had swum into a trap. A huge shark was waiting for him. The shark opened his mouth and grabbed Arnold's tail. He probably would have been killed if he hadn't cried for help. He shouted and shouted until Aunt Janet and Cousin Cody came and pulled him free. But he left half his tail in the shark's mouth.

Kevin listened very carefully, but he wasn't too impressed with Uncle Arnold. He thought Uncle Arnold was a bit of a sardine because he had called for help. 'And he let girls help him, he must be a real wimp,' Kevin decided. 'I wouldn't cry out for help, I'm not a wimp.'

Kevin wasn't so clever. I hope you know by now that, when you're in trouble, it's important to cry out for help.

That night Kevin decided that he would go and get something to eat. He wandered around outside until he saw the biggest looking worm on the seabed. He swam over, grabbed it and was on his way back to his hole when he swam straight into the largest shark he had ever seen. He began to swim away but was so busy swimming he never noticed the rocks behind him. Before he knew it, he was trapped. His tail was stuck in the rocks.

What should he do? He was caught by his tail and, try as he might to escape, he couldn't. The shark swam closer. He thought about calling for help, but then he thought, 'I'm not a sardine.' The shark came closer and closer. He knew that, if he didn't call for help, the shark would get him, but he refused. The shark kept getting closer. Kevin still refused to call for help. Kevin was foolish. He was in trouble and refused to ask for help.

Kevin's mum became very worried when he didn't come home. She went to look for him. There he was stuck in the rocks with a shark coming closer. Why didn't he cry for help? Kevin's mum swam towards the huge shark. She bit at his tail for all her worth then hid behind a rock. The shark was furious and turned to see who had dared bite him. Kevin's mum took her chance and swam towards Kevin. She pulled him free.

When they eventually arrived home Kevin's mum asked him, 'Why didn't you ask for help?'

But Kevin was still shaking too much to answer. He was foolish, not asking for help when he was in trouble. Smart people know when to ask for help.

3 God Wants To Punish People

	Programme	Item
Section 1	Welcome	
	Rules	
	Prayer	
	Praise	
	Game 1	Piggyback Tag
	Praise (x2)	
	Fun Item (2)	
	Game 2	Malteser Hunt
	Fun Item	
	Bible Text	John 3:16
	Announcements	
	Interview	
	Worship (x2)	
Section 2	Bible Lesson	Jonah 3 And 4
Preaching	Illustration 1	God With a stick
Time	Illustration 2	The Perfect Father
	Illustration 3	The Birth Certificate
	Story	Kevin The Cod Swims Away
	Prayer	

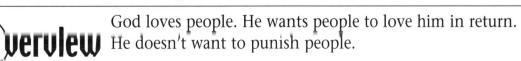

Overview God loves people. He wants people to love him in return. He doesn't want to punish people.

games

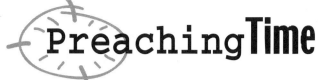

Game 1

Piggyback Tag

PREPARATION	None needed.
PLAYERS	Four people from each team and two leaders.
SET-UP	Each set of players must be in a 'piggyback' position.
OBJECT	The two leaders try and tag the players. If the team is tagged they must sit down.
WINNING	The team with the last pair tagged wins.

Game 2

Malteser Hunt

PREPARATION	Hide three Maltesers in three separate piles of flour positioned at B.
PLAYERS	Three from each team.
SET-UP	Players line up in relay formation at A.
OBJECT	The first player runs to B, removes a Malteser without using their hands, returns to A and tags the next player who repeats the process.
WINNING	The team that finds all the Maltesers, returns to A and sits down first wins.

 **BIBLE LESSON** ## JONAH 3 and 4

'God loved the people of this world so much that he gave his only Son, so that everyone who has faith in him will have eternal life and never really die.' (John 3:16)

Jonah had eventually arrived in Nineveh. The belly of a fish was not the normal way to travel, but he was there. But would the people listen to him?

Jonah began to tell the people what God had told him. He began to tell them that, unless they repented – stopped doing the bad things they were doing – and started to serve King Jesus, they would be totally destroyed. Jonah walked through the city of Nineveh shouting out his message.

The people listened. They stopped doing wrong and started to do what was right.

You'd think Jonah would be happy. But far from being happy, this made him miserable. He wanted God to kill all the people of Nineveh for being bad. Jonah made another foolish mistake. He thought God wanted to punish these people, when God just wanted them to stop doing wrong things.

Jonah was upset. He went and sat on the hillside and fell asleep. When he woke the sun was burning his face so God made a huge plant grow above him to shelter him from the sun. Jonah felt better sitting in the shade. Then God sent a worm to kill the plant and Jonah was once again in the sun. Jonah was furious.

Then God spoke to him and said something Jonah would never forget: 'Jonah you care more about that plant than you do about the thousands of people in Nineveh.'

Jonah wanted God to punish the people, but God doesn't want to punish people. He wants them to stop doing wrong and to believe in him. God loves people.

God With a stick

Object needed: *Stick.*

When I was in school our headmaster used to have one of these. *(Show them the stick.)* He didn't just have one, he used it as well. I remember one day standing outside his door because I had been naughty in class (hard to believe, I know).

The boy before me was there because he had made rude signs at an old lady on the school bus on the way home from school, and someone had told on him. He walked in before me and I could tell the headmaster was angry. Actually, he always looked angry. Everyone was afraid of him. The door closed and all I could hear was the sound of a stick going crack again and again and again. The boy walked out crying and he was fifteen years old. The head walked out behind him holding a stick that had snapped in two.

That headmaster liked to punish people who did things wrong. I was next and I was scared.

Some people think God is like that. They think he stands in heaven with a big stick waiting to punish us when we do things wrong. It's just not true. My old headmaster might have enjoyed punishing us, but God loves to forgive. He loves to forgive those who are truly sorry. He doesn't want to punish anyone.

Well, as I walked into the headmaster's office, I was shaking. He knew I was afraid. He simply held up the broken stick and said, 'Behave, or I'll break the next one on you.' Then he sent me back to class. I was so glad!

The Perfect Father

Object needed: *A large sheet of paper or card.*

It's really hard to know what God is like. But the best word I can find to describe him is one that God uses himself. The word is 'Father'. *(Write the word 'Father' at the centre of the sheet of paper.)*

King Jesus taught us, when we pray to pray to our Father who is in heaven. The word 'Father' is used to describe God. Let me show you what I mean. Call out some words that describe the perfect father. *(You will hear words such as 'caring', 'giving', 'spending', 'kind', 'gentle', etc. Write these words around the word 'Father'.)*

God is like this. He's the perfect father. *(Read out the list.)*

The Birth Certificate

Object needed: *Birth certificate.*

This is my birth certificate. It tells you something about me. It tells you my father's name and his job. It tells you my mother's name and her job. It tells you where I was born. It tells you the date I was born. In fact, it tells you quite a lot about me.

God doesn't have a birth certificate because he was never actually born. But we do have something that tells us a lot about him. It's why I know that God loves you and only wants to forgive the wrong things you've done. It's called the Bible. It tells us about how God looked after a nation called Israel. It tells us about how the Church started and how it grew. And it tells me something incredibly important. It tells me how King Jesus (who is God) came to die on a cross so that the wrong things I've done can be forgiven. Amazing! That's how I know that God loves me and doesn't want to punish me. He loved me so much he let King Jesus die for you and me.

● STORY – Kevin The Cod Swims Away

Kevin was having a really rough time. He'd been grounded for stealing from the shops for a whole month. He'd been grounded for not asking for help when the shark was about to eat him – for another month. And now, with only a day to go before he could finally go back out to play after two whole months, disaster had struck.

It was a complete accident; a real accident for a change. He had seen this tiny fish on the windowsill. It was swimming about and annoying him. He'd taken a rolled-up newspaper and tried to splat it. But, that sneaky old fish had taken off as the newspaper came closer and he'd missed and knocked over a vase. He'd dived to catch the vase but missed and knocked it into another vase. Both of them had smashed. And Kevin knew that they were worth lots of money.

'I'm going to get grounded for a year,' he moaned, 'or maybe even longer. Why didn't I watch what I was doing?'

Kevin hated being grounded. He hated having to stay in the house while all his friends were outside playing. He could see them through the window, chasing starfish and having a great time. He was very sad. He'd taken his punishment. He'd stayed in for two months and now because of a little accident he was going to get grounded for a year.

'Why do mum and dad hate me?' he wondered. 'I'm going to swim away. I'm not staying here a moment longer. They just want to punish me all the time.'

He opened his front door and off he swam. He was going to swim as far away as he could. He wasn't going to stay at home a moment longer with parents who were going to punish him for no reason. After swimming for a long time he came to a part of the ocean he had never seen before. He kept going. But, before long, he knew that he was completely lost.

He swam this way and that way but there was no sign of anyone. Except – what was that moving behind that rock? Oh no! It was that shark again, the one he'd only just managed to escape from. And another. And another. And another. He was in deep trouble. He had swum right into the middle of the sharks' home. What was he going to do?

He knew what to do. He screamed for help. The sharks saw him and swam towards him. He wasn't going to escape this time. This little cod was long overdue on the shark menu. He called for help again. Out of nowhere a whale appeared, the biggest whale he had ever seen. The sharks had seen the whale too and began to back off.

The cod swam over to the whale and the whale protected him. Good job he learned to cry out for help. The whale wanted to know why he was there. 'Why are you in these deep waters?' it asked.

Kevin was embarrassed but blurted out, 'Because my mum and dad like to punish me for things I didn't mean to do.'

Some people think that God is like that, that he likes to punish us. But God's not like that. He loves us. Sometimes we need to say sorry and ask for forgiveness for the things we do, but that doesn't change the way he feels about us. God loves us and doesn't want to punish us.

The whale began to explain the same thing to Kevin: 'Your parents love you very much and certainly don't enjoy punishing you. But sometimes, when you do things that are wrong, they have to ground you for your own good, so you learn. If it was an accident, then they'll understand.'

The whale took Kevin home. Kevin's mum had been so worried she was in floods of tears.

As soon as Kevin saw her, he blurted out, 'Sorry for breaking the vase. It was an accident.'

His mum smiled. 'Thank you for apologising. But we were much more worried about you than about foolish old vases.'

'So I'm not grounded then?' asked Kevin.

'Of course not! We don't like grounding you, but when you deliberately do things wrong we have to. Kevin, we love you.'

Kevin smiled. He was happy to be home. He thanked the whale for his help and went inside for his supper, happy that his parents loved him very much.

Kevin was foolish to think that his Mum and Dad just wanted to punish him.

To Boldly Go

A Series in Six Parts

Introduction

Title	Themes covered
1 Does God Answer Prayer?	What God is like
2 Does God Really Care?	Embarrassment
3 Does God Really Love Us?	Worship
4 What's Really Important	Forgiveness and forgiving
5 God Protects Us	To experience is better than to know about
6 Amy Dared	Bravery

Series Overview

A modern hero named Amy Carmichael, and an Old Testament hero called Elijah, help us to understand some very important lessons from God's word.

I first encountered Amy Carmichael's story many years ago in an account of her life published by the Child Evangelism Fellowship. It is a revolutionary account of a young woman who trusted God and left her comfortable Irish home to travel to India. She learnt many important lessons. Some of these lessons are explored in this series and at the same time are paralleled with the lessons learnt by Elijah.

 # Does God Answer Prayer?

	Programme	Item
Section 1	**Welcome**	
	Rules	
	Prayer	
	Praise	
	Game 1	Where's Wally?
	Praise (x2)	
	Fun Item (2)	
	Game 2	Super Memory
	Fun Item	
	Bible Text	James 5:16
	Announcements	
	Interview	
	Worship (x2)	
Section 2	**Bible Lesson**	Elijah (1 Kings 16:29–17:2)
Preaching	**Illustration 1**	How To Pray
Time	**Illustration 2**	What To Pray
	Illustration 3	Where To Pray
	Story	God Always Answers Prayers
	Prayer	

 Overview God always answers prayers. But it is difficult to understand that sometimes he says 'no'.

games

PreachingTime

Game 1

Where's Wally?

PREPARATION	Three acetates containing a 'Where's Wally?' picture.
PLAYERS	The whole team.
SET-UP	Project the acetates – one at a time.
OBJECT	To spot Wally first.
WINNING	First team to see Wally in each acetate wins.

Game 2

Super Memory

PREPARATION	Photocopy a collage of items (cut them out of a catalogue or magazine) and display them on acetate.
PLAYERS	One leader from each team.
SET-UP	The leader stands facing the front while the acetate is shown behind them.
OBJECT	The OHP is switched on for thirty seconds and the team memorises the items. The teams must then shout the items to their leaders who, thirty seconds later, must recount as many items as possible.
WINNING	The team whose leader remembers the most objects wins.

BIBLE LESSON **ELIJAH
(1 Kings 16:29–17:2)**

'The prayer of an innocent person is powerful and it can help a lot.' (James 5:16)

Ahab became king of Israel. He was one of the most evil men who ever lived. He had a wife whose name was Jezebel. Ahab was evil but his wife was even worse. They killed innocent people and were incredibly cruel at all times.

Elijah was God's friend. God spoke to Elijah and told him to go to the royal palace. Elijah wasn't sure about going into the palace of such wicked people. But God had spoken, so Elijah set off. God had told him what to do.

Elijah walked into Ahab's throne room and prayed a prayer to God. He prayed, 'God, let no rain fall on this land again until I pray and ask you.'

From that time on, no more rain fell on the land. God stopped the rain because his friend Elijah had asked. Ahab hated what Elijah had done and so did his wife Jezebel. From that time on, they wanted nothing more than to see Elijah killed.

Illustration 1

How to pray

Objects needed: *Pen, paper, telephone.*

Mr Geeky (see notes on characterisation at the end of the introduction) walks on.

MR GEEKY:	*Begins to write a letter, reading as he does so.* Dear God, my granny is not very well, so, if you can find the time, I'd really appreciate it if you could heal her.
NARRATOR:	What are you doing?
MR GEEKY:	I'm praying, like you said I should. My granny's not well.
NARRATOR:	But you don't need to write letters to pray to God.

Mr Geeky pretends to send a fax. He turns his back and makes screeching sounds.

NARRATOR:	Mr Geeky, what are you doing now?
MR GEEKY:	I'm sending God a fax to let him know about my granny.
NARRATOR:	But why don't you just talk to God?
MR GEEKY:	Well, I suppose you're right. You usually are. *Geeky goes to the telephone and pushes some numbers.* Hello, directory enquiries? Yes, I'd like the number for God. Where? In heaven, I guess. *Replaces telephone.*
NARRATOR:	Come here! When I said you just talk to God, I meant you just talk to God. Let me show you. *Closes his eyes, bows his head and prays.* Dear King Jesus, please help Mr Geeky's granny because she is not well. Amen.
MR GEEKY:	Is that all? It's much easier than I thought.

Illustration 2

What to pray

Toby Christian kneels in the corner and begins to pray.

TOBY:	Dear Celestial Being, creator of man's first respiratory movements, I beseech thee at this early time…
NARRATOR:	Toby, what on earth are you talking about?
TOBY:	I'm praying. It's really difficult. You have to use big words and say 'thou' and stuff.
NARRATOR:	Oh, Toby! You just have to speak in English. A Christian is God's friend. So you can just talk to God in the same way you talk to a friend.
TOBY:	Really?
NARRATOR:	Yes. Just tell God how you feel. Talk about what sort of a week you've had. Stuff that you would normally talk to your friends about.
TOBY:	Oh! Well that sounds easier. I'll give it a try. Hi, King Jesus. This has been a bit of a tough week. John keeps picking on me. I'm trying to be kind, but it's not easy. Help me to do the right thing.

Illustration 3

Where to pray

PC BLOB:	Hello, hello and hi there! My name is PC Blob and I'm here to arrest someone. There's the person right there.
NARRATOR:	Morning PC Blob. How are you?
PC BLOB:	Don't you 'good morning' me. You're a criminal and I'm arresting you.
NARRATOR:	Me? Why?
PC BLOB:	Don't you play innocent with me. You know fine well. Where's my notebook?

Monday:	Prayed in a car
Tuesday:	Prayed in garden
Thursday:	Prayed in bedroom
Friday:	Prayed in bathroom

	Don't even try to deny it. You are guilty of praying!
NARRATOR:	It's not against the law to pray, at least not in this country.
PC BLOB:	Yes, but you weren't in church. You must pray in church not in the garden or in the bath.
NARRATOR:	Ah. PC Blob, it doesn't matter where you pray. God is everywhere.
PC BLOB:	Ha, ha, ha. That was very funny. *Pauses.* You're serious aren't you?
NARRATOR:	Yes!
PC BLOB:	So I can pray in the park, on the train, walking up the street or riding my bike? I can talk to God anywhere?
NARRATOR:	Yes!
PC BLOB:	Oh! Well, in that case, you're not under arrest.
NARRATOR:	Thanks.
PC BLOB:	Hello, hello and goodbye.

● STORY – God Always Answers Prayers

Amy Carmichael was born the week before Christmas in 1867 in a little village on the coast of Northern Ireland. She was the eldest of seven children. There she lived with her mother and father in an old cottage.

Amy loved colours and sounds. Most of all she loved blue. Her mother had the bluest of blue eyes and Amy began to wish for blue eyes. Her own eyes were full of mischief, often sparkling, but they were brown.

Now Amy had always heard of God's Son, the Lord Jesus, and his love for her. She knew that he had come from Heaven to earth to die on a cross for her sins. Amy heard this in church every Sunday. 'God always answers prayer.' She had been reminded of this again and again.

So one evening when she was only three years old she made her way upstairs, cleaned her teeth, washed her face, knelt beside her bed and prayed, 'God, I would like blue eyes, like my mother's, by the morning. Amen.'

She climbed into bed, pulled the blankets over her head and was quickly fast asleep, confident that when she woke up in the morning she would have blue eyes.

She woke just after the sun came up and went straight to the bathroom to look at her new blue eyes. She was too small to see the mirror so she reached for a nearby stool and stood on it. Opening her eyes very slowly, she stared into the mirror. There staring back at her were a pair of bright, sparkling, mischievous eyes. But they were still brown.

Amy burst into tears and ran into her mother's bedroom. 'Mother, mother, wake up. You told me a lie. God doesn't really answer prayer.' She told her mother about the prayer and how God hadn't answered it.

Her mother smiled, not a cruel smile but a kind, understanding smile. She explained to Amy that God always answers, but sometimes he says 'no'. Amy was confused. Why did God say 'no'? She knew that her mother sometimes said 'no' to her when she had eaten too many sweet things and wanted more. Her mother would say, 'No. If you eat any more, you'll be sick.'

Her mother said 'no' because she knew what was best for her. Maybe God had also said 'no' for a reason.

Many years later, Amy travelled to India as a missionary. She found the language difficult to learn, the customs unusual and the food very strange. Most of all, she found it hard to talk to the Indian people. Whenever Amy came close to them they would turn away. She had a white face and they didn't want to talk to anyone with a white face.

Amy was struggling. How could she help these people if nobody would talk to her? Then she had an idea. She took some coffee powder and some water. She mixed the two together and smeared it onto her face. She dressed in the clothes that Indian women wore and looked at herself in the mirror. She looked exactly like an Indian woman. She walked towards the door. But, as she reached for the handle, a missionary friend arrived and stared at her. The friend couldn't believe how Indian Amy looked.

As Amy departed, her friend made one comment, 'It's a good job you have brown eyes, Amy. That would never work otherwise, because everyone here has brown eyes.'

Suddenly Amy remembered her prayer from when she was still a very young girl. She now knew why God had said 'no'.

Does God Really Care?

	Programme	Item
Section 1	Welcome	
	Rules	
	Prayer	
	Praise	
	Game 1	Basketball Relay
	Praise (x2)	
	Fun Item (2)	
	Game 2	Bizarre
	Fun Item	
	Bible Text	Matthew 6:31
	Announcements	
	Interview	
	Worship (x2)	
Section 2	Bible Lesson	Elijah And The Ravens (1 Kings 17:1–6)
Preaching	Illustration 1	Flowers
Time	Illustration 2	Stones And Snakes
	Illustration 3	Mr Geeky (Mind Reader)
	Story	God Really Does Care
	Prayer	

 We are told not to be anxious. That is easier said than done. But it becomes much easier not to be anxious when we understand that God really does care for us.

games

 PreachingTime

Game 1

Basketball Relay

PREPARATION	One basketball for each team.
PLAYERS	Six players from each team.
SET-UP	The teams line up in relay formation at A.
OBJECT	This is a straightforward relay race. They simply have to, in turn, carry the basketball from A to B and back again and pass the ball to their team mate.
WINNING	The first team to complete and sit down wins.

Game 2

Bizarre

PREPARATION	Piles of clothes.
PLAYERS	Three players and a team leader from each team.
SET-UP	Leaders stand in front of the three players.
OBJECT	To dress their leader in the most bizarre outfit in one minute.
WINNING	The most bizarre outfit wins.

 **BIBLE LESSON** ELIJAH AND THE RAVENS (1 Kings 17:1–6)

'Do not worry.'
(Matthew 6:31)

What was Elijah going to do? He'd upset the King and Queen of the land and they wanted him dead. And worse than that, he had prayed that no rain would fall and now he couldn't get anything to eat because the land was in famine.

What was he going to do? More to the point, if God really cared for him, what was God going to do? He prayed and asked God.

God really did care. He wanted to take care of Elijah and said to him, 'Go to the Chereith Brook, I will provide food for you there.'

Elijah did as God said and God kept his promise in an amazing way. The brook provided him with plenty of water to drink, but the food came in an incredible way. Every day ravens would fly to the brook and bring food in their beaks for Elijah. Now that's a miracle because the ravens would usually eat all the food themselves, but they did what God told them and God had told them to look after Elijah.

 Illustration 1

Flowers

Object needed: *A flower.*

What's this? *(Hold up the flower.)*

That's right, it's a flower. Jesus used a flower to show us something very special. He said, look at the flower. Look how beautiful it is. It didn't have to work hard to be so beautiful. It belongs to God, so God made it beautiful. The flower didn't need to worry about being beautiful because God was looking after it.

Flowers don't worry, but people seem to worry all the time. They worry about their houses, about their clothes, about their children. You don't worry about things like this, I hope. As people get older they worry about more and more things. Remember, as you grow up, the

same God who looks after the flowers of the fields thinks you're much more important than them and will always look after you.

Stones And Snakes

Object needed: *Picture of a baby.*

(Hold up a picture of a baby.)

I have a little baby girl. She's only five months old. She can't talk yet, so she just makes really strange sounds. But I sort of know what she wants. She has a bear called 'Porridge' and a rabbit called 'Rabbit'. When she wants Porridge she looks at him and makes strange sounds. I'm her father and I'm not going to give her something nasty when she wants her cuddly bear. I'm her father and I do my best to give her good things.

When we become Christians, God promises to be our father. He never gives us bad things. The Bible says, if we ask for bread he doesn't give us stones.

God is our father and he wants to give us good things: things that will make us happy and successful.

Mr Geeky (Mind Reader)

Objects needed: *Two chocolate bars.*

Mr Geeky walks in. The Narrator is holding two chocolate bars. Mr Geeky starts to make strange high-pitched screechy sounds.

NARRATOR: What are you doing?

Mr Geeky continues to stare and make strange noises.

NARRATOR: What are you doing?
MR GEEKY: I was trying to get a chocolate bar.
NARRATOR: Well, why didn't you just ask?

Narrator hands Geeky the chocolate.

MR GEEKY: I never thought of that!
NARRATOR: Some people are like that with God. God has told them not to worry, to ask and he would provide for their needs. But they just sit there sad and making strange noises. The Bible says that sometimes we don't have because we don't ask.

● STORY – God Really Does Care

When she was very young Amy Carmichael decided to help an orphanage that was near her house in Ireland (an orphanage is a place where children who have no mothers or fathers live). She thought it would be a good idea to go to the richest man in the village and ask him to donate some money to the orphanage. He refused. Amy was very confused. He had all that money and yet he wouldn't give any away. What was she to do? She thought about it long and hard until she realised that God owned the entire universe. Maybe she should just pray and ask God. That's what she did. And on that day she learnt an important lesson: God could supply all her needs.

During her time in India, Amy had to ask King Jesus again and again to supply her needs and the needs of her ever-increasing family. Amy had started her own orphanage in India and more and more children kept coming. In one year alone forty-two children arrived. Amy needed money to feed the children; money to pay the helpers; money to travel to places to rescue children who were in trouble; money to build new buildings; money for everything. But, whenever Amy needed money to provide for the children at the orphanage, she would pray and ask God to help her.

She knew that God loved her very much and had given Jesus to everyone who had asked. She knew the verse in the Bible that said, 'If God did not hold back his own son but let him die on the cross, how could he possibly withhold anything from us?'

One day Amy needed £100. She asked God and waited for the mail to arrive. She opened the letters one by one expecting to find the money that God would supply. But when the last envelope was open there was no money. What were they to do? Life in India was harder than here. If God didn't meet their needs then there would be no money to buy food and they would all starve to death.

She noticed that one letter remained and

opened it quickly. It was from England. God had spoken to someone and asked him or her to send £66. Good! But that still left £34 to find. There was only a parcel left. All the children looked at the package. It probably contained clothes or books. Amy began to open it. When she had pulled the final wrapping loose, she found a note saying that £51 was on its way. The children were so excited. God had met their need.

When they needed a holiday for some of their workers, they didn't tell anyone. They just prayed to God, who they knew cared for them. Some days later a letter arrived saying, 'Here is the money for the holiday.'

They needed a car because it took too long for them to get to children who were in danger. They needed to be able to rescue them faster.

Again they told no one but just prayed and asked God for a Ford car. They knew God cared for them, so they asked God. Three months later a letter arrived, saying, 'Dear Amy, here is the money for the Ford car.'

Amy learnt that God didn't want her to ask people for the things she needed: no matter how much money they may have had, she was to ask God to supply her needs.

(Personal Note: During the telling of this particular story we had asked the children to join with us to pray for a video projector for the children's work. Several weeks later somebody handed us a cheque for £2,000 for a video projector. It worked better than any object lesson I could think of.)

Does God Really Love Us?

	Programme	Item
Section 1	Welcome	
	Rules	
	Prayer	
	Praise	
	Game 1	Fox, Chicken And Corn
	Praise (x2)	
	Fun Item (2)	
	Game 2	Words
	Fun Item	
	Bible Text	Luke 4:18b
	Announcements	
	Interview	
	Worship (x2)	
Section 2	Bible Lesson	Elijah (1 Kings 17:10–16)
Preaching	Illustration 1	Plasters And Bandages
Time	Illustration 2	Valentine Card
	Illustration 3	Newspapers
	Story	Preena's Story
	Prayer	

 We know that God loves us, but sometimes he does extraordinary things to show just how extraordinary his love is.

games

Game 1

Fox, Chicken And Corn

PREPARATION Two pieces of carpet or newspaper for each team.

PLAYERS Three children and a leader from each team.

SET-UP Set the teams up at A (front of hall) with the carpet/newspaper.

OBJECT The carpet is a boat. Point A is an island. Point B is another island. They must transport the corn, chicken and fox (ie the three children) to the other island. The farmer can only take one item besides himself on the boat. If the corn is left alone with the chicken, the team is disqualified because the chicken will eat the corn. If the fox is left with the chicken, the team is also disqualified because the fox will eat the chicken. The teams have three minutes to work out a solution.

WINNING The team that demonstrates how to solve the problem wins the points. Each team will be asked to demonstrate their idea. Team leaders must be honest and not change their solution after seeing if another team tries it and it doesn't work.

Game 2

Words

PREPARATION None.

PLAYERS The team leaders choose as many as they need.

SET-UP None.

OBJECT To form the word which is called out, using the people available, e.g., if the word is 'love', one child might stand up straight while another lies at his feet to form the 'L'.

WINNING Each word completed and recognizable is worth a point. The team with the most points wins.

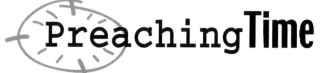

PreachingTime

BIBLE LESSON **ELIJAH (1 Kings 17:10–16)**

'The Lord's Spirit has come to me to free everyone who suffers.' (Luke 4:18b)

Eventually the brook where Elijah was getting his water dried up and God told him to go to a place called Zarephath where a widow would look after him.

The widow looked after Elijah for some time. She was very kind to Elijah and did everything she could for him. She even prepared a special room for him at the top of the house.

The woman had a son whom she loved dearly. One day the son came in from the field with a bad headache, he went to his bed and lay down for a rest. But something terrible happened: the boy died.

The woman didn't know what to do. She was sure Elijah was a friend of God and she knew she had been kind to him. She knew that God loved her, but why had he let her little boy die? She became angry with Elijah: 'Have I treated you badly? No, I have not! Then why has my son died?'

Elijah didn't know the answer. He knew that God loved children and couldn't understand what had happened. He prayed and God sent him to pray for the boy. Elijah knew that the boy was dead, but did as God had instructed. He prayed and something spectacular happened – a miracle – the boy came back to life.

Sometimes God does amazing things just to show us how much he loves us.

Illustration 1

Plasters And Bandages

Objects needed: *Plasters and bandages.*

These are used when people hurt themselves. Let me show you how they work. (*Put some plasters on some of the leaders. Wrap some children up in the bandages.*)

When you fall and get a cut, a plaster helps. When you twist your ankle, a bandage helps. But sometimes people are hurt, not outside but inside. Sometimes something bad happens: their mum and dad get a divorce and they get hurt inside; someone says something nasty to them and they get hurt inside. We can't put plasters or bandages there. That's why Jesus came to help people who have been hurt on the inside.

Valentine Card

Object needed: *A valentine card.*

This is a valentine card. I had to make it myself. Nobody sent me one of these this year. Sad really! People like to get these though, don't they? It makes them feel special; it makes them feel cared for; it makes them feel loved. It's important to feel loved. And you know something? Even if nobody else in the entire world loves us, God loves us. We are all loved by the Creator of the entire universe. King Jesus, who is God, loves us.

Newspapers

Objects needed: *A newspaper and a Bible.*

Newspapers like these often make me miserable. They are filled with pages and pages of bad news. Let me read you some. *(Read some of the headlines from today's paper.)*

This is my Bible. *(Hold up your Bible.)* I like this more than the newspaper. It's full of good news. It talks about how King Jesus loved us so much that he actually came and died for us so that the wrong things we've done could be forgiven. He also did it to show us just how much he loves us.

● STORY – Preena's Story

Today's story is about a little girl named Preena. She lived in one of the many Indian temples. It was cold and damp and very uncomfortable. She stayed there with lots of other boys and girls but they were all very sad.

One day Preena decided to run away back to her mother. She ran for a long time. It took her three whole days before she eventually reached home.

'Please, mother,' she pleaded. 'Please, let me stay. Please, don't send me back to that horrible temple. Please, let me stay. I'll be good. I'll clean. I'll do anything. Please, don't send me back.'

Her mother looked at Preena with cold eyes and said to her, 'I don't want you and I don't love you. I sold you to the temple when you were younger and that is where you belong.'

Preena's mother took her straight back to the temple. The women in charge of the temple were furious and decided to punish Preena. They took a metal poker, placed it in the fire and waited until it was red hot. Then they took the red hot poker and placed it on Preena's hand. The burn would leave a mark to show that she had tried to run away.

Preena screamed with the pain and tears ran down her cheeks. She was left alone. Late into the night her hand was still hurting. She walked over to the green statue that she had been told was a god and began to pray: 'Oh, Shiva. Oh, Vishnu. Help me. Take the pain away.'

Now the Bible says these statues are not really gods: they have eyes but cannot see; legs but cannot move; they are totally useless. Only King Jesus is the real God who loves people enough to take away pain. But Preena didn't know about King Jesus yet.

After two more hours of crying, Preena decided she would run away again. The temple woman had told her that if she ran away again she would be killed. But, although Preena was only seven, she didn't care. She would rather be dead than have to live the rest of her life in the temple.

But where would she go? She had heard of a woman across the river that she should never go near, a woman called Amy who ate little children. Preena thought, 'Right, I'm going to run to the monster, Amy.'

She set out, trying hard not to be seen by the temple guards, and headed for the river. Preena crossed the river, but one of the guards had seen her and the chase was on. She ran and ran until, just as the sun was rising, she arrived at Amy

Carmichael's house. She knocked on the door expecting a monster to open the door and gobble her up. She waited.

The door opened and there before her was no monster, but a beautiful white lady with big brown eyes. They were kind and gentle eyes.

'Hello,' said Amy, 'Who are you?'

Amy picked Preena up, took her into her house and gave her a doll. Preena had never seen a doll before. In fact, she had never seen toys before. She burst into tears and told Amy the story of how she had been sold to the temple.

Amy looked at Preena's hand and saw the scar in the centre of her palm. 'Preena,' she began, 'Someone else had a scar on his hand and on his other hand and on his feet and side; someone who got those scars because he died on a cross because he loved you so much. His name was Jesus.'

Preena began to cry, then to sob, then to weep uncontrollably.

'What's wrong?' asked Amy.

Between her sobs, Preena blurted out, 'That means the only person who ever loved me is dead!'

Amy smiled a very kind smile. 'No, Preena. Because three days later he rose from the dead.'

Preena was very excited that someone loved her. But her excitement was short-lived because outside she heard a voice, many voices. 'Where is Preena? Bring out Preena now.'

It was the temple guards. Preena began to cry again. Amy picked her up and said, 'Don't be afraid.'

Then Amy walked outside, looked at the guards and said, 'Preena is with me now. She won't be going back to the temple with you. She is staying with me.'

The temple guards didn't know what to do. They wanted to take Preena away, but they were just a little bit frightened of Amy, so they turned and slowly walked away, saying that they would be back one day.

Amy just smiled at Preena. 'You can live with me, if you want.'

Preena was very happy and became the first of many children that Amy would rescue from the temple.

What's Really Important

	Programme	Item
Section 1	Welcome	
	Rules	
	Prayer	
	Praise	
	Game 1	Gourmet Mars Bars
	Praise (x2)	
	Fun Item (2)	
	Game 2	Snakes
	Fun Item	
	Bible Text	1 Corinthians 3:13
	Announcements	
	Interview	
	Worship (x2)	
Section 2	Bible Lesson	Elijah's 'Mission Impossible'
Preaching	Illustration 1	Toby Saves His Pocket Money
Time	Illustration 2	Bodies And Spirits
	Illustration 3	What's Really Important?
	Story	People Laughed!
	Prayer	

Overview We often don't realise what's truly important. Eternal things, things which last forever, are of ultimate importance.

games

Game 1

Gourmet Mars Bars

PREPARATION	One Mars bar for each team and one fork for each person.
PLAYERS	Three people from each team.
SET-UP	The teams line up at A. The Mars bars are on plates at B.
OBJECT	This is a simple relay race. The players take turns to run to the Mars bar, scoop off a part with the fork, eat it and return. They carry on until the Mars bar has gone.
WINNING	The first team to finish the Mars bar and sit down wins.

Game 2

Snakes

PREPARATION	None needed.
PLAYERS	Six players and a leader from each team.
SET-UP	The teams line up in relay formation at A.
OBJECT	The first player runs from A to B and back. The second player puts their hands on the first player's hips and they both run. This is repeated until the entire team forms a human chain (or snake).
WINNING	The first team back and sitting down wins. If anyone breaks the chain, their team is disqualified.

Preaching Time

BIBLE LESSON ELIJAH'S 'MISSION IMPOSSIBLE'

'Whatever we build will be tested by fire on the day of judgement.'
(1 Corinthians 3:13)

God has told Elijah to go to Mount Carmel and to invite the priests of Baal, King Ahab and Queen Jezebel.

Elijah was afraid. He knew that people would think him mad; he knew that Ahab would be there to kill him. But he also knew what really mattered: what God wanted was more important than what people said.

Elijah was still afraid. But he knew that what God wanted was more important than his fears. So he marched towards Mount Carmel and the 450 priests of Baal; towards King Ahab and Queen Jezebel.

Illustration 1

Toby Saves His Pocket Money

Objects needed: *Two £1 coins.*

LEADER: Hey, Toby! Your dad told me to give you this.

TOBY: Wow! It's my pocket money. I like getting my pocket money. I'll go and sort out what I can spend, now that I have my £2. *Toby pretends he's writing down his week's spending.* OK. I always give 10% to the church, so I'll do that: 20p to church. I need money to go to children's church, so 50p for children's church. I need to give mum the 75p I owe her. That leaves me 55p. I'll keep it for when I go to heaven.

LEADER: Why 55p for heaven?

TOBY: Well, there's going to be lots to do in heaven, right? I'll need some money to pay for things, so I'm saving now.

LEADER: Toby, aren't you listening at all? We don't need money in heaven. You can't spend money in heaven. And you certainly can't take money to heaven. There's no chance.

TOBY: Oh! Well, I guess that's another 55p for chocolate. Bye, then.

Bodies And Spirits

Draw a line and a circle. Alternatively, use a piece of string and a hula hoop.

We are made up of two parts: our bodies and our spirits.

We spend a lot of time looking after our bodies. We exercise them – that's a good thing. We feed them – that's a good thing as long as we don't eat too much. We put make-up on them – that's a good thing as long as you're a girl. In fact, we spend hours and hours looking after our bodies. But when we die, our bodies will rot and decay – ugh! Our bodies are like this line: they have a beginning, but they also have an end.

We spend very little time looking after our spirits. We don't pray much, we don't read our Bible much, we don't spend too much time with other Christians and we spend very little time telling others about King Jesus. But when we die, it's our spirits that will live forever. Like this never-ending circle.

What's Really Important?

Take some flash paper* and write on it some of the things which will not last. Take some ordinary paper and write on it some things which will last. For example,

LAST	NOT LAST
Souls	Money
Kind Acts	Houses
	Cars
	Bodies

* See note on p. 43.

Call the items out in turn. Set fire to those things which do not last.

● STORY – People Laughed!

It was a very wet and windy day in Belfast. Amy was a little girl making her way home from church. She was wearing her best Sunday clothes and was doing her best to stay as close as possible to her mother who held the umbrella. Across the road Amy saw an old lady struggling with a heavy bag of groceries. She obviously hadn't been to church, her clothes were torn and old and she looked very wet. Many people from the church simply stared at the old lady as they walked past.

Amy left her mother's side and ran over to the old lady. She picked up the old lady's heavy bag, took the old lady by the arm and began to escort her home. The lady for her part was very surprised but glad of the young girl's help. As the odd couple walked on, they were met with disapproving glances. The people on their way home from church laughed and pointed. Amy began to get embarrassed, the people stared and the red glow on Amy's cheeks grew.

She felt like walking away, she felt like leaving the old lady, but instead she decided that what she was doing was more important than what people thought of her. This would be remembered in heaven after she had died. This was an eternal thing. This was truly important.

Amy had learnt a very important lesson: what God thinks of us is more important than what people think of us.

In the years that followed, Amy helped lots of people. She carried pots of soup to old people; she sat beside sick people's beds and talked to them. She knew that many people thought she was wasting her time but she also knew that King Jesus saw what she was doing and knew it was important.

Many years later, when Amy moved to India, she continued to help people. Many people decided to become Christians just because Amy's example showed them how kind Christians could be. Amy worked long and hard and every night she would come home to Preena. Amy would disguise herself and enter the temples to try and rescue the children who were held there.

Amy worked hard at finding out how and why the temple children ended up in the temple. One night she sat in a local inn in her disguise. She heard some men talking and discovered that some of the children were sold to the temple when their mothers had died and their fathers didn't want them. Sometimes a mother who wanted to gain favour with the temple people would sell her children.

Amy really wanted to reach these children; to show them some love; to tell them about King Jesus who loved them. The other missionaries told her that she was wasting her time; that she should be concentrating on the adults not on these children. But Amy was convinced that this was what King Jesus wanted her to do. The other missionaries told her that she wouldn't be a proper missionary if she only spent time with the children. But Amy knew something very, very important: eternal things are the most important.

Telling these children about Jesus would mean the difference between them going to heaven or going to hell. She had to tell them.

She raised enough money to build a house called Dohnavur and, as the years went by, hundreds of children were rescued from the dark, damp temples and brought to Dohnavur, a place of love where they could learn more about King Jesus. Amy didn't care what people said about her.

Telling children about Jesus is an eternal thing; one of those things that would remain forever. God would be pleased with her.

5 God Protects Us

	Programme	Item
Section 1	**Welcome**	
	Rules	
	Prayer	
	Praise	
	Game 1	Newspaper Search
	Praise (x2)	
	Fun Item (2)	
	Game 2	Rummage
	Fun Item	
	Bible Text	Psalm 27:5
	Announcements	
	Interview	
	Worship (x2)	
Section 2	**Bible Lesson**	Elijah On Mount Carmel
Preaching	**Illustration 1**	Angels
Time	**Illustration 2**	Protect Those We Love
	Illustration 3	Shield
	Story	Amy And The Outlaw
	Prayer	

Overview Sometimes God asks people to do things which appear dangerous. It's good to know that God protects us when we're in difficult situations.

games

PreachingTime

Game 1

Newspaper Search

PREPARATION	One newspaper for each team. (Thy must be copies of the same newspaper.)
PLAYERS	Five people from each team.
SET-UP	Set teams up at B with a newspaper each.
OBJECT	The game leader will call out a headline or an advert or a picture. The teams must find the article/picture and return it to the team leader. The game leader will repeat this for several articles/pictures.
WINNING	The team that returns the most articles first wins.

Game 2

Rummage

PREPARATION	A black bag full of scrap paper for each team. Pieces of card bearing the word 'Rummage' are placed inside each bag of scrap paper.
PLAYERS	Two players and a leader from each team.
SET-UP	Both players stand beside the black bags.
OBJECT	The team must search for the word 'Rummage', replace all the scrap paper in the bag and hand the word to the game leader.
WINNING	The first team to find the word 'Rummage', hand it to the leader and return all the scrap paper to the black bag wins.

BIBLE LESSON

ELIJAH ON MOUNT CARMEL (1 Kings 18:19–23)

'In the times of trouble you will protect me.' (Psalm 27:5)

Elijah came to Mount Carmel. Waiting for him were 450 priests of Baal who hated him. King Ahab and Queen Jezebel were there as well and they wanted to see him dead. But Elijah wasn't afraid. He knew that God had sent him and would defend and protect him.

There was to be a competition. Elijah would compete with the priests of Baal to discover whether God or Baal was in charge.

Elijah asked for two dead bulls to be brought up and placed in front of the groups. Firewood was assembled around the bulls and the people waited. Elijah issued his challenge, 'If Baal is in charge, then let him send fire to consume the bull.'

The priests of Baal prayed all day long, calling out to Baal, but nothing happened.

'Now it's my turn,' said Elijah. 'But first cover the bull with water. Let's make this a little more difficult.' Elijah prayed and fire fell. The bull was consumed. God was victorious and Elijah had been protected.

Illustration 1

Angels

Object needed: *Steering wheel.*

A lady was driving on a very busy motorway. She had been a missionary in a foreign country for many years, telling people about God, and had only recently returned home to the country where she was born.

She had been away in the foreign country since before motorways had been built. In her time as a missionary she had seen many frightening things but she had never felt more scared than she did right then. She was caught in the fast lane; cars were shooting past her; cars

behind her were beeping their horns; people were shouting things at her.

She was very scared and didn't know what to do. If she slowed down the people behind would crash into her. She couldn't pull across to the slow lane because cars were now driving past her in that lane as well. She panicked and took her hands off the wheel. It was clear she was going to crash and she was certain she was going to die.

As she sat there, tears streaming down her face, an amazing thing happened. Two arms reached out from behind her and took the wheel. The indicator came on and the car moved to the middle lane. The indicator came on again and the car moved to the slow lane. She was in shock. Her hands were still in the air. The car turned off the motorway onto a small country road where it pulled over and stopped. The hands let go of the wheel and the arms moved back. The woman didn't know what to do.

She eventually turned round. Nobody was there. The woman had heard about angels. She believed that angels were protecting her, but she had never seen an angel – until now. God's heavenly angels who protect those who love God help us all the time, even when we don't know about it.

Protect Those We Love

On a certain mountain in Switzerland there is a path that winds around the mountain. On one side of the path is the bare mountain. On the other side is a steep slope leading to a 200-metre drop.

One day a man was walking up the path which was only about a metre wide. He heard a scream and looked back to see that a small boy had slipped off the path onto the slope. It was winter and the ground was covered in snow, so the boy started to slide very quickly towards the edge and the massive drop. As the man watched, another man jumped off the path and ran down the slope towards this small boy. The boy was getting closer and closer to the edge but the man kept running. Just as the boy was about to fall off the edge, the man dived and caught him.

The boy was saved and all the people cheered the brave hero. They couldn't believe someone was prepared to risk his life to save the boy. However the man did have a good reason. He risked his life because the boy was his son.

We all protect the ones we love. That man protected his son. Our parents protect us. And King Jesus, who loves us very much, wants to protect us. It's an exciting thing to know that the King of the universe is protecting us.

Shield

Object needed: *Shield.*

This is a shield. People used to use them to protect themselves against the attack of an enemy. If someone attacked me with a sword I could use my shield to stop the sword from striking and possibly harming me. A shield is very useful when you have an enemy that wants to kill you.

There's a verse in the Bible which reads, 'God is our shield, a help in times of trouble.'

God is like this shield because he protects me. He stops the enemy from hurting me. And I do have an enemy. The Bible says the Devil wants to steal from me, destroy me and kill me. So I'm glad that God protects me. God is my shield.

● STORY – Amy And The Outlaw

When Amy Carmichael was young she helped build a welcome house for the poor girls who worked in factories. The girls were called 'shawlies' because of the shawls they wore over their heads as they rushed to work very early each morning. The girls were rough and bad mannered, so they were not made welcome in the posh churches in Ireland at that time. They thought that nobody cared for them or what they did.

But someone did care. God cared. He loved the young women and wanted to save them from their lives of sin. He wanted to forgive all the bad things they had done and become their friend. Some of God's servants cared too. Amy cared. She wanted to make friends with them; she wanted to get to know them; she wanted to be able to tell them about King Jesus.

The only way to do this was to go and live among them. Amy moved into a flat where the 'shawlies' lived. It was cold and damp; it had bugs crawling on the walls and spiders on the floors; it was dark and dusty. But she was determined to stay. 'God wants me here,' she reasoned, 'and he will protect me.'

It was a good thing that God was protecting her because one evening, as Amy travelled back to her flat, a gang of boys surrounded her. She knew she was in trouble but she knew that God would protect her. She tried to keep walking but the young men stopped her. The gang of boys was growing larger and getting rougher. Amy was in real danger.

People who serve King Jesus are often in danger. But God always looks after his people. God doesn't keep us away from danger but he protects us in danger.

Suddenly a door along the row of houses opened. A woman's hand reached out and pulled Amy inside. She was safe. That night Amy knew for certain that God would always protect her.

When Amy worked as a missionary in India, many children escaped from the cruel temples and came to her. The people who worked in the temples and the children's parents who had sold them to the temple were usually very angry and would try and get them back. Once a young girl escaped from the temple and ran away to Amy. Amy, knowing that the temple guardians would come looking, hid with the girl all night at the top of a church in the bell tower. On another occasion a girl called Kohila ran away to Amy. Her guardians were so unhappy that Amy sent her hundreds of miles away to a missionary friend where she knew she would be safe. The guardians took Amy to court and Amy could have been locked up for kidnapping. But God protected her and she was freed.

Amy didn't only spend time with children. In India in those days there lived a man who was known as the Red Tiger. He was a lot like Robin Hood: he would take things from the rich and give them to the poor. That might sound good but we must remember that stealing is wrong even if we are stealing from those who have a lot. On one occasion the Red Tiger came to see Amy.

He had with him his three children. He was afraid they were in danger because he was on the run from the police. Amy agreed to look after his children and also told him about King Jesus who loved him very much and wanted to forgive the things he did. He listened very hard and was touched that King Jesus loved him but he wasn't ready to leave his life as an outlaw.

Five days later Red Tiger was captured by the police. They beat him so badly that he was put in hospital. Amy went to visit him, even though others who had visited him had been arrested and thrown in jail. She knew that God would protect her. She talked to Red Tiger some more about King Jesus. This time he gave his life to King Jesus and asked him to forgive the wrong things he had done.

When Red Tiger was well enough he was moved to a prison and nobody was allowed to visit him. Amy was very concerned because he was only a new Christian. But she believed that God would protect him.

Red Tiger was only a new Christian and he didn't know that God would protect him in prison so he escaped. When Amy heard about this, she left a light in her window each night, hoping that he would come and talk to her. She wanted him to give himself up to the police and trust King Jesus to keep him safe. Eventually he did visit her, but he wouldn't give himself up.

Later that week the police found him and surrounded him. He fired several shots in the air to frighten the police off. When that didn't work he threw down his gun, held up his hands and surrendered. The police showed no mercy. They shot him as he stood there with his hands raised.

Many bad things were said about Amy because she had helped Red Tiger. Many people wanted to hurt her too, but King Jesus kept her safe.

Red Tiger had done many bad things, he had stolen from many people. But, because he had asked King Jesus to forgive the wrong things he had done, he instantly went to be with King Jesus in heaven when he died.

6 Amy Dared

	Programme	Item
Section 1	Welcome	
	Rules	
	Prayer	
	Praise	
	Game 1	Target Practice 1
	Praise (x2)	
	Fun Item (2)	
	Game 2	Target Practice 2
	Fun Item	
	Bible Text	2 Thessalonians 2:13
	Announcements	
	Interview	
	Worship (x2)	
Section 2	Bible Lesson	Elijah
Preaching	Illustration 1	Isaiah
Time	Illustration 2	Jeremiah
	Illustration 3	You
	Story	Amy Dares
	Prayer	

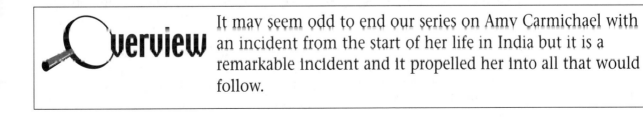

Overview It may seem odd to end our series on Amy Carmichael with an incident from the start of her life in India but it is a remarkable incident and it propelled her into all that would follow.

games

Game 1

Target Practice 1

PREPARATION	A wide sheet of cardboard with six holes in it, numbered 1 to 6. Six bean bags for each team.
PLAYERS	Three players from each team.
SET-UP	The players line up at A with two bean bags each. The cardboard target is placed at B.
OBJECT	The players run in turn from A to a point two metres in front of B. Here they throw their first bean bag at the target and return to tag the next player. The process is repeated until all the bean bags have been thrown.
WINNING	The team with the highest score wins.

Game 2

Target Practice 2

PREPARATION	A wide sheet of cardboard with six holes in it, numbered 1 to 6. Six bean bags for each team.
PLAYERS	Three players from each team.
SET-UP	The players line up at A with two bean bags each. The cardboard target is placed at B.
OBJECT	The players run in turn from A to a point two metres in front of B. Here they throw their first bean bag at the target and return to tag the next player. The process is repeated until all the bean bags have been thrown.
WINNING	The team with the lowest score wins. To prevent cheating, warn the players that every bean bag to miss the target will be worth seven points!

BIBLE LESSON **ELIJAH**

'It is only natural for us to thank God for you. God chose you to be the first ones to be saved.'
(2 Thessalonians 2:13)

We don't know anything about Elijah before he suddenly confronts King Ahab in 1 Kings 17 and announces that there will be no rain. We are given some clues as to who his father was and where he lived but the rest of Elijah's life is a mystery.

In spite of that, I think I know when God decided to get Elijah to do the amazing things he did. God actually decided what he wanted Elijah to do before he even began to put the world together. Before he spoke the words that would create light or cause thousands of varieties of trees and plants and animals to grow and develop, God had already decided what Elijah would look like. He had already decided what he wanted Elijah to do for him.

How do I know this? Mainly from today's Bible text. You see it's not just Elijah, it's everyone. Before the world even began God chose what we would look like and what he wanted us to do for him. Let me show you some more examples.

Isaiah

Isaiah was an amazing person used amazingly by God. Isaiah knew that he was a prophet – someone who would tell others what God wanted them to know – but it wasn't until the day he entered the temple and God appeared to him that he realised how much God wanted to do with his life.

You see God had already decided that he wanted to use Isaiah before the world was even started, but there had to be a point where Isaiah would come and say, 'God I want to do what you want me to do.'

Then God could use him in amazing ways. Isaiah would tell kings what God wanted.

Jeremiah

Object needed: *A picture of a baby scan (try your local hospital or maternity clinic).*

It's actually amazing what doctors can do now. This is a picture of a baby inside a mother's tummy. It doesn't look like much, but that's what we all looked like once: tiny little baby shapes.

God actually said that before Jeremiah was born God had already chosen him to be a prophet to the nations. Isn't that amazing? Before the man was even born, God had already chosen him to tell others about Jesus. Before he saw the face of his mother; before he took his first breath in this world, God had already chosen him to do a job for him.

Illustration 3

You

Object needed: *A picture of yourself.*

What's even more amazing is that God chose this next person before he was born as well. Even before he began to make the world God chose him to do a job. Let me show you a picture of him. *(Display your picture.)*

Before the world began God chose me. It gets even more interesting. Before the world began, God chose you as well. Now that really is amazing! Before anything existed you were one of God's plans. Cool, hey?

Now maybe, like Isaiah, God wants to take you to the place where you say, 'God I want to do the job that you have for me, please use me. I want to do amazing things for you.'

● STORY – Amy Dares

Amy Carmichael travelled all the way to India to speak for Jesus in that foreign land. She gave up all she had just to do what God wanted her to do. God had chosen her long before the world started, but there was a special point that Amy came to before everything fell into place.

One day Amy found herself outside one of the Indian temples. There she saw some of the little Indian girls who had been sold into slavery in the temples. She began to pray, but a different voice came into her head. It was the voice of the Devil and he said to Amy, 'Do you really dare to believe that you can take these children from me?'

Amy was surprised to hear the Devil speaking to her and felt very afraid. The voice was cold and menacing. She knew that, if she was going to try and rescue these children, the Devil would do all that he could to stop her; he would do all he could to hinder her; he would do all that he could perhaps even to the point of taking her life.

Amy began to think. Then, with the boldness and courage that only Jesus can give, she made the statement that would change everything; that would turn her life upside down and see her become what God wanted her to be. She said to the devil, 'Devil, I dare! I dare to take these children from you and there's nothing you can do or will ever be able to do that can stop me. I dare!'

And God really has chosen you before you were born. He really has chosen you before the world was actually put in place. He is just waiting now, just waiting for that time when he speaks and you respond, 'I dare!'

These are exciting times for people who really love Jesus and are prepared to do whatever he wants.

The Story Of Noah And His Ark

A Series in Three Parts

Introduction

Title	Themes covered
1 Floods	God is fair and just
2 Doves And Ravens	Purity
3 Rainbows	God keeps his promises

Series Overview

The story of Noah and his ark is the one story that most children will know. The story itself is packed full of lessons that we can learn from: the God of justice who floods the world even though he loves people; the insight into God's character we obtain from a study of the dove and the raven; the almost 'Hollywood' ending with the animals emerging from the ark with rainbows in the sky. All these combine to make the story of Noah an incredible source of learning and entertainment.

1 Floods

	Programme	Item
Section 1	Welcome	
	Rules	
	Prayer	
	Praise	
	Game 1	Wiggle
	Praise (x2)	
	Fun Item (2)	
	Game 2	Boxed In
	Fun Item	
	Bible Text	Psalm 45:7
	Announcements	
	Interview	
	Worship (x2)	
Section 2 Preaching Time	Bible Lesson	Noah And The Ark
	Illustration 1	Love
	Illustration 2	Sowing And Reaping
	Illustration 3	Where's The Water?
	Story	Teddy The Toff
	Prayer	

Overview God loves people deeply and intensely. The phrase 'God was sorry he had made them,' in Genesis 6:6, is an attempt to translate a very difficult Hebrew text. The words God uses here have no real English translation that communicates the weight of emotion in God's heart. But God had to be just and fair. He had to destroy the world.

Game 1

Wiggle

PREPARATION	A balloon for each team (plus spares).
PLAYERS	Five from each team.
SET-UP	Players line up in relay formation at A with the front member of the team holding the balloon between their knees.
OBJECT	The first person runs from A to B and back with the balloon between their knees. On return they pass the balloon to the next player.
WINNING	The first team to complete the relay and sit down wins.

Game 2

Boxed In

PREPARATION	A big box full of junk (old newspaper, tissue, etc.) containing five table tennis balls for each team is placed at B.
PLAYERS	Five from each team.
SET-UP	The players line up in relay formation at A.
OBJECT	The first person runs from A to B, searches for a table tennis ball and returns to A with it. On returning to A, they tag the next player who then repeats the process.
WINNING	The first team back and sitting down wins.

BIBLE LESSON

NOAH AND THE ARK

'You [God] love justice and hate evil.' (Psalm 45:7)

God looked down at the world he had made. He loved the people who lived in his world. He loved them very much but they had become steadily worse. They were doing all sorts of things that made him very sad. When God looked at the world he felt as sad as it is possible to feel.

Many people don't realise that God has feelings. They don't understand that God has emotions. The Bible says we were created to be like God. We have emotions and feelings because God has emotions and feelings. And the people in the world had made God feel really sad.

God felt so sad that he actually regretted creating people in the first place. God loves us very much and wants to forgive us but he can't ignore forever the wrong things we do. Eventually he has to do something about it.

The people in the world had become so bad God couldn't wait any longer. There was one exception – a man called Noah. Noah still loved God. God decided to send a terrible flood all over the world. But, before it happened, God told Noah to build a huge boat – God called it an ark. Noah was to put into the boat all sorts of animals and also to gather together his family.

Noah did what God said. Noah always did. That's how we know that he loved God.

When the ark was ready, Noah and his family went inside with all the animals and God closed the doors. Then the rains began. God loved the people, but people can't keep doing wrong things forever and expect God to ignore it. The people who did wrong all drowned in the amazing flood that covered the whole world.

God loves people but, if we keep doing wrong things, God must do something about it.

Love

Object needed: *Music cassette (choose your own song, but Bryan Adams 'Everything I do' will work well).*

I am going to show you the greatest act of love the world has ever seen:

Options:
- Invite a mime artist to act out the crucifixion scene.
- Show the crucifixion scene on a video.

God loved the world so much that he let Jesus die on a cross for the wrong things we've done. God doesn't want to punish us, but he can't let the bad things we do go unpunished.

Sowing And Reaping

Objects needed: *Seeds and bulbs of various types.*

Here is a daffodil bulb. If we plant this, I'll have a daffodil in a few months. Here is an apple seed. If I plant this, it will eventually grow into an apple tree and one day it will produce apples. Here are various seeds. Whatever I plant is whatever will grow. You get what you sow. If a farmer sows wheat he expect to get, or reap, wheat. If he sows corn he expects to reap corn. He can't sow barley seeds and expect to pick a melon harvest. You reap what you sow.

The Bible says the same thing: you reap what you sow. If you sow bad things, bad things will happen to you. If you sow good things, good things will happen to you. If you spend all your time being nasty to people, eventually people will be nasty to you. If you're kind, people will be kind to you. God makes sure this happens. Eventually bad people get what they deserve unless they've asked God to forgive the bad things they've done.

And God makes sure good people also get what they deserve. But remember, we don't go to heaven by being good. We can only go to heaven by asking Jesus to forgive the wrong things we've done, because no matter how good we are, we can never be good enough to get to heaven without God's help.

Where's The Water?

Object needed: *A cup of water.*

The world is bad. People are doing wrong things. Why doesn't God flood the world again? *(Throw the cup of water, making sure to move your arm rapidly from left to right so that each child only gets tiny droplets.)*

God made a promise to Noah, a promise we'll talk about in a couple of weeks. A promise never to flood the world again. So does that mean that we can do what we like and never be punished?

No! The Bible talks of something called judgement. One day we will all stand before King Jesus and he will look at our lives. If we are Christians, if we have asked God to forgive the wrong things we've done, then King Jesus won't see any sins, bad things, on us. We will be clean because he has forgiven us. If not, we will not be allowed into heaven. We will go to a place the Bible calls hell.

God loves people, but he can't ignore bad things for ever.

● STORY – Teddy The Toff

Teddy the Toff was very, very posh and very, very rich. He wore a big black top hat all the time, even when he slept, even when he was in the bath. He lived in a huge mansion at the edge of Green Acres.

One morning Teddy woke up as usual and wandered around his huge mansion. He looked in every room, slid down the banister, went into the garden, walked back to the house and sat down in his big chair. He was rich, posh and bored. What was he going to do? He had to find something interesting to do or he would go crazy. He wandered back out into the garden and looked over the wall. He decided he'd go for a walk down into the town. But when he arrived he still felt fed up.

'I need some excitement,' he thought. 'What can I do?'

He walked into the supermarket and there in front of him was a huge sign: 'Thieves will be prosecuted.'

'Now that could be fun,' he thought. With that, he grabbed a loaf of bread and ran for the door. A security guard saw him and gave chase, but Teddy easily outran him, hat and all, and leapt over a wall into a nearby garden to eat the bread. He didn't need to steal the bread. Teddy was very rich. He just wanted some excitement.

'Anyway,' he thought, 'they'll never catch me, I'm Teddy the Toff.'

It wasn't long before Teddy was bored again. He jumped back over the wall and started to walk down the street. He passed the jewellers and there in the window was a huge diamond ring. He walked into the shop and asked to see the ring. The assistant smiled because she knew how rich Teddy was. She reached into the window and handed the ring to Teddy. But she stopped smiling when Teddy turned and ran out of the door. She shouted for help. A policeman gave chase, but Teddy was soon over the wall and away down a back alley.

Very soon he was bored again. He went into the shoe shop and ran away with some new Nike trainers. Then it was the turn of the clothes shop and off he set with a new suit. Then it was the turn of the record shop, followed by the sweetshop and the computer shop. Teddy stole things from shops all over the town. He was having a great time. Eventually all the shops closed for the evening and Teddy, feeling quite happy with himself, made his way home carrying bags of food, clothes, jewellery, CDs, computer disks, chocolates and a whole range of other bits and pieces. He was sure he wouldn't get caught.

Maybe we all think we won't get caught. Maybe we all think we can get away with bad things. We can't. Maybe the people in Noah's day thought they could get away with doing bad things. But God knows and can't allow us to keep doing bad things. And Teddy was about to discover that he couldn't get away with it either.

Teddy turned the corner into his drive and there standing on his doorstep was the jeweller, the grocer, the computer man, the record shop owner, the security guard, lots of other people and, worst of all, a big policeman.

Teddy had to return all the things he had stolen, except the bread that he'd eaten, which he had to pay for. And worse still the policeman gave him a huge fine for stealing things. He was very lucky he wasn't sent to jail. Teddy had to pay out over £5,000 in fines. Now he wasn't so rich!

2 Doves And Ravens

	Programme	Item
Section 1	Welcome	
	Rules	
	Prayer	
	Praise	
	Game 1	Woof Woof
	Praise (x2)	
	Fun Item (2)	
	Game 2	Fetch
	Fun Item	
	Bible Text	Matthew 5:8
	Announcements	
	Interview	
	Worship (x2)	
Section 2	Bible Lesson	Ravens And Doves
Preaching	Illustration 1	Blockage
Time	Illustration 2	Dirty Dishes
	Illustration 3	Hearts
	Story	Teddy The Toff
	Prayer	

Overview The raven and the dove were both sent out. The clean dove found nowhere to land and returned. The unclean raven landed on the rotting animals. The Holy Ghost comes as a dove. Will he find clean lives to land on?

games

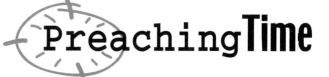

Preaching Time

Game 1

Woof Woof

PREPARATION	A plate containing a melted Mars bar and several forks for each team (plus spares).
PLAYERS	Six players from each team.
SET-UP	The players line up in relay formation at A with each member of the team holding their forks. The plates of melted Mars bars are placed at B.
OBJECT	The first person runs from A to B, takes a piece of chocolate, eats it and returns to A. On return the next player sets off. The twist in the 'tail' is that the teams are told they are eating dog food.
WINNING	The first team to complete the relay and sit down wins.

Game 2

Fetch

PREPARATION	A squeeky rubber bone for each team, placed at B.
PLAYERS	Five players from each team.
SET-UP	The players stand in relay formation at A.
OBJECT	The first person runs from A to B and squeezes the bone. On hearing the bone the next player sets off to join them, until all the players are at B. When they are all at B they run together back to A.
WINNING	The first team back and sitting down wins.

 **BIBLE LESSON** **RAVENS AND DOVES**

'God blesses people whose hearts are pure. They will see God!' (Matthew 5:8)

Noah and his family had been in the ark for a long time. At last the ark came to rest on the very top of a mountain called Ararat. Noah wanted to know if the flood had finally gone down enough for him to let the animals out, so he opened the door and let a raven out.

The raven is a big black bird. But it is also an unclean bird. It left the ark and flew around. Seeing the carcasses of dead animals floating on the water, it began to fly from one to another plucking out pieces of rotten meat. The raven never flew back to the ark. It was perfectly happy landing on dirty, decaying, smelly, rotting animals.

Noah still wanted to know if the floodwaters had gone down, so he sent out a dove.

The dove is a clean bird. It flew over the floodwaters and looked at the rotting animals. The dove wouldn't land on something unclean. It circled and then returned to the ark.

In the Bible, God sometimes comes in the shape of a dove. He looks for clean hearts and clean lives that he can come and live in but sometimes our hearts and lives are so clogged up with bad things that he can't get through.

I wonder which bird would be more comfortable with your life? The unclean raven or the pure dove?

Illustration 1

Blockage

Objects needed: *A metre length of pipe, a bucket and a jug of water.*

Pour the jug of water into the pipe so that it lands in the bucket and say, God wants to come into our lives. He wants to pour himself into us, like I'm pouring this water into this bucket.

But, sometimes, God can't do that because

he gets blocked. *(Put your hand over the end of the pipe to block the flow of water.)* The things that block God from coming into our lives are called sins. They are things such as lying and cheating and thinking bad thoughts. They block God coming into our lives. There is a way to get rid of the blockage. We have to ask God to come and clean out our lives. We have to ask him to forgive our sins. Only God can clear away the blockage. *(Take away your hand and let the water flow freely again.)*

Illustration 2

Dirty Dishes

This illustration takes the form of a solo narrative. The customer pretends that he can hear the water's voice.

Waiter! What do you call this? *(Holds up a dirty plate.)*

This is absolutely disgusting. You expect me to eat off this? I wouldn't let my dog eat off this. It's disgusting! It looks like it hasn't been washed for months. It's got bits of beans and pieces of leftover potato and ketchup stains. It is disgusting. What on earth do you think you're doing getting me to eat off this?

What do you mean, 'If you think my plates are a mess, you should look at your heart?'

There is absolutely nothing wrong with my heart. I go jogging every day. I have a very good heart. It's a very fit heart. It will keep going for years and years.

What are you talking about?

Who'd want to live inside someone's heart?

Who?

God?

How can he live in my heart? If he lives in my heart, then he won't be able to be anywhere else.

He can't be everywhere at the same time, can he?

Well, I guess that's one of the advantages of being God. So, why won't he live in my heart?

Mine's a very fit heart!

It's not very clean! What do you mean?

It's full of sin!! Oh!!

Anyway, what's my heart got to do with you? I bet mine's better than yours!

You don't think so? Well, you don't know a thing!

How can your heart be cleaner?

Because God's cleaned it out?

And why would he do that? Because you asked him and said sorry for all the wrong things you'd done?

Oh!

I've had enough of this! Just fetch me a clean plate will you?

Illustration 3

Hearts

Objects needed: *Cardboard heart, washing powder, washing-up liquid, soap.*

Today I'm washing my heart. I've done so many wrong things over the last couple of weeks I need to get it really clean again. I swore at that man in the street! I thought some nasty thoughts, and I even got angry with my mother. So, I'm just cleaning my heart.

The only problem is, I don't seem to be able to get it clean. I'll try soap. *(scrubs away with the soap)*

That doesn't seem to be working. Maybe washing powder will work. *(scrubs away with the powder)*

That doesn't seem to work either. Maybe this washing-up liquid will do the trick. It gets my dishes really clean. *(tries the liquid)*

It just doesn't seem to work. I guess the Bible was right: only God can make dirty hearts clean.

● STORY – Teddy The Toff

Teddy the Toff was very, very posh and very, very rich. He lived in a huge mansion at the edge of Green Acres. But he wasn't in his mansion today. He'd just bought a new business called 'Sparkly Springs', a huge lake in the middle of the loveliest countryside in the world. Sparkly Springs was very, very popular. Hundreds of people came to it every day. They ate in the café overlooking the lake, bought pictures from the shop, sat at the picnic tables and watched the swans swimming. Sparkly Springs made a lot of money every week from all the people that visited, but Teddy the Toff was going to make even more. Or so he thought!

His first idea was to put all the prices up. But after looking in the café, and walking around the shop, he soon realised that would be impossible. Then he thought about charging people to come in, but he didn't think that would be a very popular idea. Eventually he came up with another idea. He would get rid of some of the staff. There seemed to be too many anyway. He would save money by paying fewer people and he would become even richer.

The very next day he called each of the staff into his office in turn and asked them to explain what they did.

'I'm Cathy. I'm the cleaning lady. I mop the café and clean your office.'

'I'm Siobhan. I sell things in the shop.'

'I'm Percy. I make sure all the cars are parked properly in the car park.'

'I'm Cathleen, I cook things for the café.'

Teddy listened to fifteen different people explaining their jobs. They all sounded incredibly important. He didn't think he'd be able to sack anyone. But then Larry walked in. 'I'm Larry. I collect the rubbish which is left around near the lake.'

'That's it,' thought Teddy. 'If I put up a sign saying "Please take your rubbish home", I can sack Larry.'

That's what he did. He put up the signs and sacked Larry. But it didn't work out as he had planned. The next week, everything seemed to go well. Most people took their rubbish home. One or two people forgot, but that wasn't so bad. Teddy saw a couple of old crisp bags at the side of the lake, but nothing much really. The following week was the same, and the week after that. Teddy was very pleased with himself, he was becoming richer and richer every week.

But the lake had started to change. A small stream flowed into the lake and a small stream flowed out the other side. But slowly the way out of the lake became blocked. The water had nowhere to go and the rubbish began to pile up. After another six months the lake began to smell. It smelt disgusting. People stopped coming to the lake. They started going elsewhere. Teddy was losing lots and lots of money and he didn't understand what was going on. In the end, he was so upset that he called all the staff together and asked them, 'What's going on? Why is the lake smelly?'

All the staff agreed, 'It's because you sacked Larry. Larry did an important job.'

'No he didn't,' Teddy protested. 'He just picked up the odd crisp bag every now and then. He hardly did anything.'

The staff explained to Teddy: 'It all builds up. A little today and a little tomorrow and a little the next day and before long the lake is blocked and begins to smell. Our hearts are the same,' they said. 'They don't get full of bad things straight away, but if we keep doing bad things and never ask God to forgive us and take the bad things away, eventually our hearts are full of rotten, horrible things.'

Teddy hated to admit he was wrong, but he hated to lose money even more. 'Where is Larry?' he shouted. 'Bring me Larry!'

Eventually Larry was found and agreed to come back to work, as long as Teddy paid him twice as much money as before.

Within a month everything was back to normal and all the people started to come back. The only thing that had changed was Larry now had much more money.

Rainbows

	Programme	Item
Section 1	**Welcome**	
	Rules	
	Prayer	
	Praise	
	Game 1	Piggyback Racer
	Praise (x2)	
	Fun Item (2)	
	Game 2	Journalist
	Fun Item	
	Bible Text	Hebrews 13:5
	Announcements	
	Interview	
	Worship (x2)	
Section 2	**Bible Lesson**	Rainbows
Preaching	**Illustration 1**	Breaking The Stick
Time	**Illustration 2**	Friends
	Illustration 3	Everywhere
	Story	Teddy The Toff
	Prayer	

Overview God never breaks his promises.

games

 **Preaching**Time

Game 1

Piggyback Racer

PREPARATION	None.
PLAYERS	Six players and leader (who can carry the children) from each team.
SET-UP	The players line up in relay formation at A with their leader at the front of their team.
OBJECT	The leader carries the first person from A to B and back. When they return to A they collect the next player and so on.
WINNING	The first team to complete the relay and sit down wins.

Game 2

Journalist

PREPARATION	An identical newspaper for each team placed at B.
PLAYERS	Six players from each team.
SET-UP	The players line up in relay formation at A.
OBJECT	Each person has a certain article to recover from the paper. The first person runs from A to B, searches for the article and brings it back with them. On returning to A they tag the next player who then repeats the process.
WINNING	The first team back and sitting down wins.

 **BIBLE LESSON** ## RAINBOWS

'I will never leave you or forsake you.' (Hebrews 13:5)

Noah, his family and a zoo full of animals waited in the ark until God told them it was time to leave. They were very excited. The animals made their way out of the ark into the strange new world that awaited them. There was much joy and excitement.

But Noah could see dark clouds in the sky. Was God about to flood the earth again? Noah felt the droplets of rain on his cheeks and wondered if he should try and get everyone back into the ark. He was worried and concerned. Then God said, 'Noah, I will never flood the earth again and I will display rainbows in the sky to remind you of my promise. Noah, don't worry. I will never flood the earth again.'

Noah looked up and there in the sky was a rainbow: red, orange, yellow, green, blue, indigo and violet. It was the first rainbow that Noah had ever seen.

God had made a promise. Noah felt safe. He knew that people sometimes make promises and don't keep them, but God had made a promise and God never breaks his promises.

 **Illustration 1**

Breaking The Stick

Objects needed: *A very thick stick and a very thin stick.*

There are two types of promises: the type that people make and the type that God makes.

When people make promises, they sometimes break them. You all know people who have broken their promises. The promises people make are like this thin stick: they are easily broken.

When God makes a promise, he doesn't break it. God's promises are like this thick stick: no matter how hard I try, I cannot break it. God never breaks his promises. God never let us down.

This is great news because God has made us several promises. One of the greatest was when he said, 'I will never leave you or forsake you.'

Illustration 2

Friends

Put your hand up if you have friends. Put the other hand up as well if you have ever made promises to those friends.

At some time we have all made promises. And I'm sure that sometimes we've broken a promise. Maybe you promised to meet someone at 7 o'clock and didn't show up until 7:30. Maybe you didn't show up at all. I know that I sometimes make promises to be home at a certain time and I end up talking with someone and break the promise. We all do it. If we're good people, then we don't break promises on purpose.

We do our best to keep our promises. And we hope that our friends try and keep their promises to us as well. But we all know that sometimes our friends break their promises.

Wouldn't it be amazing if we had a friend who never, ever broke a promise? A friend who had never broken a promise and who never would break a promise? God is like that and King Jesus is like that. When God promised Noah that he would never flood the earth again, he kept his promise. And, when he says to us, 'I will never leave you or forsake you,' he really means it.

Illustration 3

Everywhere

Object needed. *A map or globe.*

PERSON 1: Tell me. Will King Jesus really never leave me or forsake me?

PERSON 2: That's what he promised, and he never breaks his promise.

PERSON 1: So, look at this map. This is us right here. Is God with us right here?

PERSON 2: Of course.

PERSON 1: But what if I went over to France?

PERSON 2: He promised he'd still be with you.

PERSON 1: And what about if I went to this place? Australia?

PERSON 2: Yes, he'd be there too.

PERSON 1: How about up here in the Arctic Circle where it's really cold? Would he be there with me?

PERSON 2: Yes.

PERSON 1: But, what if I left the world altogether and went to Mars or Jupiter?

PERSON 2: Yes, there too.

PERSON 1: That really is amazing. He really never breaks that promise. He really is always there, looking after me and helping me.

PERSON 2: It gets even more amazing. When you die he's still with you. And he takes you into heaven to be with him. When you give your life to King Jesus, he is there with you always from then on.

PERSON 1: Wow!

● STORY – Teddy The Toff

Teddy loved to make money. He had lots of different businesses that made him lots of money. But the one that made him the most was his building business. He had built buildings all over the world. He started off with little houses on the west side of his home town. When he sold them he built bigger houses and then mansions. Now he was about to begin his largest building ever. He had been given one hundred million pounds to build the largest hotel in the whole world. Teddy was very excited. He thought he must be the richest person in the world: so much money just for him.

Teddy the Toff really was doing well for himself and he really was quite a nice person. But he had a problem. Teddy found it very hard to keep promises.

When Teddy started to build small houses he hired ten men. He promised them that he would pay them £200 every Friday. But it was nearly two months before Teddy got around to paying the men and even then he didn't give them as much as he'd promised. When Teddy started building bigger houses, he promised the man who was delivering the bricks that he would pay him at the end of the month. Six months later, the man had to go to Teddy and ask for his money. Teddy reluctantly gave it to him. When

Teddy started the mansions he promised the men he would pay them £300 every Friday, he promised the man who delivered the cement that he would pay him every month and he promised the man who brought the bricks that he would pay him every six weeks. It was nearly a year before they got paid!

Teddy became richer and richer. But those who worked for him became more and more annoyed with him. He just didn't keep his promises. He had lots of excuses such as, 'I forgot!' But the people who worked with him weren't very happy.

God keeps all his promises and because of this he can be trusted all the time. Teddy just didn't.

Now he was starting his one hundred million pound deal. He still had a lot of materials left from the mansions, so he started with them. The men who worked for him worked from very early in the morning to very late at night. Before long the men were really tired and needed a break and all the materials had run out.

He phoned for more men. But nobody came. He had broken so many promises that nobody would trust him. He phoned the company for more sand. But nobody would come. He tried the cement and brick companies. But he'd broken so many promises that nobody would come. He had started the biggest hotel in the world and nobody would help him. Nobody trusted him. The man who gave him the one hundred million pounds wanted it back. The hotel would be finished but not by him.

Teddy went from being one of the richest men in the world to one of the poorest. He would eventually recover and build his business back up, but the next time he would understand the importance of keeping his promises.

We need to learn from a God who never ever broke a single promise; the God who promised, 'I will never leave you or forsake you.'

Fruit Of The Spirit

A Series in Nine Parts

Introduction

Title	Themes covered	Fruit
1 Love	'Agape' love	Plum
2 Joy	More than a feeling	Pear
3 Peace	Peace is more than the absence of war	Grape
4 Patience	God does things in his perfect time	Orange
5 Kindness	Consistent kindness. Kindness as a way of life	Lemon
6 Goodness	Not just doing good, but being good	Lime
7 Faithfulness	Trust! Can we be trusted?	Strawberry
8 Gentleness	Meekness is not weakness	Apple
9 Self-control	Can we control ourselves?	Banana

Series Overview

The characteristics of Jesus are listed for us in Galatians 5:22–23. They are more commonly referred to as the fruit of the Spirit. In a generation where gifts, talents and abilities are elevated, very often at the expense of good character, a study of Galatians will certainly prove worthwhile.

The stories at the end of each lesson all fall under the heading 'Tales from Around The World'. A series of tales both traditional and modern is presented to reinforce the message.

This nine-part series will work through each 'fruit of the Spirit' in turn. A summary is printed towards the end of part nine.

1 Love

	Programme	Item
Section 1	**Welcome**	
	Rules	
	Prayer	
	Praise	
	Game 1	Plum Stones
	Praise (x2)	
	Fun Item (2)	
	Game 2	Plum Lost
	Fun Item	
	Bible Text	Galatians 5:22-23
	Announcements	
	Interview	
	Worship (x2)	
Section 2	**Bible Lesson**	1 Corinthians 13
Preaching	**Illustration 1**	Philia
Time	**Illustration 2**	Eros
	Illustration 3	Agape
	Story	Olle And The Troll
	Prayer	

Overview Jesus didn't ask us only to love the lovely; he asked us to love everyone unconditionally. God wants us to love the unlovable.

Game 1

Plum Stones

PREPARATION	You will need twenty or so plums, and a bucket for each team.
PLAYERS	Six players from each team.
SET-UP	Players line up at A. The plums are placed on a table at B, with a knife and fork for each team.
OBJECT	The first player runs from A to B, uses the knife and fork to remove the stone from the plum, and then returns to A with the plum stone. At A they drop the stone into the bucket and the next player sets off.
WINNING	The team with the most plum stones in the bucket after three minutes wins.

Game 2

Plum Lost

PREPARATION	You will need twenty or so plums.
PLAYERS	Five players from each team.
SET-UP	The players line up in relay formation at A. The plums are hidden so that the teams can tell where they are, but the players cannot.
OBJECT	The first person runs from A, finds a plum and returns. Player two then runs. This continues until one of the teams has seven plums.
WINNING	The first team with seven plums and every player sitting down wins.

FRUIT

Today's fruit is **plum**, representing God's gift of love (for summary see end of part nine, 'Self-control').

 ## 1 CORINTHIANS 13

'God's Spirit makes us loving, happy, peaceful, patient, kind, good, faithful, gentle, and self-controlled.'
(Galatians 5:22–23)

Some of us have some strange ideas about what love is. This is what the Bible says:

> Love is kind and patient, never jealous, proud or rude.
> Love isn't selfish or quick tempered.
> It doesn't keep a record of wrongs that others do.
> Love rejoices in the truth, but not in evil.
> Love is always supportive, loyal, hopeful, and trusting.
> Love never fails.

The New Testament part of the Bible was written in a language called Greek. There are several different words for love in Greek. Let's look at three of them.

Invite three volunteers to come and hold three cards with the words 'Agape', 'Philia', and 'Eros' written on them.

Philia

This is the first type of love we are going to talk about. It is love for our friends.

It's great to have friends who love us and who don't leave us when things get hard. It's the sort of love where you look out for each other and take care of each other. I hope that we are like that and that we have friends like that: *philia* love.

Illustration 2

Eros

This is romantic or 'slushy' love, the love between a boy and a girl.

Major overacting is necessary to make this work well. The narrator stands off-centre while Romeo and Juliet 'prance about' in the centre of the stage.

ROMEO: If I profane with my unworthiest hand,
This holy shrine, the gentle fine is this,
My lips, two blushing pilgrims, ready stand
To smooth that rough touch with a gentle kiss.

NARRATOR: This is *eros* love.

JULIET: Good pilgrim, you do wrong your hand too much,
Which mannerly devotion shows in this;
For saints have hands, that pilgrims' hands do touch,
And palm to palm is holy palmers' kiss.

NARRATOR: It's pretty slushy stuff!

ROMEO: Have not saints lips, and holy palmers too?

NARRATOR: It's from *Romeo and Juliet*, a play about love by William Shakespeare.

JULIET: Ay, pilgrim, lips that they must use in prayer.

ROMEO: O, then, dear saint, let lips do what hands do;
They pray, grant thou, lest faith turn to despair.

NARRATOR: All these words just so he can kiss her!

JULIET: Saints do not move, though grant for prayers' sake.

ROMEO: Then move not, while my prayer's effect I take.
Thus from my lips, by yours, my sin is purged.

The couple move towards each other as if to kiss. The narrator runs across the stage and stops them.

NARRATOR: This is the second kind of love. The Greek word is *eros*. It's the love between… Well, you saw for yourself.

Agape

Object needed: *Acetate with picture of Jesus on the cross.*

This is the third type of love. It's called *agape* love. It's the love that keeps loving no matter what. It's very different from the rest.

> If I love with *philia* love and my friend is horrible to me, I will stop loving them.
> If I love with *eros* love and my girlfriend is horrible to me, I will stop loving her.
> If I love with *agape* love and you are horrible to me, I will keep on loving you.

The best example is this *(display acetate)*:

Two thousand years ago Jesus was nailed to a cross for no reason at all. He had never done a thing wrong. While he hung there, the sins of the entire world, the wrong things anyone had ever done, were placed on him. His hands were pierced with nails, as were his feet. He had long thorns stuck into his head. He was whipped with a whip made of ropes with metal and bones stuck on.

And, in spite of this, Jesus still loved the people who did it. Who did it? We did. It was because of the wrong things that we had done that Jesus had to die. Jesus loved with a special love, a love called *agape* love. No matter what happened Jesus kept on loving.

Jesus wants us to have this sort of love; a love which doesn't just love the people we like or the people who are kind to us, the sort of love that loves everyone; the sort of love that even loves our enemies.

● STORY – Olle And The Troll

(Today's story comes from Norway.)

Olle had never seen a troll. He was only five years old.

'Trolls are ugly!' said his mother. 'They have noses like turnips and eyebrows like blackberry bushes.'

'They are scary!' said his father. 'Their mouths are like caves with huge gleaming teeth.'

'Trolls are dangerous!' said his parents together. 'They put our best goats into sacks and took them away with them to the mountains. You must be careful of trolls, or they will put you into a black bag and take you to the mountains as well.'

Olle had never seen a troll but, if he did, he knew exactly what he would do. He would take the sword that he had made by nailing two pieces of wood together and he would cut the nasty thing to pieces. 'I'll chop him to pieces,' boasted Olle. 'No trolls had better show their faces around here.'

'You'll do no such thing,' commanded his father. 'If you see a troll, you are to call for help and keep the front door locked.'

Olle had never seen a troll. He was only five years old. He had never seen a troll, but the troll of the great mountain had seen him and decided one day to stuff him in his sack and take him back to the mountain. So he waited for Olle's parents to start their day's work, then he tramped down the big mountain to Olle's house.

The troll disguised himself. He pulled a hood over his head, picked up a stick and pretended to limp. When he arrived at Olle's front door he knocked on it and called out in a croaky voice, 'Hello, I'm an old man and I'm lost. Can you come and help me?'

Olle looked out of the window. Olle had never seen a troll but he was sure that they wouldn't look like this. This was an old man with a limp. He shouted, 'I can't open the door. The troll from the mountain might put me into a sack and take me back to troll mountain if I open the door. He's already taken our goats.'

'Maybe I can help,' replied the disguised troll. 'I've seen some goats on the mountain. I could take you there.'

'But that's where the troll lives,' replied Olle. 'Not that I'm scared, I've got my sword.'

'Well, come on then,' retorted the disguised troll.

Olle was convinced. He came out of the door and followed the troll up the mountain, stopping only to butter a piece of bread. Olle had never seen a troll, even though he was walking up the mountain with one. He was only five years old.

Olle decided to stop and eat some of his bread. He offered the troll some but, as everyone knows (except Olle), if a troll accepts food from you, he can't harm you. The troll refused. He was looking forward to eating Olle. Olle continued to offer the bread to the troll. He really was a very kind and loving five year old.

The troll smiled. 'What if I wasn't a nice old man, but really a troll?'

Olle smiled. 'Don't be silly. You're a kind old man who's helping me to find my goats.'

The troll was so impressed with himself and his disguise that he began to laugh out loud. Soon he would be ready to eat Olle. But Olle, seeing the troll's mouth open wide in laughter, thought it would be a great opportunity to share his lunch with him and tossed some bread into his mouth. The troll coughed and spluttered but swallowed the bread. And, as everyone knows (except Olle), if a troll takes food from you, they can't harm you.

The troll was really upset. But what could he do? He knew the rules. He was so sad that he took Olle to the goats and helped him take them home again. Olle's parents were so pleased to see Olle and their goats that they threw a great celebration.

Olle had shown love – even to a troll. And because he showed nothing but love, even to those who wanted to hurt him, everything turned out for the best. For his part Olle was very disappointed. He had been to the top of Troll Mountain and not seen a troll (so he thought). Then again, he was still only five years old.

2 Joy

	Programme	Item
Section 1	**Welcome**	
	Rules	
	Prayer	
	Praise	
	Game 1	Pear(fect) Meal
	Praise (x2)	
	Fun Item (2)	
	Game 2	Pear(fect) Man/Woman
	Fun Item	
	Bible Text	Galatians 5:22–23
	Announcements	
	Interview	
	Worship (x2)	
Section 2	**Bible Lesson**	The Cross
Preaching	**Illustration 1**	Roller-coaster Emotions
Time	**Illustration 2**	Things That Make Us Happy
	Illustration 3	God's Happiness See-Saw
	Story	The Skaters
	Prayer	

 **Overview** When God makes us happy, it's different from the emotion we call happiness. God's happiness elevates itself above feelings. It makes us happy even in the tough times.

games

Preaching Time

Game 1

Pear(fect) Meal

PREPARATION	Make up some pear and place it in a dish. Do this for each team. You will also need three spoons and bibs.
PLAYERS	Two players from each team.
SET-UP	One player wears the bib and sits on a seat with the plate of mashed pear. The other player kneels behind the chair with the spoon.
OBJECT	To feed as much pear to the player with the bib as possible.
WINNING	The team that eats the most pear in three minutes wins.

Game 2

Pear(fect) Man/Woman

PREPARATION	Some pickles, cocktail sticks, buttons; lots of other bits and pieces. Six pears.
PLAYERS	Two players from each team.
SET-UP	The six players stand behind tables, facing the audience.
OBJECT	When someone shouts go, they must (using the various food items, and bits and pieces) make the most pear(fect) man/woman pear.
WINNING	The best pear man/woman after two minutes wins.

FRUIT

Today's fruit is **pear**, representing God's gift of happiness (for summary see end of part nine, 'Self-control').

 **THE CROSS**

BIBLE LESSON

'God's Spirit makes us loving, happy, peaceful, patient, kind, good, faithful, gentle, and self-controlled.'
(Galatians 5:22–23)

There is an amazing verse in the Bible. It says, 'for the happiness to come, Jesus endured the cross'. *(Display the acetate of the Crucifixion from the last lesson.)*

It's amazing how anyone could think about happiness while they were being crucified.

There's another amazing verse. It says, 'God's happiness makes us strong.'

You see, the happiness God gives us is nothing to do with the way we feel. God wants us to be happy inside even when everything is going wrong: when our teacher shouts at us; when we have toothache; when our team is coming last; when we're grounded for being naughty.

It doesn't seem possible to be happy when all that stuff is happening, does it? But God wants us to have a happiness that is deep inside. It's the happiness that comes from knowing that, whatever happens, God loves us and one day we'll be in heaven with him.

 **Illustration 1**

Roller-coaster Emotions

Object needed: *Picture of a roller-coaster.*

Who's ever been on one of these? *(Show the picture of the roller-coaster. Then invite someone who has to come and describe the experience. You're looking for lots of ups and downs to be mentioned.)*

Some of us have feelings that are just like that roller-coaster. One day you're happy, you feel up; the next you're sad, you feel down. One minute happy, the next sad: feelings that just go up and down.

The happiness God gives us should not be like that. We should have this happiness inside, no matter what we feel outside.

Things That Make Us Happy

Objects needed: *A fairly large piece of paper and a marker pen.*

Divide the paper up as follows:

Things that make us feel happy	Things that make us feel sad

Let me have some ideas of things which make you feel happy and which make you feel sad.

What we need to learn is that, even when we are not doing the things in the happy column, God still wants to give us his happiness inside.

The happiness God gives is stronger than our feelings. We may not feel happy but inside we can know God's happiness.

God's Happiness See-Saw

Object needed: *A plank of wood with nails in it and some pieces of paper listing some of the things from the 'Things which make me sad' column above. Also, another piece of paper with the words, 'God loves us very much, died on the cross for us and one day we'll be with him in heaven' written on it.*

Construct a pivot for the plank or ask someone to hold the plank at the central point. Begin to place the sad labels onto the see-saw, so you have this effect:

The sad things we do affect us. They try and stop this happiness which we have inside. Sad feelings are very strong feelings. But we must always remember this: *(Hang on the other text… 'God loves us…')*

The see-saw now swings the other way. If we can keep reminding ourselves of this, the sad feelings will always lose out to the happiness God has placed inside. And, if we keep reminding ourselves of the happiness God has placed inside, it will eventually shine out and we'll be happy all through. We will have happy feelings coming from the inside out.

● STORY – The Skaters

Today's story is a modern tale from England.

Once upon a time there was a magical land where the oddest creatures you have ever seen lived. They were called the Skaters. They had thin bodies, long dangly legs, crash helmets in various colours on their round heads and pads the same colour as their crash helmets on their arms and legs. Now all that sounds strange enough, but the weirdest part of all was that instead of feet they had wheels which meant they could travel very fast and do all sorts of marvellous tricks.

But no one was travelling around very fast or doing all sorts of marvellous tricks today! In fact, no one had been travelling around and doing marvellous tricks for the past year! An evil man had played a trick on the Skaters and taken all their cans of oil away. This meant that when it rained the Skaters' wheels began to rust until at last the Skaters couldn't move at all. Then, to upset the Skaters even more, the man, whose name was Evendoo, placed the cans of oil just metres away from the Skaters. They could see the oil they needed, but could never actually reach it.

People didn't come to the Skaters' land very often and those who did were usually friends of Evendoo and did nothing to help the Skaters. So, there they had stood, extremely miserable, for a whole year. They would probably still be there now if a friendly man named Billy Bearing had not turned up. Billy was very unusual: he wore tartan trousers, had bright red hair and spoke with a strong Scottish accent. But the most amazing thing about Billy was the huge smile he wore on his face. His entire face seemed to shine. Billy was happy on the inside and this happiness shone out. Billy was a Christian of course – you don't get this sort of thing otherwise.

Billy took one look at the Skaters and knew what to do. He reached for a can of oil and began squirting. 'Och! A wee bit of oil here and a wee bit there and they'll be as good as new.'

Before long all the Skaters were moving very fast and doing marvellous tricks again. They were so happy they just couldn't stop themselves. Billy became an instant hero and was presented with his very own skateboard. But, after falling on his bottom several times, he decided, 'Och! This skating lark is no' for me. I'll stick to walking, if you don't mind.'

The Skaters were overjoyed at being able to skate again and it wasn't long before their cries of fun reached the ugly castle on the hill where Evendoo lived. He looked out of his window and saw the Skaters going very fast and doing marvellous tricks, and he was furious. He grabbed his bag of special stones that one of his evil friends had found for him and set off to sort out whoever had released the Skaters from his nastiness.

Evendoo walked into the middle of the Skaters' town and shouted, 'Who did this? Who oiled you? Who did it?'

The Skaters slammed on their brakes and looked at Evendoo. Some began to shake; others began to cry (but soon stopped for fear of rusting their wheels again); others looked at the floor and tried not to look at Evendoo's piercing eyes. The Skaters knew how evil and nasty Evendoo could be.

'Who did this?' Evendoo demanded.

'Och! I think you'll be looking for me mister. Nice to meet you. I'm Billy Bearing.'

Evendoo spun round and turned his piercing eyes on Billy. He expected Billy to be afraid, maybe even to run away, but instead, Billy reached out his hand and said, 'Nice to meet you, sir!'

Evendoo just stared. Billy smiled and Evendoo was sure he was glowing with happiness.

'Well, I'll teach you to meddle in my affairs,' said Evendoo as he pulled a special stone out of his bag.

He lifted the stone but Billy smiled and said, 'Och! You don't want to be doing that sir. It will nay work.'

Evendoo didn't listen. He grabbed the stone that would make Billy cry for a month, threw it at Billy and waited. As Evendoo watched, tiny little flowers floated down around Billy. Evendoo gasped.

Evendoo tried another. This one would make Billy feel as sad as it was possible to feel. But instead, a huge box of chocolates appeared in Billy's hand. The happiness inside Billy was protecting him.

Finally Evendoo went for his worst magic. This would make Billy think that all his relatives had died; that all the people he knew were ill; and that his pets had all run away. This was surely going to get Billy. Just for good measure, Evendoo grabbed another stone as well. This one would turn Billy into a wobbling jelly.

Evendoo threw the stones. There was a huge explosion and where Billy had been there now stood a big red Jelly. Evendoo began to dance and shout and celebrate. The Skaters began to cry, even though their wheels would rust. Evendoo was delighted. But then the jelly began to change shape. Something was happening. Billy's happiness wasn't just on the outside. It was all through him. He was full of happiness; he knew that Jesus loved him; he knew how much Jesus had done for him. The jelly exploded and there stood Billy. He began to laugh. Evendoo hated laughter especially when it came from happiness inside, the happiness he knew King Jesus was giving Billy.

Evendoo turned and ran. He knew he was no match for real happiness.

Billy had happiness inside, the type only Jesus can give, the happiness that isn't about how we feel. Eventually Billy left the Skaters and set off again. I don't know where. The Skaters, well, they lived happily ever after, going very fast and doing marvellous tricks.

3 Peace

	Programme	Item
Section 1	Welcome	
	Rules	
	Prayer	
	Praise	
	Game 1	Grape Expectations
	Praise (x2)	
	Fun Item (2)	
	Game 2	The Grape Wall Of Cupland
	Fun Item	
	Bible Text	Galatians 5:22–23
	Announcements	
	Interview	
	Worship (x2)	
Section 2	Bible Lesson	The Storm
Preaching	Illustration 1	War And Peace
Time	Illustration 2	Peace And Quiet
	Illustration 3	God's Peace
	Story	The Wind In The Willows
	Prayer	

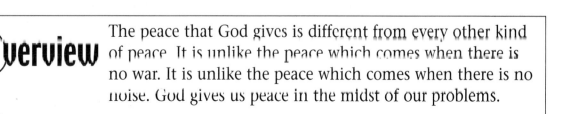

Overview The peace that God gives is different from every other kind of peace. It is unlike the peace which comes when there is no war. It is unlike the peace which comes when there is no noise. God gives us peace in the midst of our problems.

games

PreachingTime

Game 1

Grape Expectations

PREPARATION	A bucket and a bunch of grapes for each team.
PLAYERS	Five players from each team.
SET-UP	The players line up in relay formation at A. The buckets are placed at B.
OBJECT	The first person runs from A with a grape to a point two metres in front of the buckets. They throw the grape at their bucket and return to A. Player two repeats the process and so on.
WINNING	The team that gets the most grapes in the bucket after three minutes wins.

Game 2

The Grape Wall Of Cupland

PREPARATION	Three piles of paper cups, or old pop cans set up in pyramid fashion on tables at B and a bunch of grapes for each team.
PLAYERS	Five players from each team.
SET-UP	The players line up in relay formation at A.
OBJECT	The first person runs from A with a grape to a point two metres in front of the pyramids. They throw the grape at their pyramid and return to B. Player two then runs.
WINNING	The team that clears their pyramid off the table, or clears the most after five minutes, wins.

FRUIT

Today's fruit is **grape**, representing God's gift of peace (for summary see end of part nine, 'Self-control').

BIBLE LESSON **THE STORM**

'God's Spirit makes us loving, happy, peaceful, patient, kind, good, faithful, gentle, and self-controlled.'
(Galatians 5:22–23)

One day Jesus and his disciples got into a boat and he said, 'Let's cross the lake.' They started out and, while they were sailing across, he went to sleep. Suddenly a storm struck the lake and the boat started sinking. They were in danger so they went to Jesus and woke him up. 'Master, Master! We are about to drown!'

Jesus got up and ordered the wind and waves to stop. They obeyed him and everything was calm. Then Jesus asked the disciples, 'Don't you have any faith?'

They were frightened and amazed. They said to each other, 'Who is this? He can give orders to the wind and waves and they obey him.' The disciples were amazed. They hadn't yet learnt that Jesus is the only one who can bring calm to the storm; the only one who can bring peace into chaos.

We have lots of different ideas about peace. Let's look at three.

Call up three volunteers and hand them pieces of card with 'War and Peace', 'Peace and Quiet' and 'God's Peace' written on them.

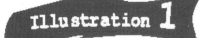

War And Peace

Objects needed: *An army hat, some combat clothes.*

Take the first piece of card, send the child back to their seat and continue.

In many different parts of the world right now wars are being fought, guns are being fired, innocent people are being killed or hurt. We are fortunate to live in peace. It's very important that we all pray for the innocent who are being killed.

But, as a famous man called Martin Luther King Junior once said, 'Peace is more than the absence of war.' We may not be at war but many people still don't feel at peace. Peace comes from inside. Peace is more than the absence of war.

Peace And Quiet

Object needed: *A drum or tambourine or loud horn*

Someone walks onto the stage banging a drum, or shaking a tambourine and singing in their loudest voice, 'I love noise, I love riot, I love the sound of the big bass drum.' (If you don't know the tune, make it up.)

Take the second piece of card. Send the child back to their seat. The drummer continues in the background.

Some people think that peace is when there is... *(Tap the drummer on the shoulder.)* 'Excuse me! I'm trying to talk.' *(The drummer stops.)* That's much better. Now, where was I? Yes, some people think that peace is when there is no noise. But even when it's very quiet, people don't feel peace inside. That's where real peace needs to be – inside.

The drummer walks off singing his song.

God's Peace

Take the third piece of card. Send the child back to their seat and continue.

There are lots of things that stop us feeling peace inside. Let me tell you a poem about some of them.

Whatif

Last night while I lay thinking here.
Some Whatifs crawled inside my ear
And pranced and partied all night long
and sang their same old Whatif song:

Whatif I'm dumb in school?
Whatif they've closed the swimming pool?
Whatif I get beat up?
Whatif there's poison in my cup?
Whatif I flunk the test?
Whatif green hair grows on my chest?
Whatif nobody likes me?
Whatif a bolt of lightning strikes me?
Whatif I don't grow taller?
Whatif my head starts getting smaller?
Whatif the wind tears up my kite?
Whatif they start a war?
Whatif my parents get divorced?
Whatif the bus is late?
Whatif my teeth don't grow in straight?
Whatif I tear my pants?
Whatif I never learn to dance?

Everything seems swell, and then
The night time Whatifs strike again!

(Quoted from *Helping Children Handle Stress*
– Author unknown)

But God talks about peace that is beyond understanding. Now that sounds complicated so let me explain. If I was being picked on in school by some bullies I should feel worried. But, if we spend time with King Jesus by praying and tell him about it, we can feel peace inside. Peace which is beyond understanding is peace that we get when we think we shouldn't be feeling peace.

Perhaps mum and dad are arguing or for one reason or another a lot of people are shouting at each other in your house, but it's still possible to feel God's peace, if we just go to him and pray and ask him to give us his peace.

Maybe the story will help you understand it a bit more. It's a story about being in the presence of God and feeling the peace that he can bring.

● STORY – The Wind In The Willows

Today's story is from a very famous English story. It comes from a chapter entitled 'The Piper at the Gates of Dawn'.

Slowly, but with no doubt or hesitation whatever, and in something of a solemn expectancy, the two animals passed through the broken, tumultuous water and moored their boat at the flowery margin of the island. In silence they landed, and pushed through the blossom and scented herbage and undergrowth that led up to the level ground, till they stood on a little lawn of a marvellous green, set round with Nature's own orchard-trees – crab-apple, wild cherry, and sloe.

'This is the place of my song-dream, the place the music played to me,' whispered the Rat, as if in a trance, 'Here, in this holy place, here if anywhere, surely we shall find Him!'

Then suddenly Mole felt a great Awe fall upon him, an awe that turned his muscles to water, bowed his head, and rooted his feet to the ground. It was no panic terror – indeed he felt wonderfully at peace and happy – but it was an awe that smote and held him and, without seeing, he knew it could only mean that some august Presence was very, very near. With difficulty he turned to look for his friend, and saw him at his side cowed, stricken, and trembling violently. And still there was utter silence in the populous bird-haunted branches around them; and still the light grew and grew…

'Rat!' he found breath to whisper, shaking. 'Are you afraid?'

'Afraid?' murmured the Rat, his eyes shining with unutterable love. 'Afraid! Of Him? O, never, never! And yet – and yet – O Mole, I am afraid!'

Then the two animals, crouching to the earth, bowed their heads and did worship.

(From Kenneth Grahame:
The Wind in the Willows.)

4 Patience

	Programme	Item
Section 1	Welcome	
	Rules	
	Prayer	
	Praise	
	Game 1	Orange Dribble
	Praise (x2)	
	Fun Item (2)	
	Game 2	Orange Bowls
	Fun Item	
	Bible Text	Galatians 5:22–23
	Announcements	
	Interview	
	Worship (x2)	
Section 2	Bible Lesson	David
Preaching	Illustration 1	Baby
Time	Illustration 2	Coming Back
	Illustration 3	Michael J. Jordan
	Story	Tortoise Brings Food
	Prayer	

Overview Most of us want everything now. We don't want to wait. But God's dealings with us require patience. He takes us step by step.

Game 1

Orange Dribble

PREPARATION	An orange for each team.
PLAYERS	Five players from each team.
SET-UP	The players remove their shoes and line up at A in relay formation.
OBJECT	The first player dribbles the orange from A to B and back. The next player then repeats the process.
WINNING	The team that finishes first and sits down wins.

Game 2

Orange Bowls

PREPARATION	Five oranges for each team marked with the team colour, a tennis ball.
PLAYERS	Five players from each team.
SET-UP	The players line up in relay formation at A. The tennis ball is placed five metres beyond point B.
OBJECT	The first person runs from A to B with an orange. At B they bowl the orange underarm to try and land it as close to the tennis ball as possible. They return to A and player two repeats the process.
WINNING	The team with the orange closest to the tennis ball wins.

FRUIT

Today's fruit is **orange**, representing God's gift of patience (for summary see end of part nine, 'Self-control').

 **DAVID**

'God's Spirit makes us loving, happy, peaceful, patient, kind, good, faithful, gentle, and self-controlled.'
(Galatians 5:22–23)

In an earlier series we talked of a man called David. Samuel came to him when he was a young man and poured a very special oil over him to show that one day he would be king.

David could not have been king there and then, even though he knew God had chosen him. God had to teach him many lessons before he was ready to be king. This is the way that God deals with us. He teaches us and trains us as we follow him, as we pray to him and as we learn to read the Bible, God's book. And the more we learn the more God trusts us with.

David had to learn to forgive those who were bad to him, to overcome enemies, to lead a gang of outlaws, and always do the right thing. He had to learn all these things before God made him king, so David also had to learn to be patient.

We too have to learn to be patient. God gives us different things to do so that we may learn more about him. He teaches us all the time to trust him and be patient. God won't give us things to do that we aren't ready for.

In our world today there are people whom God has chosen to stand in front of tens and hundreds of thousands to speak about him. But God didn't trust them to do that until they showed that they could be trusted with five people, or twenty people. They had to be patient.

We must learn to be patient, and learn to trust God.

Baby

Object needed: *A photograph of a toddler (preferably a relation).*

This is a picture of my daughter *(substitute your relationship with the person in the photograph).* In the photograph she's a toddler. She's just learned to walk and it took some time. She had to have a lot of patience. We take being able to walk for granted but she was only a year old and just couldn't get the hang of it.

It was the funniest thing to watch. She would take a couple of steps, wobble and fall backwards onto her bottom. It was the most amazing thing. Now I know why nappies are so thick. It's so that when the babies fall backwards, they don't hurt themselves but just bounce. And then she would sit there and giggle. You'd think she'd be upset because she'd just fallen over, but no, she just giggled. I think it was bouncing on her nappy that made her laugh.

You would not believe what she'd do next. She'd get back up and try again. And she would do that for most of the day: walk, wobble, fall, bounce on her nappy, giggle and start again. Amazing, hey?

She fell a lot, but she had to learn to be patient. She got the hang of it eventually. If she had stopped trying because she had no patience, she'd be your age and still crawling. But she knew better than that. She kept trying and she was patient.

And we learn by being patient. God wants to teach us more and more but we won't learn it all today. We must be patient.

Coming Back

Object needed: *A Bible.*

In the Bible there's a book called Acts. In chapter 1 Jesus says goodbye to his disciples and goes back to heaven. Let me read it to you. *(Read Acts 1:9–11.)*

In this part of the Bible, two men or, more probably, two angels appear to the disciples and promise them that Jesus is definitely coming back to earth. This was a promise made nearly 2,000 years ago and Christians still believe that Jesus will return very soon.

But only a few years after Jesus made this promise lots of Christians were becoming impatient and wanted to know why Jesus had not come back yet. Paul had to write a letter to explain that Jesus is coming again, but nobody knows when. He told the people to be patient but to make sure they were ready for when Jesus came back.

We too need to be patient because Jesus is coming back to this earth. But we must also make sure that we are ready; that we've asked Jesus to forgive our sins, the wrong things we've done; and that we're living as Christians should.

Michael J. Jordan

Object needed: *Michael Jordan video (available from most stores including Woolworths, Tesco, Safeway, HMV). If you prefer to use football as the analogy, footage from Ronaldo the Brazilian is also available at these stores.*

Let me show you some video shots of one of my heroes. *(Play an extract from the video.)*

Michael Jordan is probably the best basketball player in the entire world. He can win games almost by himself. He can get the ball into the basket from almost anywhere on court. He has won many championships, received many awards and earns millions of pounds each year in sponsorship deals. He really is a great player.

Michael Jordan hasn't always been a great basketball player. It took years of practice, years of standing in his garden throwing the basketball through the hoop, years of playing with his friends in nearby basketball courts. It took hours of practice every week when he was in college. But Michael was patient, he kept going. He never stopped practising. He knew that one day he would be the best if he was patient.

God wants to do amazing things in our lives. Let's learn to be patient and see what God can do through us.

● STORY – Tortoise Brings Food

Today's story comes from Africa.

The sun was hot, the earth was dry. There had been no rain for many months. There was no food. The animals were very hungry.

Lion, the king of the beasts, called his friends together under a tall, gnarled tree. 'The legends say that this tree is a special tree and will give us all the food we need if we can just say it's secret name. But there is only one person who knows that name, the old man who lives at the top of the mountain.'

'Then we must go at once,' said Elephant, 'as quickly as we can, before we all starve to death.'

'I'll go,' said Tortoise slowly.

They all stared at him. 'Don't be so silly,' roared Lion. 'You can't go. You're too slow and we'll all starve to death. No, we must send Hare. He will be back in no time.'

Hare hurried up the side of the mountain, his long ears pulled back in the wind. He leapt, he scampered, he raced until very soon he was standing in front of the old man. 'Please,' said Hare, 'tell me the name of the special tree.'

The old man looked, the old man listened and then he said, 'Worn-del-hay-ma.'

Hare said, 'Thank you,' and then he hurried back down the mountain. He leapt, he scampered, he raced all the time saying the word, 'Worn-del-hay-ma'.

But just as he reached the bottom of the mountain, he ran straight into a huge anthill and knocked himself silly. By the time he reached the rest of the animals he had forgotten the special word.

'We will have to send someone else,' said Lion.

'I'll go,' said Tortoise slowly.

This time they all laughed at him.

'Don't be so silly,' roared Lion, 'You can't go. You're too slow and we'll all starve to death. No, we must send Elephant. He will be back in no time.'

Elephant hurried up the side of the mountain, his long trunk swinging back and forth. He stamped and he tramped and he marched until very soon he was standing in front of the old man. 'Please,' said Elephant, 'tell me the name of the special tree.'

The old man looked, the old man listened and then he said, 'I have already given the name to Hare, but I suppose I can tell you. The name is Worn-del-hay-ma.'

Elephant said, 'Thank you,' and then he hurried back down the mountain. He stamped and he marched, all the time saying the word 'Worn-del-hay-ma'.

But just as he reached the bottom of the mountain, he ran straight into a huge anthill and knocked himself silly. By the time he reached the rest of the animals he had forgotten the special word.

'This is ridiculous,' said Lion. 'We will have to send someone else.'

'I'll go,' said Tortoise slowly.

They all sighed. 'Don't be so silly,' roared Lion, 'I will go myself.'

Lion hurried up the side of the mountain, his mane blowing in the wind. He leapt, he charged, he pounced until very soon he was standing in front of the old man. 'Please,' said Lion, 'tell me the name of the special tree.'

The old man looked, the old man listened and then he said, 'I have told Hare and I have told Elephant but I will tell you as well. It is Worn-del-hay-ma.'

Lion said, 'Thank you,' and then he hurried back down the mountain. He leapt, he pounced, he charged, all the time saying the word, 'Worn-del-hay-ma'.

But just as he reached the bottom of the mountain Lion ran straight into a huge anthill and knocked himself silly. By the time he reached the rest of the animals he had forgotten the special word.

'What will we do now?' chorused the animals together.

'I'll go,' said Tortoise slowly.

Nobody said a word. Tortoise set off. He made his way up the mountain. He never hurried, for that is not the tortoise way. He waddled up the side of the mountain. Eventually he stood in front of the old man. 'Please,' said Tortoise, 'tell me the name of the special tree.'

The old man looked angry, the old man listened and then he said, 'I have already told Hare and Elephant and Lion. I will tell you but, if you forget, I will not tell anyone else. The word is Worn-del-hay-ma.'

Tortoise said, 'Thank you. I will not forget.' Then he waddled back down the mountain. He walked slowly around the huge anthill and joined the rest of the animals.

All the animals looked very anxious. Tortoise spoke slowly, 'The word is Worn-del-hay-ma. It is not such a hard word really.'

The tree delivered all the food they needed and Tortoise became a hero. Tortoise had saved everyone by being patient. Sometimes we achieve more with patience than we do by rushing about.

 **Kindness**

	Programme	**Item**
Section 1	Welcome	
	Rules	
	Prayer	
	Praise	
	Game 1	Lemon Squeezes
	Praise (x2)	
	Fun Item (2)	
	Game 2	Lemon Passes
	Fun Item	
	Bible Text	Galatians 5:22–23
	Announcements	
	Interview	
	Worship (x2)	
Section 2	Bible Lesson	The Woman Caught In The Act Of Sin
Preaching	Illustration 1	When?
Time	Illustration 2	Who?
	Illustration 3	Why?
	Story	The Happy Prince
	Prayer	

**verview** We are all kind sometimes; we are all kind when it suits us. This is not the fruit of the Spirit called kindness. The kindness that comes from the Spirit is consistent; it enables us always to be kind to those who need our kindness.

games

Game 1

Lemon Squeezes

PREPARATION	A lemon cut into two and a glass for each team.
PLAYERS	Six players from each team.
SET-UP	The players line up in relay formation at A with the front person holding the lemon halves. The glasses are placed at B.
OBJECT	The first player runs from A to B, squeezes as much juice as they can into the glass in fifteen seconds and then returns to A where the next player repeats the process.
WINNING	The team with the fullest glass after all the players have run wins.

Game 2

Lemon Passes

PREPARATION	One lemon for each team.
PLAYERS	Five players from each team. (You may need to choose only girls!)
SET-UP	The five players stand side by side. The first player has the lemon tucked under their chin.
OBJECT	The first person passes the lemon from their chin to the next player without using their hands or the hands of the next player. This repeats until the lemon reaches the end.
WINNING	The team whose lemon reaches the end first wins. If the lemon drops, it must go back to the start.

Preaching Time

FRUIT

Today's fruit is **lemon**, representing God's gift of kindness (for summary see end of part nine, 'Self-control').

BIBLE LESSON

THE WOMAN CAUGHT IN THE ACT OF SIN

'God's Spirit makes us loving, happy, peaceful, patient, kind, good, faithful, gentle, and self-controlled.' (Galatians 5:22–23)

Note: this passage was also used – but with a different emphasis – in the first section, 'Encounters with the King'.

In our series called 'Encounters with the King' we talked about some of the people Jesus met. Today we're going to remind ourselves of one of them: the woman who was caught in the act of sin.

One day Jesus was at the temple when a commotion erupted outside. The Pharisees (the religious rulers in Jerusalem) burst into the temple and threw a young woman to the ground. She was crying and clearly very upset.

They said, 'We've caught this woman doing wrong things. She was sinning. What shall we do to her? Our law says we should throw stones at her until she's dead. What do you say?'

They were trying to trap Jesus. Instead of answering their question, he knelt down and began writing in the sand.

'What shall we do?' they demanded.

Jesus looked at the men and said, 'If any one of you has never done anything wrong, then let him throw the first stone.'

The Pharisees looked at each other. They didn't know what to do. They began to walk away feeling embarrassed. They knew that they had all done things wrong.

When all the men had left, Jesus looked at the woman. She was still very upset. 'Where are the men who accused you?' he asked.

'They have all gone,' she replied.

'Well, if not one of them accuses you, then neither do I. Now go and don't sin any more.'

The woman had been doing wrong. Jesus could have asked that she be punished. But Jesus showed nothing but kindness.

When?

A person dressed up as an old lady with a stick enters and stands at the edge of a pretend road. Toby Christian enters.

LADY:	Hello, love. Can you help me across the road?
TOBY:	Of course. *Toby helps the old lady across the road.*
NARRATOR:	Toby is showing 'kindness', one of the fruits of the Spirit. But watch what happens the following day.
LADY:	Hello, love. Can you help me across the road? I can't see too well. I need someone to help me.
TOBY:	But I'll be late for my girlfriend. She hates it when I'm late.
LADY:	Please help me.
NARRATOR:	If we only show kindness when it suits us, that's not the fruit of the Spirit. We have to be 'consistent'. That's a big word. It means 'all the time'. We must be kind all the time. What will Toby do?
TOBY:	But my girlfriend will go crazy. I'm supposed to be going shopping.
LADY:	But it's a long way across this road.
TOBY:	OK! I'll help.
NARRATOR:	Well done, Toby. Let's be kind all the time.

Who?

Objects needed: *A fairly large piece of paper and a marker pen.*

Divide the paper up as follows:

People to be kind to	People not to be kind to
❖ John	❖ Harry
❖ Simon	

Most people think like this. They have in their minds two groups of people: one group to be kind to and another not to be kind to. John is my friend. Yes, I'll be kind to him. Simon is my friend. Yes, I'll be kind to him. Harry tripped me up in the playground. I'm not being his friend. And this is the way we go on. When we are kind in this way, it is not the fruit of the Spirit called kindness. Anyone can be kind to the people who are kind to them.

- Think about all the people who are kind to you. It's easy to be kind to them.
- Think about all the people who are not kind to you. We still need to be kind to them.

Why?

Object needed: *The picture of Jesus on the cross from the earlier lessons.*

Jesus was very different. He was kind to everyone. He had the fruit of the Spirit called kindness. Some people loved Jesus very much and Jesus in return was kind to these people. But some people were horrible to Jesus. Some people called him names and wanted to kill him. Jesus was kind to these people as well. He taught us that we should love even our enemies. Jesus was always kind.

In fact, Jesus was even kind to the people who crucified him. Can you imagine that? He was even kind to the people who nailed him to a cross. He asked his Father to forgive them. Now that's the fruit of the Spirit called kindness.

The main reason that we need to have the fruit of the Spirit called kindness is that Jesus had it. Jesus was kind all the time. And we too must learn to be like Jesus and learn to be kind all the time.

● STORY – The Happy Prince

Today's story comes from Ireland.

High above the city on a tall column stood the statue of the Happy Prince. Now this wasn't any ordinary statue. His eyes were made of bright blue sapphires and at his side he wore a sword with a bright red ruby at its hilt. From the bottom of his feet to the top of his head he was covered with the finest gold. And there he stood looking over the city.

Far away a swallow decided it was time to fly south for the winter. He knew that if he didn't leave soon winter would come and he would die. So the swallow set off. After several hours of flying it began to get dark and the swallow had to find somewhere to spend the night.

By this time he was high above the city. Far below he could see the statue of the Happy Prince. 'That'll make a fine bedroom,' he thought. 'It will be nice to sleep in a bedroom with golden walls high above a city.' The swallow flew down, positioned himself at the feet of the prince, pulled his wing over his head and dropped off to sleep.

A few minutes later he felt drip, drip, drip on his head. 'Oh, no!' he thought. 'Winter has come already and it's raining.' As the swallow looked up, the sky was clear. There wasn't a cloud to be seen, just a bright autumn moon.

He lowered his head, pulled his wing over it and tried to go to sleep again. A few minutes later he felt drip, drip, drip on his head.

'What is going on?' He looked up, but again the sky was clear. Then he looked into the face of the Prince and there, running from his eyes, were the biggest tears you have ever seen.

'Who are you?' asked the swallow, being a very inquisitive little bird.

'I'm the Happy Prince,' the prince replied.

'Well, you don't look very happy. Why are you crying?' the swallow wanted to know.

'You see,' the prince began, 'when I was alive and had a heart of flesh instead of the heart of lead which I now have, I lived in the finest castle. The walls were of the finest gold. The floor was covered with the loveliest rugs and it was always cosy and warm. I wore the finest clothes and always had the best food to eat. And I thought everyone else was exactly the same. I thought everyone had fine homes, lovely clothes and plenty of food to eat. But now that I can see the entire city, I know that isn't true. Only today I looked out over the city and saw a little boy who is very ill. He was asking his mother for medicine to make him better, but she didn't have any money to buy medicine. He asked for something to drink but all she had was water from the river. So tonight the little boy is crying and his mother doesn't know what to do.'

'That's really sad,' said the swallow. 'Is there something I can do to help?'

'Would you help, kind swallow? Would you?'

'Of course. But tomorrow I must fly south or the winter will come and I will die. But, for tonight, what can I do?'

The Prince instructed the sparrow to fly up onto his sword and remove the ruby from its hilt. 'Take it and fly with it to the boy's mother. With it, she will be able to buy lots of medicine.'

The swallow did as he was asked. He flew and dropped off the ruby. The mother picked it up and was very excited. She had never seen a ruby before and knew that she could now buy all the medicine she needed. The swallow flew back to the prince and reported all that had happened. The prince smiled. It was now beginning to get quite cold. But the swallow felt very warm inside.

'Prince, it is too late for me to fly south now, so I will spend one more night with you. But tomorrow I must fly south for the winter.' So the swallow pulled his wing over his head and began to drop off to sleep. Just then he felt drip, drip, drip on his head. 'Now what?' he thought. He looked up and there running from the face of the Happy Prince were great big wet tears.

'Prince, now what's wrong?' asked the swallow.

The prince began to unfold his new story. 'Today I looked over the city and in a little attic room was a young man who was trying to finish a play for the theatre. But, he won't be able to finish it now. It's too cold and he can't afford firewood until he finishes the play. So there he sits shivering in his attic room.'

The swallow really did need to fly south soon, but he was a very kind-hearted bird and so again he offered to help. 'What can I do, prince?'

The prince said, 'Swallow, please fly onto my shoulder and take out one of my sapphire eyes and fly with it to the young man.'

The swallow was horrified. He protested but

eventually gave in and, taking the sapphire, he flew with it to the young man. He dropped the sapphire through a gap in the window and flew off. The young man had no idea where the precious stone had come from but he knew that, with it, he could buy all the firewood he needed and finish his play.

The swallow flew back to the prince. 'Dear prince, I have done what you wanted. But tomorrow I must fly south. It is getting too cold for me now.' With that the swallow pulled his wing over his head and began to drop off to sleep. However, very soon he felt the same old drip, drip, drip on his head. He tried to ignore it but again he felt drip, drip, drip on his head.

He looked up at the prince and shouted, 'Prince, I don't care what's wrong! I'm not helping!' With that he pulled his wing back over his head. But the tears continued: drip, drip, drip, drip, drip, drip…. Eventually the swallow looked up. 'OK, prince. Tell me what's wrong. But I'm not going to help.'

So the prince began. 'Today, dear swallow, I looked over the city and saw a little girl selling matches in the marketplace. She comes there every day to sell her matches. She's an orphan and has no one to look after her, so every night she sleeps on someone's doorstep and every day she sells her matches to get enough money to buy food and to buy more matches. But today she dropped all her matches into the water and now she has no matches to sell and she is trying to sleep but she is very hungry.'

The swallow was nearly crying himself and, although he knew that he should be flying south, he offered to help the prince just one more time.

'Hop onto my shoulder again, dear swallow, and take my remaining sapphire eye to the little girl.'

The swallow really didn't want to take the prince's last eye. But the prince commanded him so he took the eye and flew to the little girl. She was asleep so the swallow placed the sapphire gently in the little girl's hand and flew back to the prince. When she woke up, the little girl was very excited. She could now buy food and more matches and even get somewhere to live. But she didn't know where the gift had come from.

The swallow flew back to the prince and said, 'Prince, now you have no eyes and cannot see the city, so I will stay and be your eyes for ever.'

The prince thanked the swallow and then said to him, 'Now, swallow, fly over all the city and come back and tell me what you see.'

The swallow set off and came back and reported to the prince. 'I have seen many rich people with fine clothes, but I have also seen many poor people who are hungry and have nowhere to live and who are dressed in rags.'

The prince sighed and asked the swallow, 'Swallow, covering my body is the finest gold. Will you take it off piece by piece and fly with it to the people who need it?'

The swallow set to work at once and worked until everyone in the city had money to buy food and houses and nice clothes. But nobody ever knew where the gold came from.

Then winter came. The swallow flew back to the prince and, looking up into the prince's face, he said, 'Prince, it's getting cold now, far too cold. Too cold for me. Goodbye.' And, with that, the little bird fell over and died. At the same time the lead heart inside the prince broke in two. And there they stayed, the prince with the broken heart and the dead bird far above the city. Until one day the Lord Mayor walked down the main street.

'What a fine city,' he thought. 'Everyone has nice houses and plenty of food and they all wear such nice clothes.' He didn't know it was because of the swallow and the prince. Nobody knew.

Then he came to the statue of the prince. He was not impressed. 'Look at that statue, so old and green and mouldy. I'm sure it used to be a nice statue. And what's that? It looks like there's a dead bird up there. We must build a new statue.'

So the Lord Mayor ordered the statue to be pulled down. Workmen came with hammers and smashed it into little pieces until there was hardly anything left.

A workman came to the Lord Mayor and in his hands he held the lead heart of the prince and the dead swallow. 'This is all that's left, Lord Mayor. What shall I do with them?'

The Lord Mayor found the objects disgusting. 'Throw them outside the city onto the rubbish tip,' he ordered.

And that's where they lay until one day God was talking with one of his angels. 'Go to the city and bring back the two most precious things you can find.'

The angel left at once and began his search of the city. 'What can I find?' he wondered. He searched and searched, but he couldn't find anything. Eventually he came to the rubbish tip and from the rubbish tip he took the heart of the prince and a little dead swallow and, with them, he flew back to God.

God looked at the objects and said to the angel, 'You have chosen very well for the most precious things in the city are those who helped others even when they received no thanks.'

And the most precious people in any city are those who help others even when they receive no thanks.

God commanded the bird and the prince to live and so they spent all eternity in God's garden in heaven.

(Adapted from the original story by Oscar Wilde.)

6 Goodness

	Programme	Item
Section 1	**Welcome**	
	Rules	
	Prayer	
	Praise	
	Game 1	Lily The Lime
	Praise (x2)	
	Fun Item (2)	
	Game 2	Sub-Lime
	Fun Item	
	Bible Text	Galatians 5:22–23
	Announcements	
	Interview	
	Worship (x2)	
Section 2	**Bible Lesson**	David Does The Right Thing
Preaching	**Illustration 1**	Holiday Rock
Time	**Illustration 2**	Good Is God
	Illustration 3	Blue Pop
	Story	Antonio The Juggler
	Prayer	

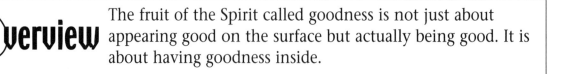

Overview The fruit of the Spirit called goodness is not just about appearing good on the surface but actually being good. It is about having goodness inside.

 games

 PreachingTime

Game 1

Lily The Lime

PREPARATION	You will need several drawing pins, several cocktail sticks, a number of grapes and five limes for each team.
PLAYERS	Two players from each team.
SET-UP	The players line up at A. All the items mentioned above are at B.
OBJECT	The players run together from A to B where they have 45 seconds to build their very own Lily The Lime. When the time is up the players walk Lily back to A for judging.
WINNING	The loveliest Lily wins.

Game 2

Sub-Lime

PREPARATION	Three black bags full of lots of different things including many round things and one lime.
PLAYERS	Two players from each team.
SET-UP	The players line up at A. The bag is at B.
OBJECT	The players run from A to B, search through the black bag until they find the lime, put everything else back into the bag and return to A.
WINNING	The first team back with the lime and sitting down wins.

FRUIT

Today's fruit is **lime**, representing God's gift of goodness (for summary see end of part nine, 'Self-control').

 **BIBLE LESSON**

DAVID DOES THE RIGHT THING

'God's Spirit makes us loving, happy, peaceful, patient, kind, good, faithful, gentle, and self-controlled.' (Galatians 5:22–23)

Note: this passage was also used – with a different emphasis – in the third section, 'The Shepherd Boy Who Became King'.

David was forced to live as an outlaw. Saul was searching for him everywhere.

On one occasion Saul and his army of 3,000 men set up camp in the desert as they searched for David. In the middle of the night David crept into the middle of the camp and into Saul's tent. Saul was fast asleep and so was the man who should have been guarding him.

What was David to do? He was in the tent of the man who had been hunting him for months and had tried to kill him on many occasions.

What would you do? The man is trying to kill you, surely it's OK to kill him?

But David had learnt something very important. Even if others did wrong things to him, he would still do the right thing. Murder was wrong even if the other person was trying to kill him. David had learnt always to do the right thing. David didn't just pretend to be good; he was good.

David took Saul's spear to prove that he had been there and left. In the morning he would return Saul's spear and embarrass the man who was supposed to guard the king.

David always did what was good. Do we always do what is good? Do we always show the fruit of the Spirit called goodness? Or do we do wrong things when things are against us or when we don't feel like doing the right thing?

God could make David great because he always did what was good.

Holiday Rock

Object needed: *A stick of rock (usually available from a seaside resort).*

Here's a stick of rock. You'll notice it has lettering on the top. This one says 'Blackpool' *(or whatever it says)*. The amazing thing is that if I cut the stick of rock in two it still says 'Blackpool'. It has the word 'Blackpool' running right the way through, not just on the surface.

It should be the same with the fruits of the Spirit. We should have them right the way through, not just on top. If you only appear to be good, you're just pretending and you don't really have the fruit of the Spirit called 'goodness'. We must have goodness running right through us. We should be good at all times, wherever we are and whatever we are doing.

Good Is God

Objects needed: *Four letters 'G' 'O' 'O' and 'D' written on four pieces of card.*

Ask four children to stand behind you with a letter each.

It's hard to be good. In fact, since I know most of you, I know that some of you find it almost impossible to be really good, with goodness right inside you.

The Bible says something interesting about this. It says, 'Only God is good.'

Actually, the word God is inside the word Good. Let me show you. *(Ask one of the people holding the 'O' to sit down.)*

Now we have God. It is impossible to be good without God's help. But with God's help, it is possible. We must learn to ask God to make us good, not just on the outside, but right the way through.

Blue Pop

Object needed: *A bottle of blue pop.*

Here is a bottle of blue pop. I know lots of you drink this. I'll try some. *(Drink some pop.)*

Interesting taste. Not nice, just interesting. Some things taste nice and they're not really good for you. Other things taste horrible and they are good for you.

Some things look good on the surface. Some berries are beautiful colours, but actually they are poisonous to eat. Some people are very pretty or very handsome but, when you get to know them, they are quite horrible. It's hard to tell what someone's like from the surface. It's easier with this pop. I can read the list of ingredients. *(Read the list on the side. There should be a lot of E numbers.)*

I can tell from this list that this pop isn't very good for you. If you had a list of ingredients, I wonder if they would be fruits of the Spirit? Or would they be things such as spitefulness, meanness and jealousy? I wonder, if you had a list of ingredients, would one of them be goodness?

● STORY – Antonio The Juggler

Today's story comes from Italy.

You will need juggling balls and a clown mask to help you.

This story happened hundreds of years ago in the little village of Sorrento in Italy. Now in those days Sorrento had hardly anything. It had a market and a church and very little else.

The market was always very busy: people buying things, people selling things. The stall-holders would sell anything and the people would buy anything.

The church was beautiful. It had tall stained-glass windows and, when the sun shone through the windows, wonderful colours glimmered around the great hall. At the front stood a statue of Mary and in front of Mary was a statue of Jesus as a child. The statue showed Jesus as a very sad seven-year-old.

In Sorrento there lived a young boy. His

name was Antonio and when our story begins, he is six. Antonio was an orphan. He had no mother or father and would sleep every night in doorways. He was dressed in rags and had no money. But he was happy and he could do something very special. *(Begin to juggle and then ask the question, 'What do you call this?')*

He would juggle apples and oranges and potatoes. He would juggle tomatoes, pears and even cucumbers. He could juggle anything.

One day a troupe of travelling performers came to Sorrento. Everyone clapped and cheered as first the acrobats stepped forward and did cartwheels and handstands, then other performers came out and sang, and finally a man stepped forward to do some magic tricks.

Antonio thought, 'It must be great to be a performer. This is the life for me.' He went to the leader of the performers and asked to join.

'But we don't need a beggar. Go away,' came the stern reply.

'But I can do something special. I can juggle,' replied Antonio. And that is just what he did.

The leader smiled. 'Not bad. With a bit of practice, you may turn out to be quite good. You may join us, but don't expect to be paid. We will give you one meal a day and the company of the finest performers in Italy.'

Antonio practised long and hard until he became very good. Then one day the lead performer gave him a clown outfit and let him juggle in front of an audience. *(Put the clown mask on a volunteer. He stands beside you and acts the parts.)*

He juggled with sticks, then with plates, then with rings, then with burning torches and finally he threw a red ball into the air, then an orange one, a yellow one, a green one, a blue one and a purple one. 'And now, ladies and gentlemen,' he proclaimed, 'it's time for the sun in the heavens.' And up it went, a big golden ball. All the people cheered and cheered.

Before long Antonio was famous. 'He's the best juggler in all of Italy,' they would say.

He left the performers and began to travel by himself. He would enter a town and very quickly the people would gather around. He juggled with sticks, then with plates, then with rings, then with burning torches and finally he threw a red ball into the air, then an orange ball, a yellow ball, a green ball, a blue ball and a purple ball. 'And now, ladies and gentlemen,' he proclaimed, 'it's time for the sun in the heavens.' And up it went, the big golden ball. All the people cheered and cheered.

He performed in front of dukes and princes,

kings and queens and always did the same thing: first the sticks, then the plates, then the rings, then the burning torches and finally the red, orange, yellow, green, blue and purple balls. 'And now, ladies and gentlemen, the sun in the heavens.' Up would go the golden ball and all the people would cheer. Antonio became very rich and very famous.

One day he sat between two villages eating his lunch in a field. Two priests walked by. 'Sirs, why don't you join me for some lunch?' Antonio called. 'I have plenty.'

'Thank you very much,' the priests replied.

'Where are you going?' Antonio asked.

'We're going throughout Italy spreading the joy of God. Maybe you could come with us?'

Antonio smiled, 'That's good for you. But I'm just a juggler. I go from town to town making people laugh.'

'Maybe it's the same thing,' one of the priests said. 'Maybe, when you bring happiness to people, you bring happiness to God.'

'That may be so,' Antonio smiled. 'But I must be on my way.' With that he collected his things and off he set.

Many years went by, Antonio grew old and times became hard in Italy. Nobody had time for the juggler any more. 'We've seen your tricks before, old man,' they would say. 'Go away.' He went from town to town and no one wanted to see his juggling.

And then, one day he was juggling when he dropped the sun in the sky. The crowds laughed, but not with joy. They drove him out of the town, laughing and calling him names. 'The clown who can't juggle,' they all laughed.

Antonio walked away feeling very sad indeed. He came to a stream, sat down, removed his clown mask and put his juggling things in a bag. He wandered around not knowing where to go. All his money had gone, his clothes became rags again and, when the cold weather came, Antonio decided it was time to go home.

He walked for many days, eventually arriving in Sorrento in the middle of the night. Everywhere was locked up, except the church. He went in and, finding a corner at the back, he went to sleep.

He was woken the next morning by the sounds of singing. As he looked around he saw that the old church was full of people. They were singing and taking turns to bring gifts and place them in front of the statue of Mary and Jesus.

'What is going on?' Antonio asked.

'Old man, don't you know anything?'

someone replied. 'It's harvest festival. They're bringing their gifts to God.'

Antonio stood and watched. At last everyone went home. Antonio walked to the front and looked at the statue of Jesus. 'You look so sad,' he said to the statue. 'All these gifts and still you look so sad. I wish I had a gift I could bring you... Maybe I have, I used to make people happy.'

He opened his bag, knelt before the statue, put on his clown mask and began to juggle. He juggled with sticks, then with plates, then with the rings, then with the burning torches. He had never juggled this well in his life. His heart was beating very fast.

'This is for you, little child.' He threw a red ball into the air, then an orange ball, then a yellow one, then a green one, a blue one, a purple one and, 'Now ladies and gentlemen,' he proclaimed, 'it's time for the sun in the heavens.' And up it went, the big golden ball.

When he had finished, he lay down in front of the statue.

Next morning two priests came in and saw Antonio still lying there. They rushed up to him. One of them knelt beside him, then turning to the other priest he said, 'He's dead, his heart has stopped.'

But the other priest wasn't listening. His mouth was wide open and he was pointing at the statue. There on the face of Jesus was a great big smile and in his hands he held a large golden ball.

And if you visit the little Italian town of Sorrento today and go into the little church, you'll see a statue of Mary and Jesus. And, if you look at the statue of Jesus, you'll see he's smiling and in his hands he holds a golden ball.

Antonio may have had tough times, but he was good right through. He was full of goodness.

Faithfulness

	Programme	Item
Section 1	Welcome	
	Rules	
	Prayer	
	Praise	
	Game 1	Strawberry Noses
	Praise (x2)	
	Fun Item	
	Game 2	Strawberry Picker
	Fun Item (2)	
	Bible Text	Galatians 5:22–23
	Announcements	
	Interview	
	Worship (x2)	
Section 2	Bible Lesson	Rainbows
Preaching	Illustration 1	Boyfriend And Girlfriend
Time	Illustration 2	Precious Stones
	Illustration 3	The Promise
	Story	Polly And The Frog
	Prayer	

 Being faithful is closely linked to being trusted and keeping our promises. Today we look at a faithful God who looks for faithful followers.

Game 1

Strawberry Noses

PREPARATION	You will need a strawberry for each team.
PLAYERS	Three players from each team.
SET-UP	The players line up at A in relay formation.
OBJECT	The first player gets on his hands and knees and pushes the strawberry from A to B and back again with his/her nose. When they return to A the next player begins.
WINNING	The team that completes the race first and sits down wins. After the game their noses should make an interesting sight!

Game 2

Strawberry Picker

PREPARATION	Ten strawberries and a bucket for each team.
PLAYERS	Six players from each team.
SET-UP	Five players line up in relay formation at A with two strawberries each. The sixth player stands two metres beyond B with a bucket.
OBJECT	The first person runs from A to B, tosses one strawberry towards the person holding the bucket, returns to A and the next player begins. This continues until each player has been twice.
WINNING	The team with the most strawberries in the bucket wins. If it is a tie, the team that finished first wins.

FRUIT

Today's fruit is **strawberry**, representing God's gift of faithfulness (for summary see end of part nine, 'Self-control').

BIBLE LESSON **RAINBOWS**

'God's Spirit makes us loving, happy, peaceful, patient, kind, good, faithful, gentle, and self-controlled.'
(Galatians 5:22–23)

A lesson from our series on 'Noah and his ark' may help us here.

Noah, his family and a zoo full of animals waited on the ark until God told them it was time to leave. They were very excited. The animals made their way out of the ark into the strange new world that awaited them. There was much joy and excitement.

But Noah could see dark clouds in the sky. Was God about to flood the earth again? Noah felt the droplets of rain on his cheeks and wondered if he should try and get everyone back into the ark. He was worried and concerned. Then God said, 'Noah, I will never flood the earth again and I will display rainbows in the sky to remind you of my promise. Noah, don't worry. I will never flood the earth again.'

Noah looked up and there in the sky was a rainbow: red, orange, yellow, green, blue, indigo and violet. It was the first rainbow that Noah had ever seen.

God had made a promise. Noah felt safe. He knew that people sometimes make promises and don't keep them, but God had made a promise and God never breaks his promises.

Boyfriend And Girlfriend

TOBY TROUBLE: See her over there? That's lovely Lucy. She is the loveliest girl in the world. *Sighs!* I love her! Well, actually, I don't think I love her. But I would like to be her boyfriend. Do you think I've got a chance? No harm in trying! *Walks over to Lucy.* Hi, Lucy. I really like you.

LUCY: I know, Toby! I can tell by the way you keep staring at me!

TOBY: Will you be my girlfriend, Lucy?

LUCY: OK. I'll be your girlfriend.

TOBY: That means you promise to be my girlfriend and nobody else's.

LUCY: I know. Don't you think I know what being a girlfriend means? I promise to be your girlfriend and no one else's. *She kisses Toby on the cheek, giggles and walks away.*

TOBY: I'm so chuffed. Lucy is my girlfriend.

Both exit. Hunky walks on, looking cool. Several seconds later, Lucy returns. Together they hold hands and walk around the stage. Toby returns and sees them.

TOBY: What is she doing? She promised to be my girlfriend. *Lucy kisses Hunky on the cheek and Hunky walks off.* Lucy! What were you doing?

LUCY: Hi Toby! What do you mean?

TOBY: I saw you with Hunky.

Lucy looks embarrassed, then giggles.

LUCY: Sorry, Toby! He's just much nicer than you. *Lucy walks off leaving a sad looking Toby.*

NARRATOR: It's bad when people make promises to us and don't keep them. People promise to be faithful and sometimes they are not. This was sad. But when mums and dads split up because one of them couldn't keep their promises, couldn't be faithful, that's even worse. Lots of you know about that stuff. But we make promises to God all the time. Some of us promised to be Christians and that means being Christians all the time. Do you think we are faithful? All I really know is that when people are not faithful, someone usually gets hurt. Like Toby! Let's remember to be faithful. It's one of the fruits of the Spirit, you know.

Lucy comes back on, takes Toby's hand and together they walk off.

Precious Stones

Objects needed: *Jewels or a treasure chest.*

These things look valuable don't they? They are probably worth a lot of money. But the Bible says, 'A good name is better than riches.'

That means being respected by others and having a good character is better than being rich. When we have as many fruits of the Spirit as possible, we become people with a good name. When we become people who keep promises, who can be trusted, who are faithful, then we become people with a good name. Remember, 'A good name is better than riches.'

Illustration 3

The Promise

Jesus died on the cross for the wrong things we'd all done. He took our punishment. But Jesus was much stronger than death, and death had absolutely no power over the Son of God. The God who became man, who had never done a thing wrong, defeated death and came back to life three days after he was killed.

After that he spent some time with his disciples and taught them many things. He told them of how he must soon return to his Father in heaven, a special event we call the Ascension. But, before he went back to be with God, Jesus made his disciples a promise, a promise which is for us as well. He promised, 'I will be with you always, right to the end of the world.'

Sometimes we make promises and, though we do our best to keep them, sometimes we break them. God is not like us. When God makes a promise, it doesn't change. When God promised that he would be with us always, right up to the end of the world, he meant it. Even though we can't see him, God is always with us.

● STORY – Polly And The Frog

Today's story is from England.

Polly had a very wicked stepmother. Her own mother had died when she was very small and the woman her father had married didn't like Polly. She made Polly do the hardest jobs around the house and, if she didn't do the jobs well, she was punished. As for Polly's father, he loved the woman so much that he wouldn't do anything to stop her.

One day the wicked stepmother called for Polly and very sternly said, 'Girl! Go to the well and fill this sieve with water. When it is full bring it back to me.'

Polly knew this was impossible. The sieve was full of holes. She couldn't do it. No one could. She walked to the well but when she arrived all she could do was sit down and cry.

'You don't look very happy, young lady. What's the matter?'

Polly turned round and to her amazement saw the fattest, slimiest, friendliest frog she had ever seen. She was so surprised to see a talking frog that she answered almost immediately, forgetting she wasn't supposed to talk to strangers. 'It's my stepmother,' she began. 'She wants me to fill this sieve with water. It's impossible, I know, but if I don't she'll punish me as soon as I get home.'

'It's not impossible at all,' the frog croaked. 'I'll tell you how to do it, if you promise me one thing, you must do anything I ask of you for one whole night.'

'All right,' Polly agreed. 'Now, tell me what I must do.'

'Take some leaves and moss and jam them into the holes,' commanded the frog. 'And then fill the sieve.'

Polly did what the frog suggested. It worked. 'Thank you. You saved my life,' she said.

'That's OK,' replied the frog. 'But don't forget your promise.'

Polly hurried home with the sieve full of water. Her stepmother was so amazed she didn't even find anything wrong with Polly's work.

That night during dinner there came a knock at the door. 'Polly! There's a frog here for you,' called Polly's father from the front door.

Polly swallowed hard and walked to the front door.

'Do you mind if I come in?' asked the frog.

Well, Polly did mind very much but she also remembered her promise and she knew how important it was to be faithful and to keep promises. 'We're just having dinner,' she began.

'That's nice,' croaked the frog. 'I feel a bit hungry myself.'

Polly returned to the dining room with the frog behind her. At first her stepmother looked angry, then a smile spread across her face as she realised this was a golden opportunity to make fun of Polly. 'Oh, I see you found a new friend,' she sneered. 'He seems a perfect match for you.'

'It's hard to see down here,' said the frog. 'Can I sit on your lap?'

Polly was very unhappy but she knew how important it was to be faithful. She knew how important it was to keep her promises, so she allowed the frog to sit on her lap. He was very slimy.

'Now, how about a bite to eat?' asked the frog.

The stepmother howled with laughter. 'Let's see you feed him, Polly,' she cackled.

Polly scooped up a bit of her dinner and fed it to the frog.

'Perhaps the little froggy would like a drink as well?' mocked the stepmother.

'No thank you,' replied the frog. 'But I do

have one more request. I wonder if Polly would kiss me, right here on my cheek?'

The stepmother laughed so much she nearly fell off the chair. 'Go on Polly. Kiss your froggy friend,' she said.

Polly was embarrassed. 'I thought you were my friend,' she said to the frog.

'I am,' said the frog. 'Trust me. Friends keep their promises.'

Polly was feeling ill but she leaned forward, shut her eyes and kissed the frog on his green, slimy cheek. When Polly opened her eyes, the frog had gone and, as happens in many of these stories, in his place was the most handsome young man she had ever seen.

'You've done it!' he shouted, jumping off her lap and dancing for joy. 'You've broken the curse and now I'm free again. Will you come with me tonight to my castle and be my princess?'

Polly looked at her father and at her stepmother. Her father looked amazed and the wicked stepmother was no longer laughing.

'Yes,' she said at last, 'I would like that very much. But what about them?'

'Well,' began the prince, looking at the stepmother. 'We do have some vacancies for cleaners.'

'No, it's all right!' said the stepmother hurriedly. 'We'll stay right here. You visit when you want.'

Polly became Princess Polly simply because she kept her promises. She was faithful. If we are faithful, we may not marry a prince or princess, but God will always bless us and look after us.

Gentleness

	Programme	Item
Section 1	**Welcome**	
	Rules	
	Prayer	
	Praise	
	Game 1	Apple Bobbing
	Praise (x2)	
	Fun Item (2)	
	Game 2	Toffee Apple
	Fun Item	
	Bible Text	Galatians 5:22–23
	Announcements	
	Interview	
	Worship (x2)	
Section 2	**Bible Lesson**	The Life of Jesus
Preaching	**Illustration 1**	The World's Strongest Man
Time	**Illustration 2**	Police Dog
	Illustration 3	Karate Kid
	Story	Pryderi And The Dragon
	Prayer	

Overview Gentleness is not the same as weakness. It is power under control.

Game 1

Apple Bobbing

PREPARATION	You will need three apples and a bowl of water for each team.
PLAYERS	Three players from each team.
SET-UP	The players line up at A. The apples are floated in a bowl of water at B.
OBJECT	The first player runs from A to B and tries to remove an apple using only their mouth. When they are successful they return to A and the next player goes.
WINNING	The team that completes the relay and sits down first wins.

Game 2

Toffee Apple

PREPARATION	You will need an apple, a stick, a bowl of water, a bowl of flour and a bowl of tiny cake sweets for each team.
PLAYERS	Five players from each team.
SET-UP	The players line up in relay formation at A. The items listed above are all placed at B.
OBJECT	The first person runs to B, picks up the stick and returns to A, handing the stick to person two; person two takes the stick and runs to B, places the apple on the stick and returns; person three takes the apple on the stick, runs to B, dips it in the water to wet it, returns and hands the items over; person four puts the apple in the flour; person five puts the apple in the sweets.
WINNING	The first team back with a completed 'toffee' apple and sitting down wins.

FRUIT

Today's fruit is **apple**, representing God's gift of gentleness (for summary see end of part nine, 'Self-control').

THE LIFE OF JESUS

'God's Spirit makes us loving, happy, peaceful, patient, kind, good, faithful, gentle, and self-controlled.'
(Galatians 5:22–23)

Can you imagine how hard it must have been for Jesus at times? Can you imagine how hard it would be to let some men called Pharisees say horrible things to your face and call you names?

But Jesus had the fruit of the Spirit called gentleness. Don't make the mistake of thinking gentleness is the same as weakness. It's not. Jesus was not weak. He had great power. He could have spoken a word and a flaming ball of lava would have fallen from the sky and destroyed whole towns and cities. He could have made the ground open up and swallow the Pharisees. As the Son of God, he could have called on an army of fiery angels with swords any time he wanted.

Jesus didn't do that. He chose to be gentle. But gentleness isn't weakness. It's controlled power. Some of you think being gentle is the same as being weak. It's not.

Jesus hung on the cross to be punished for the wrong things we'd all done. He didn't have to do that. If he had asked, a legion of angels would have come to rescue him.

He was never weak. He always had great power but, because he chose to be gentle, he didn't use that power to hurt people. Instead he used that power to help people.

The World's Strongest Man

Object needed: *A weightlifting weight.*

This is a weight. It's quite heavy but not too heavy for me to lift. The man who has lifted the heaviest weights on a bench is a Christian. His name is Anthony Clarke. At one point – in 1993 – he was actually the strongest man in the world.

I wonder what you would do if you were the world's strongest man? Maybe you'd walk down the street with your arms out wide like Arnold Schwarzenegger, pushing people out of your way as you go, looking as tough as you could?

Anthony Clarke's not like that at all. He is courteous, polite and very gentle. Does that mean that he's weak? Of course not! Gentleness isn't weakness. It's controlled power.

Police Dog

Object needed: *A picture of a dog, a toy dog or, best of all, a real dog.*

A policeman walked through the streets of a big city and walking by his side was his dog, a very large Alsatian. A group of boys, seeing that the dog was on a lead, followed behind and made strange sounds to try and scare the dog. The dog didn't move. One of the boys ran up to the dog and shouted 'Boo!' in its ear. The dog didn't move. One of the braver, or possibly stupider, boys rushed up and pulled the dog's tail. The dog still looked quite calm. The same boy went to grab the dog's nose but the dog just licked his hand.

The boys were convinced the dog was a coward. They thought it didn't react because it was afraid of them. Both the policeman and the dog ignored them as the boys followed them through a shopping centre.

Suddenly a man shouted, 'Thief!' A teenager ran out of a shop, holding a pair of jeans he hadn't paid for.

'Stop!' shouted the shopkeeper. But the teenager started to run instead. The boys watched as the policeman calmly took the dog off the lead and gave the command, 'Stop him, boy!'

The dog ran faster than the boys thought possible. He jumped into the air, knocked the teenager to the ground, gripped the teenager's hand with his huge teeth and growled until the teenager stopped struggling.

The boys were amazed. They had made the mistake of thinking that gentleness is the same as weakness. The dog was gentle but not weak. Gentleness isn't weakness. It's controlled power.

Karate Kid

Object needed: *A video clip from* Karate Kid *(alternatively, a karate top.)*

I don't know if you've ever seen *Karate Kid*. In *Karate Kid* the man who trains the hero is called Mr Miakki. He seems quiet, shy, sensitive and very gentle. He holds doors open for people, he says 'please' and 'thank you' and is always very polite.

Some people who saw him every day might assume that he was a wimp because of the soft way he talks, the clothes he wears and the gentle way he acts. That would be a mistake. Remember, gentleness isn't weakness; it's controlled power.

Whenever someone tries to hit Mr Miakki they soon regret it. Mr Miakki isn't weak at all, he's just gentle. Whenever someone tries to attack him, he shows them what he is really like – a karate master. Don't confuse gentleness with weakness.

● STORY – Pryderi And The Dragon

Today's story is from Wales.

There was once a kingdom that was glorious and beautiful. Its king was fair and just and always did the right thing. He had three sons and a daughter. Although his wife had died many years earlier, his sons and daughter brought him great happiness.

One day disaster struck. A dragon decided to make his home in the kingdom. He terrorised the people of the land, burnt down many of their houses and demanded that each family bring him a gift of their youngest daughter, starting from the beginning of the new year. That left three months before the sacrifices would begin and the king's daughter Branwen was to be first. Many of the king's bravest knights tried to fight the dragon but they were all killed.

The king didn't know what to do, so he summoned his wisest men and asked them how he was to rid the kingdom of the dragon. They consulted their old, old books and found an ancient legend. The legend spoke of a prince going to a distant castle and finding the name of the dragon. Whoever called the dragon by its name would kill it. The king's three sons were all eager to go on the quest to the castle.

Gwydion the eldest said, 'Father, I will go for I am the greatest warrior in the Kingdom.'

Callum the middle son said, 'Father, I will go for I am the greatest hunter in the Kingdom.'

Pryderi the youngest said, 'Father I will go…'

But before he could say any more his brothers started laughing. 'What will you do?' they jested. 'Tell the lord of the castle one of your poems?' And they laughed so much tears flowed down their cheeks.

Gwydion the eldest set off on his quest. He travelled for some time over mountains, through rivers, into valleys and around great forests until eventually he arrived at the castle spoken of by the legend.

Gwydion knocked hard on the castle doors and they slowly opened. An old woman stood in his path. 'Stand aside woman,' he demanded. 'I am on an important quest.'

The woman did as she was ordered. Gwydion walked into the castle. Swirling mists engulfed him, strange shapes filled the air and strange noises bombarded his senses. He looked straight ahead and there in front of him was a golden king sitting upon a stone throne.

'Who dares approach me?' came the booming voice of the king.

Gwydion began to say, 'It is I, Gwydion…'

But before the sentence was completed, the king looked up at the prince, a strange light came from the king's eyes and Gwydion was turned to stone.

Many weeks went by and then Callum, the middle son, went to his father to ask permission to attempt the journey. After some preparation he set off. He travelled for some time over mountains, through rivers, into valleys and around great forests until eventually he arrived at the castle spoken of by the legend.

Callum knocked hard on the castle doors and they slowly opened. An old woman stood in his path. 'Stand aside woman,' he demanded. 'I am on an important quest.'

The woman did as she was ordered. Callum walked into the castle. Swirling mists engulfed him, strange shapes filled the air and strange noises bombarded his senses. He looked straight ahead and there in front of him was a golden king sitting upon a stone throne.

'Who dares approach me?' came the booming voice of the king.

Callum began to say, 'It is I, Callum…'

But before the sentence was completed, the king looked up at the prince, a strange light came from the king's eyes and Callum was turned to stone.

More weeks went by and Pryderi went to his father to ask permission to attempt the journey. His father wouldn't listen to him. 'Your brothers are both lost. Your sister is to be sacrificed to the dragon and, if I lose you as well, I will surely die of a broken heart.'

Pryderi loved his father very much. But he wanted to bring his brothers back and save his kingdom, so he disobeyed his father and set off in search of the castle. He travelled for some time over mountains, through rivers, into valleys and around great forests until eventually he arrived at the castle spoken of by the legend.

Pryderi knocked hard on the castle doors and they slowly opened. An old woman stood in his path. 'Hello. My name is Pryderi,' he said.

After meeting his brothers, the woman was surprised to hear Pryderi being so polite.

Pryderi was a prince just like his brothers. He too could have commanded the woman to do what he wanted. But he had the fruit of the Spirit called gentleness. He wasn't weak; he was gentle. He knew how to control his power.

She was even more surprised when Pryderi continued, 'Is there any way you can help me with my quest?'

The woman had never been treated so kindly and courteously. She explained to Pryderi that anyone who looked directly in the face of the king would be turned to stone. She gave him a special mirror. 'Approach him backwards,' she said. 'Then make your request when he asks.'

Pryderi walked into the castle armed with the mirror. Swirling mists engulfed him, strange shapes filled the air and strange noises bombarded his senses. He looked straight ahead and there in front of him was a golden king sitting upon a stone throne.

'Who dares approach me?' came the booming voice of the king.

Pryderi replied, 'It is I, Pryderi.' But he did not directly face the king. He kept looking in the mirror.

'Ah!' said the king. 'I see that you are a wise young man. What is your request?'

Still without making eye contact Pryderi made his request. 'I have two requests O King. I would like to know the name of the dragon who is destroying my kingdom and I would also like you to release my brothers.' For Pryderi had seen the two stone statues of his brothers in the courtyard.

'I will grant your requests,' replied the king. 'Your brothers are fortunate that at least one of the family knows how to be kind and courteous. As for the name of the dragon, it is Browg. He is an old and particularly bad tempered dragon.'

The king clicked his fingers and Pryderi's brothers turned back to flesh and blood. The three brothers rode home together.

On arriving in the kingdom, Pryderi rode straight for the dragon. The dragon laughed as he saw Pryderi approach. 'Who are you? Such a young man to die,' scoffed the dragon.

Pryderi looked straight at the dragon and said, 'It is not I who will die today, but a dragon named Browg.'

Horror filled the dragon's face. His name had been spoken. He exploded right in front of Pryderi. The rule of the dragon had been broken. The kingdom would recover and one day Pryderi would be its wisest and noblest king ever.

Self-control

	Programme	Item
Section 1	Welcome	
	Rules	
	Prayer	
	Praise	
	Game 1	Banana Relay
	Praise (x2)	
	Fun Item (2)	
	Game 2	Banana Tag
	Fun Item	
	Bible Text	Galatians 5:22–23
	Announcements	
	Interview	
	Worship (x2)	
Section 2 Preaching Time	Bible Lesson	Self-control
	Illustration 1	Body
	Illustration 2	Balloons
	Illustration 3	Fruit Bowl
	Story	Gelert
	Prayer	

We come to the final and probably most important fruit of the Spirit – self-control. Through the lack of it, kingdoms have fallen and lives have been ruined. God wants to teach us to control ourselves.

Game 1

Banana Relay

PREPARATION	You will need a banana for each team.
PLAYERS	Five players from each team.
SET-UP	The players line up at A with the first player holding the banana.
OBJECT	The first player runs from A to B and back. On their return, they pass the banana to the next player, and so the race continues in relay formation.
WINNING	The first team back and sitting down wins, unless they have let go of their banana, in which case they are disqualified.

Game 2

Banana Tag

PREPARATION	You will need three bananas for each team.
PLAYERS	Four players from each team.
SET-UP	The players line up at A with the first three players holding bananas.
OBJECT	The first player runs from A to B and back. On their return, player two takes hold of player one's banana and they set off together. On their return, player three takes hold of player two's banana and the three set off together. And so on until all four players run together.
WINNING	The first team back and sitting down wins, unless they have let go of their bananas, in which case they are disqualified.

FRUIT

Today's fruit is **banana**, representing God's gift of self-control (for summary, turn to the end of illustration 3).

 ### SELF-CONTROL

'God's Spirit makes us loving, happy, peaceful, patient, kind, good, faithful, gentle, and self-controlled.'
(Galatians 5:22–23)

Today we come to the end of our series on 'Fruits of the Spirit'. Do you remember what the fruits of the Spirit are? They are the things we need to learn to be like, so that we can be more like Jesus.

Today we place the final fruit of the Spirit onto our tree. It fits just down here. We'll remember this fruit by using a banana. This fruit of the Spirit is called self-control.

Lots of people in the Bible had to learn about this one. Before he started serving God, Moses killed someone. He hadn't learnt about self-control. King David had a man called Uriah killed before he learnt about self-control. Peter, one of Jesus' disciples, chopped off a man's ear with a sword before he learnt about self-control. Jesus had to pray for the man so that his ear would grow back.

But eventually they all learnt self-control and they remembered to be self-controlled most of the time! Moses led thousands of people across the desert to where God wanted them to live but he wasn't allowed to go there himself because he lost his temper and forgot about self-control.

It's very important that we learn about self-control.

Body

A person walks on and stands facing the children. Suddenly their hand comes up and they begin to strangle themselves. The narrator rushes on and pulls the hand away.

NARRATOR: Oh dear! You see what happens when we lose self-control. We can't control ourselves.

The person's hand comes up again and grabs the person's throat. The narrator once again pulls the hand away.

NARRATOR: Seems crazy! But lots of you have no self-control.

The person's hand grabs the narrator's throat. The narrator pulls it free.

NARRATOR: Sometimes we do things without thinking. That's when we forget about self-control.

The person's legs begin to move, wobble, run and stop. The person tries to hold onto their legs to stop them moving.

NARRATOR: But if we pray and ask Jesus, he will help us with this thing called self-control.

Person continues desperately to keep his legs still. The narrator looks at the mime artist and repeats,

NARRATOR: But if we pray and ask Jesus, he will help us with this thing called self-control.

The person nods, looks up and pretends to pray. His legs stop moving.

NARRATOR: Jesus helps us to be self-controlled. It's very important.

The person shakes the narrator's hand and walks off.

Balloons

Objects needed: *Balloons.*

From time to time people upset us. They jump in front of us in the line to get into children's church, they call us names, they knock into us, or they just plain annoy us.

If we have self-control we react like this: *(Take the balloon and begin to blow.)* They jump in front of us in the line. That upsets us. *(Blow the balloon up more.)* They call us names. This makes us more upset. *(Blow up the balloon more.)* We lose a game. This makes us even more upset. *(Blow up the balloon a bit more.)* But, if we are self-controlled, we don't lose our tempers or have a tantrum. *(Let the balloon go…)*

But what happens if we have no self-control? We react like this: *(Take the balloon and begin to blow.)* They jump in front of us in the line. That makes us upset. *(Blow the balloon up more.)* They call us names. This makes us more upset. *(Blow up the balloon more.)* We lose a game. This makes us even more upset. *(Stick a pin in the balloon.)*

If we have no self-control we blow up like the balloon. We lose our tempers, we have tantrums and, ultimately, we ruin our lives. But, if we are self-controlled, we don't lose our tempers or have a tantrum.

Fruit Bowl

Object needed: *Fruit bowl and all the fruits mentioned in the series.*

This is a fruit bowl. Let's pretend it's like our lives. It's not very good right now; it's empty. But what if we begin to fill it up.

Here's a banana. That can be today's fruit of the Spirit, self-control. Now the bowl looks more interesting, but it needs more I think. Like our lives, self-control isn't enough, we need more.

How about a:

Plum	remember we said this one was	**Love**	our bowl's looking better and so are our lives.
Pear	remember we said this one was	**Happiness**	our bowl's looking better and so are our lives.
Grape	remember we said this one was	**Peace**	our bowl's looking better and so are our lives.
Orange	remember we said this one was	**Patience**	our bowl's looking better and so are our lives.
Lemon	remember we said this one was	**Kindness**	our bowl's looking better and so are our lives.
Lime	remember we said this one was	**Goodness**	our bowl's looking better and so are our lives.
Strawberry	remember we said this one was	**Faithfulness**	our bowl's looking better and so are our lives.
Apple	remember we said this one was	**Gentleness**	our bowl's looking better and so are our lives.
Banana	remember we said this one was	**Self-control**	our bowl's looking better and so are our lives.

● STORY – Gelert

Today's story comes from Wales.

About 750 years ago in Wales there lived a prince whose name was Llewellyn. Llewellyn had two things that he prized above everything else.

The first was his hunting dog Gelert. Gelert was the fiercest hunting dog in Wales. He stood over a metre in height and everyone in the prince's castle was frightened of him. The prince had good cause to love Gelert. On more than one occasion one of the wolves that lived in the woods around the castle had tried to kill Llewelyn but Gelert was always too fast for them and would never let them near his master.

Llewellyn loved his dog dearly but the most important person in his life was his little son. He loved his son more than he loved anyone else in his entire nation. His son was about nine months old and was the cutest baby: he would throw his food off his plate, he was sick over his nanny, he tried to throw his shoes down the toilet. But he had one of those really cute smiles that made it really hard for people to tell him off.

Gelert was the fiercest dog in Wales. Nobody would dare go within ten metres of his dog basket. Everyone was frightened of him. One growl and they would run for miles. Everyone was afraid of him, except for the baby. Nobody had told the baby to be afraid of Gelert, so the baby wasn't.

One day the baby crawled over to the dog. The dog gave a low growl but the baby giggled and moved closer. Gelert growled louder, the baby giggled and moved closer. Gelert was getting more and more annoyed but the baby crawled closer and closer, giggling the entire time. The baby looked up into Gelert's face. The dog looked down at him and gave a mighty bark but instead of crying, as you might expect, the baby grabbed the dog's ears and when Gelert stood up there was the baby hanging by Gelert's ears. Gelert didn't know what to do. Everyone was frightened of him and that's the way he liked it. How come this baby wasn't? Gelert just stood there with the baby hanging from his ears and the poor dog began to make crying sounds until the baby let go and crawled away.

The next day the baby crawled over and grabbed Gelert's tail and started swinging back and forth on it.

When he got a bit older the baby started crawling onto Gelert's back and riding around on him. It really was a sight to see.

Once the baby went missing altogether and nobody could work out where he had gone. They searched high and low in every room and still they couldn't find him. Eventually somebody spotted him. He had crawled into Gelert's dog basket and was fast asleep curled up with the dog. The nursemaid went across to pick the baby up but Gelert barked loudly which sent the nursemaid running as fast as she could. So that's where the baby stayed until he woke up and he crawled away from the dog so the nursemaid could change his nappy!

Gelert and the baby became so attached that whenever the prince went off on a hunting trip he would leave Gelert behind to look after the baby. (The nursemaid would also have to stay.

Talented though he was, Gelert just didn't know how to change nappies.)

The woods which surrounded the castle were very thick and from time to time wolves would wander into them and creep up to the castle to see if there was something to eat there.

One day a very large and hungry wolf made his way to the castle and as he approached he could smell something sweet in the air. He jumped up at one of the castle windows and looked in. Gelert was asleep just in front of the fire, so the wolf couldn't see him. What he could see excited him. There was a baby lying in a crib. The wolf licked his lips and opened his mouth, revealing his sharp teeth. He saw the nursemaid, but he was in no hurry. He could wait until the nursemaid left and then he'd pounce.

A long time went past but the wolf waited patiently. Eventually the nursemaid went to get the baby some milk. The wolf flexed his muscles and pounced at the crib. He planned to grab the baby in his massive jaws and escape back into the woods. As he flew through the air his mouth open, Gelert woke up. Gelert almost instinctively dived towards the wolf. He was aiming for his throat, but only managed to knock the wolf in the ribs and hurl him against one of the walls. The wolf was furious and ran at Gelert with all his strength. They barked and growled. The wolf jumped on top of Gelert and looked like he would kill the great dog. Then Gelert used all his strength to pin the wolf to the ground. They tumbled and turned. The furniture was knocked over; the crib was turned over so that the baby ended up underneath; the sofa was turned over; there was blood spattered on the walls. The place was a mess.

Finally, the wolf leapt at Gelert and it looked like he was going to win. But Gelert was too quick and, with the speed that only a hunting dog has, he dodged the wolf and sunk his teeth into the wolf. It was all over. The wolf was dead.

The prince returned to his castle and the first thing he wanted to do was to see his son. When he reached the nursery he could not believe his eyes. The room was a mess, there was blood everywhere and the baby was nowhere to be seen. The wolf was hidden behind the overturned sofa and there was Gelert crawling towards him with blood all over his body. The prince had the kind of temper which just exploded and the first thing he thought was, 'Gelert's killed the baby!'

His anger exploded. He drew his sword and with one mighty stroke cut off Gelert's head. The prince stood there devastated by what had happened. His son was dead and so was his best hunting dog. The two things he prized above anything else were dead.

The prince began to cry but, through his sobs, he heard a faint cry coming from somewhere in the room. He searched frantically to find where the sound had come from. He lifted up the crib and there to his amazement was his little son, lying there, giggling. The baby had loved it all. He had never seen two dogs fight before and he thought it was the funniest thing he had ever seen.

The prince picked up the baby and as he did so, he saw the body of the dead wolf. The prince realised what had happened and he was absolutely devastated.

Because he couldn't control his temper he had killed his best hunting dog, the dog who had saved his son's life.

The Example Of Paul

A Series in Six Parts

Introduction

Title	Themes covered
1 Paul Repents	Turning away from the bad things
2 Paul Begins To Preach	Telling others even when it's hard
3 Paul Persecuted	Learning to keep going no matter what
4 Paul Protected	God looks after us
5 Paul Revealing	It's the hard times which show what we're really like
6 Paul Dying	'To live is Christ, to die is gain.'

Series Overview

Paul is one of the most exciting characters in the Bible and his meeting with Jesus is one of the most dramatic stories of the New Testament. He has a very significant place in church history: the apostle to the Gentiles (the first new covenant man to take the gospel to non-Jews). Yet when the romanticism is stripped away, we are presented with a man who met Jesus, who suffered and was persecuted for his faith. He spoke about Jesus throughout the Roman empire. He pioneered churches, trained and developed leaders, and ultimately gave his life for what he believed in.

Paul is our example of radical conversion. He gave everything to Jesus. This was no lukewarm conversion.

This series is designed to see children not just won for Jesus but radically living for him, unafraid to speak what they believe. This is the radical Christianity which caused the Son of God to die a radical death: a very real conversion, a very real life lived for Jesus, a very real life lived in the service of a very real God.

1 Paul Repents

	Programme	Item
Section 1	Welcome	
	Rules	
	Prayer	
	Praise	
	Game 1	Wiggle
	Praise (x2)	
	Fun Item (2)	
	Game 2	Boxed In
	Fun Item	
	Bible Text	Romans 10:9
	Announcements	
	Interview	
	Worship (x2)	
Section 2	Bible Lesson	Paul On The Damascus Road
Preaching	Illustration 1	The Word Repent
Time	Illustration 2	Choices
	Illustration 3	Burial
	Story	The Adventures Of Fooboo Jooboo (1)
	Prayer	

Overview Paul hated Christians. He dedicated his life to the destruction of the followers of 'The Way'. But after he met Jesus he totally repented of the things he did. He turned away from his old way of living and turned to Jesus.

games

 Preaching**Time**

Game 1

Wiggle

PREPARATION	A balloon for each team (plus spares).
PLAYERS	Six players from each team.
SET-UP	The players line up in relay formation at A with the front member of the team holding the balloon between their knees.
OBJECT	The first person runs from A to B and back with the balloon between their knees. On their return, they pass the balloon to the next player.
WINNING	The first team to complete the relay and sit down wins.

Game 2

Boxed In

PREPARATION	A big box full of junk (old newspaper, tissue, etc.) containing five table tennis balls per team is placed at B.
PLAYERS	Five players from each team.
SET-UP	The players line up in relay formation at A.
OBJECT	The first person runs from A to B, searches for a table tennis ball and returns with it to A. On returning to A, they tag the next player who then repeats the process.
WINNING	The first team back and sitting down wins.

 **BIBLE LESSON** ## PAUL ON THE DAMASCUS ROAD

'God will accept you and save you, if you truly believe and tell others.' (Romans 10:9)

Paul hated Christians. He had actually gone to the rulers in Jerusalem and asked permission to imprison all Christians. He had stood by and given his approval as a man named Stephen had stones thrown at him until he was dead. Paul would have liked to see all Christians killed in the same way. He hated what they stood for. He didn't think they were right.

Maybe you know somebody like that. Maybe you yourself don't like Christians or don't believe what Christians believe.

But one day everything changed…. Paul was on his way to Damascus. He had special letters which allowed him to arrest the Christians there. He was riding along on his horse when suddenly a bright light came out of nowhere and shone in his face. The light was brighter than the sun. He fell to the ground, blinded. The men who were with him saw the bright light, but they never heard the voice that followed. This voice was for Paul only.

'Why are you hurting me Paul?' came the voice.

'Who are you?' Paul asked in his panic.

'I am Jesus who you are persecuting,' was the reply.

Paul didn't believe Jesus could possibly be alive. He thought that all the stories about Jesus were lies. But now he had met Jesus. Now he knew that Jesus existed and that persecuting Christians was wrong.

Jesus told Paul to continue his journey to Damascus. There someone would come and pray for him. Paul had to be led to Damascus because he was totally blind. His sight would come back later, but Paul would never be the same again.

Now the man who had wanted to imprison anyone who talked about Jesus, wanted only to tell as many people as possible about Jesus. Paul had repented. He had become a Christian and repented. What does repenting mean?

He was doing one thing, trying to destroy Christians. But now he was a Christian and so he turned around and started telling people about Jesus.

Illustration 1

The Word Repent

Objects needed: *Four signs reading: 'Right', 'Wrong', 'Please God', 'Hurt God'.*

Display the words 'Right' and 'Please God' on one side of the stage and the other two on the other side of the stage.

Repent is a big word. But it isn't so difficult to understand. Before we become Christians we do certain things that are wrong and hurt God *(walk towards the appropriate signs)*. We are unkind, we lie, we say bad words, we are naughty at times. But when we become Christians, we repent. We stop walking this way and doing these things, we turn around and walk the other way *(walk towards the other signs)*. We now do things which are right and please God. We are kind and caring, we help people, we say only the things God would be pleased with. We repent, we turn around and walk the other way. That's what it means.

We can't become Christians without repenting. I can't say I love God and keep on hurting him. I can't be a Christian and continue to be unkind to people. I can't be a Christian and keep on swearing. I must stop doing these things and walk the other way. To repent means to stop doing the things which are obviously hurting God and begin to live to please him.

Illustration 2

Choices

Objects needed: *Large piece of paper and a pen.*

Draw a line down the centre of the paper and write 'Hurts God' on one side and 'Pleases God' on the other.

If we're going to live to please God, it's important to decide which things please him, and which things hurt him. I have a list of different things that we do. All you have to do is put your thumb up if you think it pleases God and put your thumb down if you think if hurts God.

Write the words in the appropriate columns after you've allowed the children to decide.

Here we go:

- Use bad words, swear words
- Hit people
- Pray
- Smash windows
- Go to Children's Church
- Do what our parents ask
- Steal money
- Help people who are lonely or hurt
- Read a Bible
- Bully people

Illustration 3

Burial

Object needed: *Piece of card cut out in the shape of a tombstone.*

Repentance is about burying the bad things we used to do. So we dig a great big hole in our mind and we place into that hole all those bad things.

Pretend to dig a hole and place things into the hole, call out their names as you do so.

Bad temper, swear words, stealing, fighting, bullying...
And then we cover them over.

Pretend to fill in the hole.

It's important that we don't try and dig them back up. We've repented of those things, we're not going to do them again. We must walk away. It's finished. We're Christians now. We've turned our back on those things.

● STORY – The Adventures Of Fooboo Jooboo (1)

Fooboo Jooboo was a very odd person. He was ten years old and he wore brightly coloured clothes: green shoes, red jeans, and a blue and green stripy jumper. Together with his favourite red and yellow cap and thick red glasses they made him look very unusual indeed.

He lived with his mum and dad in a detached house just outside Bobbing Town. Fooboo Jooboo's house was as strange as him. The outside was decorated in the brightest blues and reds, the window frames were green and the door was bright yellow. Inside, the carpet was purple, the walls red and the ceiling orange. The furniture was blue and the television was yellow with white spots.

Fooboo Jooboo wasn't very kind mainly because nobody had ever been kind to him. His mum and dad were always shouting at each other and when they weren't shouting at each other they were shouting at him. 'Fooboo! Clean your room! Fooboo! Wash your face! Fooboo! Dig the garden! Fooboo! Stop doing that! Fooboo! Be quiet!'

His house was always full of noise, the noise of people shouting. He hated it but instead of trying to be different, he became (as so often happens) exactly like it. He shouted at everyone, the same way his mum and dad shouted at him. He was unkind to everyone, the same way his mum and dad were unkind to him.

He would take money from the younger children on the way to school. He would shout at his teachers and refuse to do his work. He hated his school, he hated his parents, he hated everyone. But most of all he hated Jimmy. Jimmy was so nice. It didn't matter how nasty he was to Jimmy or how many times he called him names (and he called him lots of names) Jimmy just smiled. That really annoyed Fooboo and just made him hate Jimmy even more.

Fooboo used to make fun of Jimmy but, on the day he dropped all his sandwiches on the way to school, Jimmy offered to share his with him. He used to throw stones at Jimmy but, on the day he had to play rugby for the school and forgot his boots, Jimmy lent him his. Fooboo hated Jimmy. No matter how bad he was to Jimmy, Jimmy showed him nothing but kindness in return.

One day while he sat next to Jimmy in class, Jimmy tried to tell him about a God who loved him. Fooboo didn't understand about love, he only knew about shouting and nastiness. Jimmy told him that if he asked Jesus to forgive the wrong things he'd done (Fooboo knew that he'd done lots of bad things) and repented (that is, stopped being bad, doing nasty things and hitting people and instead started being kind and caring, like Jesus wanted), then God would come and be his friend and look after him and he'd go to heaven one day. Fooboo listened to the part about God being his friend. He didn't have any friends but repenting sounded hard: he'd have to be kind. He wasn't sure he could be kind while his mum and dad kept shouting at him.

Fooboo only acted tough, he wasn't really. It was just that his mum and dad shouted so much that he couldn't stand it. He felt empty and lonely inside but, instead of telling people this, he just hit them and was nasty to them. Some people who are very cruel indeed are just very sad inside.

Some time went past. Fooboo became nastier and sadder. His parents continued shouting at each other and started shouting at him even more. He really hated being at home and one night at about midnight he ran away. He travelled far away from Bobbing Town to Laser City. Laser City was an amazing place. Fooboo arrived there the following morning after walking all night. There were so many shops and so many people. He walked for miles and still there were more shops selling everything: clothes, toys, records, pets, computers, everything.

Eventually it became very late and Fooboo walked up a back street to look for a place to sleep. He found some old newspapers and wrapped himself up. It was cold but eventually he managed to fall asleep. A little while later he felt a sharp pain in his side. He looked up into the faces of five very tough looking boys of about seventeen. They all looked very mean and very dirty. They were dressed in black, with black stripes on their cheeks.

The leader of the gang kicked Fooboo again. 'What are you doing here?' he demanded. 'This area belongs to the Basher Boys after dark. And I'm the leader of the Basher Boys.'

Fooboo was scared. He began to speak but didn't get a chance.

'Shut up!' commanded the leader of the Basher Boys. 'We don't care why you are here. We're going to kill you anyway.'

He pulled a knife out of his pocket. The blade glinted in the moonlight. Fooboo knew he was going to die. He braced himself for the stab of the knife. Just then there was a blinding flash of light.

What happened next was quite unbelievable...

(To be continued...)

Paul Begins To Preach

	Programme	Item
Section 1	Welcome	
	Rules	
	Prayer	
	Praise	
	Game 1	Box Shoes
	Praise (x2)	
	Fun Item (2)!	
	Game 2	Balloon Jumpers
	Fun Item	
	Bible Text	Romans 10:9
	Announcements	
	Interview	
	Worship (x2)	
Section 2	Bible Lesson	Paul Begins To Preach
Preaching	Illustration 1	A Story To Tell
Time	Illustration 2	What Is a Christian?
	Illustration 3	A Story To Tell
	Story	The Adventures Of Fooboo Jooboo (2)
	Prayer	

Overview Paul was completely changed. Now it was time to tell others. He had what churchgoers would call a testimony. He had something to say. He began to preach.

Preaching Time

Game 1

Box Shoes

PREPARATION	Two boxes for each team (the boxes should be large enough for the children to get their feet into them).
PLAYERS	Three players from each team.
SET-UP	The players line up in relay formation at A. The front member of the team puts the boxes on their feet.
OBJECT	The first person runs from A to B and back with the boxes on their feet. On return they pass the boxes to the next player.
WINNING	The first team to complete the relay and sit down wins.

Game 2

Balloon Jumpers

PREPARATION	A male leader per team wearing a black bag as a jumper. (The reason for a male leader will become evident as the game progresses).
PLAYERS	Five players from each team.
SET-UP	Five players stand around the leader with a pile of balloons each.
OBJECT	To blow up as many balloons as possible and put them inside the black bag that the leader is wearing.
WINNING	This is a three minute game and the winning team will be the one to make their leader look the widest!

Note: Asthmatic children should be encouraged not to take part in this game.

BIBLE LESSON **PAUL BEGINS TO PREACH**

'God will accept you and save you, if you truly believe and tell others.' (Romans 10:9)

Paul was led by the hand until he reached the city of Damascus. God had spoken to a man called Ananias and told him to go to Paul and pray for him. Ananias was afraid because he had heard the things that Paul was doing, but he knew how important it was to do exactly what King Jesus said, so he went to Paul and prayed for him. Instantly something like scales fell from Paul's eyes and he could see again.

Now Paul was a Christian he knew what he should do. He began to tell others how he had become a Christian and why they should become Christians as well. People were amazed and began to tell other people all over Damascus about God.

I've always wondered what Paul began to tell people. I know he began to preach, but what did he say? He didn't really know much about God. Like some of you he'd only just become a Christian, so what was he going to say?

He probably began to tell people how and why he became a Christian. He began to tell people what had happened to him.

He would say something like this: 'I was travelling on the Damascus road when suddenly I saw a bright light and heard a voice... I began to realise that Jesus was real and that he had died on a cross for the wrong things I had done.'

He would simply tell people what he had experienced.

If we're Christians, we need to start telling others about Jesus as well. And what do we tell them? We tell them what has happened to us.

Paul didn't stay in Damascus for long. Some people got very angry with the things he was saying and wanted to kill him.

Not everyone will like it when we tell them about Jesus. But, if we don't tell them, they will never have the chance to go to heaven.

Eventually some of Paul's friends had to lower him in a basket over the city wall one night. He left Damascus but he never stopped telling people what had happened to him or about his new friend Jesus. What Paul was doing is called preaching. We can all preach. If we are Christians we all have a message to bring.

A Story To Tell

What we are going to do now is listen to somebody who like Paul met Jesus and has become a Christian.

(Let somebody give their testimony, ideally a young adult whom the children look up to and respect.)

What Is a Christian?

The gospel is very simple. Let me explain it to you.

1. This is what the Bible – God's book – tells us about being God's friend.
2. We have all done wrong things. The Bible calls these things sin. Sin hurts God. Sins don't go away, they build up in our hearts.
3. Sin is what stops us becoming God's friend. It also stops us going to heaven when we die. People with sin are not allowed into heaven.
4. God wants to come and live inside us. But he can't when sin is there. This makes God sad. He really wants to be our friend.
5. God loved you so much that he sent Jesus – Jesus is God's son – to die on a cross to be punished for your sins. He died on the cross to take away all your sins.
6. But Jesus was stronger than death and came back to life.
7. Because Jesus died on the cross you can be God's friend. All you have to do is ask God to forgive you for hurting him.

A Story To Tell

What we are going to do now is listen to somebody else who met Jesus and has become a Christian.

(Let another person give their testimony, remembering the pointers from Illustration 1.)

● STORY – The Adventures Of Fooboo Jooboo (2)

Fooboo was scared. He began to speak but didn't get a chance.

'Shut up!' commanded the leader of the Basher Boys. 'We don't care why you are here. We're going to kill you anyway.'

He pulled a knife out of his pocket. The blade glinted in the moonlight. Fooboo knew he was going to die. He braced himself for the stab of the knife.

Just then there was a blinding flash of light. There before him stood what looked like a man, except that he was over three metres tall and held a gleaming sword in his hand. His clothes were of the brightest white and he seemed to shine in the moonlight. He smiled at the Basher Boys and moved his sword from one hand to the other.

The Basher Boys looked at each other. They were white with fear. The leader dropped his knife and they ran off into the night.

Fooboo Jooboo lay on the floor with beads of perspiration running down his face. What would happen now? Had he escaped the Basher Boys just to be cut to pieces by this giant?

The man in white put his sword back in its scabbard, stretched out his hand and pulled Fooboo to his feet. He spoke and his voice sounded like the sound of a waterfall, 'Go home! Find Jimmy. He has something to tell you.'

And, with that, the man vanished right in front of Fooboo's eyes. At first, Fooboo thought he was dreaming but this was no dream. He was standing in an alley in Laser City and he was all alone. He didn't know what to do. He didn't know who the man was or how he could possibly know Jimmy. Jimmy didn't seem the sort of person who would know a giant who dressed in white and carried a sword.

Even though Fooboo didn't understand, he did as the man said and set off home. He was still twenty kilometres from home when a police car pulled alongside and the policeman called out, 'Are you Fooboo Jooboo?'

Fooboo nodded.

'Then you'd better get in. Your mother and father have been so worried about you.'

The policeman took Fooboo home. His parents seemed really glad to see him. They hugged him and his mother told him how worried she had been. They made Fooboo promise never to do anything as silly as run away again. He promised.

'Maybe everything will be better now,' he thought as he made his way to bed.

But several minutes later, the shouting started. They were arguing over whose fault it was that Fooboo had run away. Fooboo so wished they'd stop. Eventually the shouting faded into the background as Fooboo thought about the strange couple of days he'd had. Who was that enormous man with the sword? How did he know Jimmy? And what was Jimmy going to tell him?

Fooboo couldn't wait until the morning.

(To be continued...)

3 Paul Persecuted

	Programme	Item
Section 1	Welcome	
	Rules	
	Prayer	
	Praise	
	Game 1	Wheelbarrow, Hop, Skip And Jump
	Praise (x2)	
	Fun Item (2)	
	Game 2	Egg And Spoon Race
	Fun Item	
	Bible Text	Luke 9:62
	Announcements	
	Interview	
	Worship (x2)	
Section 2	Bible Lesson	Paul In Trouble
Preaching	Illustration 1	Caterpillars And Butterflies
Time	Illustration 2	Names
	Illustration 3	Finish The Race
	Story	The Adventures Of Fooboo Jooboo (3)
	Prayer	

Overview Paul was completely changed. He began to preach. But now people were getting angry with him. Not everyone wanted to listen. So what was he going to do?

Games

Game 1

Wheelbarrow, Hop, Skip And Jump

PREPARATION	None needed.
PLAYERS	Five players from each team.
SET-UP	The players line up in relay formation at A.
OBJECT	The first two players form a wheelbarrow and go from A to B and back. The third person hops the same route, the fourth person skips and the fifth person bunny hops.
WINNING	The first team to complete the relay and sit down wins.

Game 2

Egg And Spoon Race

PREPARATION	A hardboiled egg and a spoon for each team (a couple of spare eggs might be useful).
PLAYERS	Five players from each team.
SET-UP	The players line up in relay formation at A. The front person holds the spoon with the egg on it.
OBJECT	The first player races from A to B and back with the egg on the spoon. They pass the spoon to the next player who repeats the process. If the egg falls, the player must stop and replace it. If the egg breaks, the player must wait for a leader to bring another egg before they carry on.
WINNING	The team back first and sitting down wins.

BIBLE LESSON **PAUL IN TROUBLE**

'Anyone who starts ploughing and keeps looking back isn't worth a thing to God's Kingdom.' (Luke 9:62)

Paul began to talk about Jesus in every city he visited. Sometimes people liked what he said and many people became Christians. Other times they hated what he said and refused to accept his message.

Not everyone will be happy with us when we tell them that we are Christians. Not everyone will want to hear about becoming a Christian.

Paul got into all sorts of trouble. Here's a list of some of the things that happened to Paul:

- Five times he was tied to a post and given thirty-nine strokes of the whip.
- Three times he was beaten with sticks.
- On one occasion he was stoned until the people thought he was dead.
- He was put in jail many times.

Paul never did anything wrong. He just told people about Jesus.

I'm sure Paul thought about giving up. On one occasion he writes that things got so bad in Asia that he wanted to die. Many people became Christians but people don't always stay Christians.

I wonder if you are the type of person who will stick in there no matter what or if you're going to give it all up when it gets too hard.

Paul never gave up. He kept on doing what God wanted him to do. He was beaten, jailed, whipped and stoned but he kept on going.

What about you? Are you going to keep on going no matter what?

Caterpillars And Butterflies

Object needed: *A double-sided card with a picture of a caterpillar on one side and a butterfly on the other.*

Who knows what this is? *(Display caterpillar picture.)*

That's right, it's a caterpillar. But it won't always be a caterpillar. One day it will turn into one of these. *(Display butterfly picture.)*

One day the caterpillar will form a cocoon. It will stay in the cocoon, changing shape and size, until it eventually comes out as a butterfly. It's not easy for that butterfly to come out. He has to fight and wriggle and push. It may hurt. There may be pain involved. But eventually it comes out and it is beautiful.

Being a Christian isn't easy either. Sometimes people call us names. Sometimes they will not listen to what we have to say. In some parts of the world people who become Christians are still killed. But, because we know God is with us and that one day we'll be in heaven, we keep on going.

Names

Object needed: *A large piece of paper.*

Some people make fun of Christians. They call Christians some strange names. Let's see if we can think of some of the names that Christians are called.

List the names on the sheet, eg, Bible Bashers.

So what do we do when people call us names? We ignore it. We know that what we have to say about Jesus is so important, it doesn't matter what people call us and what people say. We keep on going.

Finish The Race

Object needed: *Small trophy.*

A person dressed in shorts and T-shirt walks onto the stage.

COMMENTATOR: We're here at the Olympic Games. Over there is the person we all think is going to win. His name is Fastius Sprinticus. He's Italian. Look, he's warming up now.

The person in the T-shirt starts warming up, then acts out what the commentator says.

COMMENTATOR: The race is about to begin, Fastius is taking his position. And they're off! Fastius moves straight into the lead. He's speeding past everyone. He's coming up to the finishing line and... He's stopped! What's he doing? Fastius, you haven't crossed the finishing line.

FASTIUS: But I'm so much faster than the rest. I've won, I'm the fastest.

COMMENTATOR: But you haven't crossed the line.

FASTIUS: I don't need to. I'm the fastest.

COMMENTATOR: Look they're all overtaking you. They've all finished. Fastius, you're last.

FASTIUS: But I don't understand. I'm faster than them.

COMMENTATOR: But, to win, you must finish the race. And it's worth remembering that becoming a Christian isn't enough. It's staying a Christian until the end that really counts.

● STORY – The Adventures Of Fooboo Jooboo (3)

Fooboo found it very difficult to sleep. Who was that enormous man with the sword? How did he know Jimmy? And what was Jimmy going to tell him?

Fooboo couldn't wait until the morning. He tossed and turned all night. As soon as it was light he leapt out of bed, gobbled down his breakfast and made his way to school. He searched all over the playground for Jimmy. Where was he? Fooboo eventually caught sight of him, but it was too late to ask him anything. The bell had gone and it was time to make his way in for class.

Sums! Fooboo hated sums at the best of times. He wasn't very good at sums. But today was much worse. How could he concentrate on sums? He needed to talk to Jimmy and he wanted to know who that man with the sword was.

At last the bell went for break and Fooboo got his chance to talk to Jimmy. He watched Jimmy walk out onto the playground. He followed him over to the place where he ate his crisps and sat down beside him.

Jimmy smiled.

'A huge man with a sword and glowing white clothes told me to come and talk to you,' Fooboo blurted out.

Jimmy kept smiling and said, 'I know.'

'What do you mean, you know?' Fooboo was confused. 'It happened in Laser City. How could you know?'

'The huge man told me,' Jimmy replied calmly. Seeing how confused Fooboo was, he went on to explain, 'Fooboo, the huge man was not a man at all. His name is Asil. He is a warrior angel. He was sent by King Jesus to protect you. King Jesus loves you very much, Fooboo. I tried to explain to you before about Jesus, but you wouldn't listen. Now you have met one of his angels. King Jesus has a job for you. But, before you can do what he wants, you must repent and become a Christian.'

Fooboo just sat there with his mouth open. What was he to do? Now he knew for certain that Jesus existed because he'd met one of his angels. But he'd done so many bad things. He couldn't be like Jimmy. He couldn't be a Christian, could he?

Throughout the rest of the morning, Fooboo thought about what Jimmy had said. His teacher, Mr Harvey, was talking about Hastings and some battle in 1066 but Fooboo was miles away. What was he going to do? Eventually he reached a decision.

At lunchtime Fooboo found Jimmy and told him that he wanted to become a Christian. Together they sat on a small bench and Fooboo repeated a short prayer that Jimmy prayed, 'King Jesus, I know I've done things wrong, things the Bible calls sin. I know these things hurt you very much and I'm sorry. I don't want to do them anymore. I repent and turn away from those things. Please make me a Christian. I give my life to you, Jesus. Amen.'

Fooboo didn't feel any different. But he knew something had happened. He was a Christian and now he was going to tell everyone about it.

As soon as lunch was over Fooboo marched back to his class. He stood at the front of the class and told everyone to be quiet. They were all a bit scared of him, so they did as they were told. He then made his announcement: 'I've become a Christian. Jesus saved my life by sending an angel called Asil, a great big angel with a sword. I've realised that I've done wrong things and now I've asked God to take those wrong things away. I've repented. I'm never going to do those things again.'

The class sat in stunned silence as Fooboo continued, 'And you need to become Christians too. God loves you very much and wants to forgive all the bad things you've done. Who wants to become a Christian?'

Fooboo Jooboo stood at the front of the class waiting for everyone to put their hands up and become Christians. But what happened next was not what he expected. Somebody started laughing, and then someone else. Soon the whole class was laughing and pointing at him. Fooboo couldn't believe it. He felt so embarrassed. He leaned over and grabbed the first person he could find. It just happened to be Sam. Sam was quite small, so Fooboo lifted him straight off the chair and into the air. But Sam kept laughing. Fooboo dropped Sam and ran out of the room.

He ran all the way home. He burst into his house and, ignoring his mother's shouts of, 'What are you doing here?' he ran upstairs, dropped beside his bed and started crying.

'What have I done? I thought being a Christian would be a good thing.' He wept into his pillow. 'What am I going to do? Everyone is laughing at me. What am I going to do?'

What is Fooboo going to do? Will he stop being a Christian? Will he ever be able to face his friends in school again?

(To be continued…)

4 Paul Protected

	Programme	Item
Section 1	Welcome	
	Rules	
	Prayer	
	Praise (x2)	
	Fun Item (2)	
	Game 1	Feeding Time
	Praise	
	Game 2	Nappies
	Fun Item	
	Bible Text	Matthew 28:20
	Announcements	
	Interview	
	Worship (x2)	
Section 2	**Bible Lesson**	Paul Is Protected
Preaching	**Illustration 1**	Street Speaker
Time	**Illustration 2**	From Chair To Chair
	Illustration 3	Catherine Booth
	Story	The Adventures Of Fooboo Jooboo (4)
	Prayer	

Overview Isn't it amazing that Paul ended up in all these incredibly dangerous situations but always seemed to be protected? When we serve King Jesus we have his protection as well. King Jesus is amazing: he tells us what to do, he helps us do it and he protects us while we do it.

Game 1

Feeding Time

PREPARATION	A yoghurt, a bib and a spoon for each team.
PLAYERS	One player and one leader from each team.
SET-UP	The leader sits in a chair with his arms behind his back and the bib on. The player stands behind the leader with their arms pushed under the leader's armpits.
OBJECT	To feed the leader as much yoghurt as possible in the time allowed.
WINNING	The team with the most yoghurt consumed wins.

Game 2

Nappies

PREPARATION	A disposable baby nappy for each team. (Some children may feel overly embarrassed by this game. Choose with sensitivity.)
PLAYERS	Five from each team.
SET-UP	The players line up in relay formation at A. The front person wears the nappy and puts their thumb in their mouth.
OBJECT	The first player crawls from A to B and back with their thumb in their mouth. On return they transfer the nappy to the next player who repeats the process.
WINNING	The team back first and sitting down wins.

PAUL IS PROTECTED

'I will be with you always even until the end of the world.' (Matthew 28:20)

Paul continued to tell people about Jesus for many years. He was arrested again and again but God looked after him and he was set free. He kept telling people about Jesus until eventually the Roman governor in Jerusalem arrested Paul and sent him to Rome to stand trial before the emperor himself.

Paul was taken by armed guard aboard a ship and they set sail for Italy. But even here God showed how much he was protecting Paul.

They had just left the coast of Crete when a mighty wind called the northeaster started blowing the ship all over the place. The wind was so strong that the sailors threw ropes around the bow of the ship to try and stop the ship being ripped to pieces. The following day the storm continued and the sailors were so afraid they started to throw all the luggage over the side to stop the ship sinking.

The storm continued for three days and the sailors were convinced they were going to die. But Paul stood up. 'Listen to me!' he shouted over the noise of the storm. 'Don't give in! An angel appeared to me last night and told me that nobody is going to die. Only the ship will be lost.'

The storm continued for another eleven days, blowing the ship all over the Mediterranean. At last they saw an island. The sailors tried to get as close to land as they could but the ship smashed against some rocks and everyone was thrown overboard. But just as Paul promised, God protected them and they all swam safely to the beach.

They had arrived in Malta. They hadn't yet reached Rome, but they were all safe. God protects those who work for him.

Street Speaker

Telling people about Jesus can be a very frightening thing. Imagine you had to stand on a street corner and tell people about Jesus.

A person stands at the edge of the stage and tries to talk about Jesus. He stammers and stutters and is obviously very nervous.

It really is a very frightening experience. You think you're all alone. You think people will be laughing at you. It's not easy.

The person standing at the edge of the stage continues to look flustered but stammers through a message about how much God loves you.

But what would happen if, as you stood there, a bright light appeared behind you and a three-metre tall, warrior angel complete with sword whispered to you, 'Go for it mate! I'm with you. It'll be OK'?

Suddenly you would become fearless and start telling people. You would not be afraid, because you would know that someone was with you.

The person starts talking fluently about Jesus.

But it would be even more amazing if Jesus himself stood with you and started to help you. If the creator of the universe was with you, I'm sure you'd be very brave indeed.

But that's exactly what you have got. You have King Jesus inside you, helping you. How can Jesus be inside you and inside your friend and inside everyone who is a Christian? It's very difficult to explain but, trust me, it's true.

From Chair To Chair

Objects needed: *Two chairs about five metres apart.*

Place a child on one of the chairs and then begin.

It is your job to get from this chair to that chair. You are not allowed to touch the ground. Pretend that the floor is a swamp full of crocodiles, snakes and other nasty creatures.

Give the child a few seconds to think.

It's very difficult I know. In fact, it's impossible. Sometimes living for Jesus seems impossible. It seems that Jesus wants us to be kind and good and that is very difficult. Moving from this chair to that chair is certainly very difficult, unless someone helps you.

Pick the child up and put them on the other chair.

It's very easy when someone helps. That's what becoming a Christian is like. God tells us what to do and then he helps us do it. Isn't that great? He asks us to tell others about him and then he helps us do it. He tells us to stop swearing and telling lies and then he helps us do it.

Remember! He helps us but he doesn't do it for us. We still have to try to do what's right.

Illustration 3

Catherine Booth

Object needed: *Salvation Army hat.*

Has anyone ever heard of the Salvation Army? The man who started the Salvation Army was named William Booth. William went around the country, and eventually around the world, telling people about Jesus. His wife's name was Catherine. She wanted to go with her husband and tell people about Jesus, but she was afraid. She had seen what had happened to William when he stood on street corners telling people about Jesus: sometimes people swore at him; sometimes he was beaten up; sometimes people spat at him. But all the time he kept on telling people about Jesus. Catherine didn't know what to do, so she did what she always did when she didn't know what to do. She prayed.

As Catherine knelt in prayer, Jesus himself appeared before her. She looked up at Jesus and asked, 'Jesus, is there no other way?'

Jesus showed her the nail prints in his wrist where he had been nailed to the cross and said, 'Catherine, sometimes people who follow me suffer.'

Still looking at Jesus Catherine asked one more question, 'Then, Jesus, will you go with me?'

Jesus looked into her eyes and replied, 'Catherine, I will be with you until the very end.'

Catherine stood up and joined her husband. She began to tell people about Jesus. She didn't care what happened because Jesus was with her.

And we must never be afraid. Jesus is with us and will look after us.

● STORY – The Adventures Of Fooboo Jooboo (4)

Fooboo ran upstairs, dropped beside his bed and started crying.

'What have I done? I thought being a Christian would be a good thing.' He wept into his pillow. 'What am I going to do? Everyone is laughing at me. What am I going to do?'

What is Fooboo going to do? Will he stop being a Christian? Will he ever be able to face his friends in school again?

He sat on his bed with great big tears running down his face. He was sure he was doing the right thing. He was sure King Jesus wanted him to become a Christian and to start telling his friends about him. But why did he get laughed at?

Suddenly something strange appeared in his room. It looked like a huge television screen. Pictures started to take shape. He could see Jesus. He watched as Jesus was whipped by Roman soldiers and forced to carry a huge cross up a hill. He saw how, when the cross became too heavy for Jesus, someone else was made to carry it. But the crowd still laughed and mocked Jesus. He saw how Jesus was nailed to a cross. He saw the nails going into his wrists and into his feet. He watched as Jesus hung on that cross. He saw a Roman soldier pierce Jesus' side with a spear. He saw Jesus die.

Being laughed at in class didn't seem so serious now. Fooboo realised what Jesus had been through just for him. He cried some more. This time not for himself, but for how much Jesus had to suffer for the wrong things Fooboo had done. Jesus wasn't guilty. Jesus hadn't done a thing wrong but he had taken Fooboo's punishment and the punishment of every person in the entire world. Fooboo knew that Jesus was stronger than death and came back to life.

Then a different picture appeared. It was Jesus talking to his disciples. 'I'll be with you always, even if you can't see me,' he said.

Then Jesus turned and looked straight at Fooboo. 'And I'll be with you too, Fooboo. Always!' The big television picture disappeared.

Fooboo sat there with his mouth wide open. Jesus was with him. What would he do now? The sun had set. The house was quiet. Fooboo felt very peaceful. He got into bed and went to sleep. He didn't know what would happen in class tomorrow, he didn't know if they'd laugh, but he knew that Jesus was with him. He closed his eyes and went to sleep. What would happen in class tomorrow?

(To be continued...)

5 Paul Revealing

	Programme	Item
Section 1	Welcome	
	Rules	
	Prayer	
	Praise	
	Game 1	Goal
	Praise (x2)	
	Fun Item (2)	
	Game 2	Headers
	Fun Item	
	Bible Text	1 Samuel 16:7
	Announcements	
	Interview	
	Worship (x2)	
Section 2	Bible Lesson	Paul Revealing
Preaching	Illustration 1	Diamonds And Coal
Time	Illustration 2	What's Inside Comes Out
	Illustration 3	Flash Or Burn
	Story	The Adventures Of Fooboo Jooboo (5)
	Prayer	

Overview Paul throws what he thinks is a piece of wood onto the fire. But when it feels the heat of the fire the piece of wood reveals its true self: not a piece of wood, but a snake. Maybe we're the same. Anyone can be a good Christian without pressure or fire.

games

Preaching Time

Game 1

Goal

PREPARATION	A football for each team, a set of goal posts and a goalkeeper.
PLAYERS	Five players from each team.
SET-UP	The five players line up in relay formation at A. The goal posts are set up at B with the goalkeeper in position.
OBJECT	The players take turns to dribble from A to B, shoot, collect the ball and return to A.
WINNING	The team that scores the most goals after three minutes wins.

Game 2

Headers

PREPARATION	A football for each team.
PLAYERS	Five players and a leader who can head a ball from each team.
SET-UP	The five players line up in relay formation at A. The leaders are at position B.
OBJECT	The players take turns to run from A to B, throw the ball to the leader who heads it back, collect the ball and return to A.
WINNING	The team that gets the most headers after three minutes wins.

BIBLE LESSON

PAUL REVEALING

'People judge others by what they look like, but I [God] judge people by what is in their hearts.' (1 Samuel 16:7)

Paul and his colleagues had been shipwrecked on the shores of Malta. All the sailors were wet and cold after their ordeal. They lit a fire and tried to get warm. Paul went to collect firewood. He collected bundles of wood or, at least, what he thought was wood. It wasn't until he started to put some of the pieces onto the fire that he found out what one of the 'sticks' really was.

It's not until we face times of pressure that we find out what we're really like. Sometimes when things are really tough we find out what our friends are like.

Paul tried to throw what he thought was a stick onto the fire. The stick was a snake and, as soon as it felt the heat of the fire, it struck out at Paul and bit his arm.

We all reveal what we're really like when things get hot, when things are hard. Some of us are like that snake, when things are hard we become nasty.

The amazing thing was that, even though the snake was poisonous, God protected Paul and he never even got ill.

Illustration 1

Diamonds And Coal

Objects needed: *A diamond and a piece of coal.*

These two items are made of exactly the same stuff. They're both made of carbon. They're both made in exactly the same way by being subjected to massive pressure underground. The difference between them is the amount of pressure pushing down on them.

Some people can cope with a small amount of pressure. Others can cope with a huge amount of pressure. Some of us get angry and rude and horrible if things get tough or hard. Others are able to cope. Some people become nasty under pressure. They're like coal. But diamonds can handle a lot more without being crushed.

Are you like the diamond? Or like the coal?

What's Inside Comes Out

Objects needed: *Three cups. One containing blackcurrant, one containing orange and one containing water.*

Here are three cups full of three different liquids.

This one contains blackcurrant. When I pour it out, what comes out? Obviously blackcurrant. What's inside is what comes out.

This one contains orange. When I pour it out, what comes out? Obviously orange. What's inside is what comes out.

If you tell me you're a Christian, then I expect that, whether things go right or wrong, Jesus would be proud of what comes out of you. If someone swore at you, you would respond like Jesus responded. Last week I explained to you that we have the spirit of Jesus inside us. What comes out of you is what's inside you. When we become Christians we begin to change. If you were always fighting and swearing and being rude and horrible before you were a Christian, I would expect that to change. Now you would try not to fight or swear or be horrible, because you have become a Christian. What's inside is what comes out.

This cup contains water. When I pour it out, what comes out? Obviously water. What's inside will eventually come out. No matter how hard we try to hide it, what's inside will eventually come out.

What's inside you?

Flash Or Burn

Objects needed: *Ordinary paper, flash paper* and matches.*

These two pieces of paper both look like ordinary pieces of paper. But you can tell what they're really like when you place them near fire. Let's pretend the fire is a bad thing which has happened to us, maybe somebody just took our seat in children's church. What are we going to do? What will we be like?

Some of us will come near to the fire but deal with it calmly. *(Bring the paper close to the match. Then take it away.)*

Some of us will come near to the fire and we will explode. We will lose our temper and perhaps hit someone. *(Bring the flash paper close to the match. It will burn fiercely.)*

Which one do you think Jesus wants us to be? When the pressure's on, let's react like Jesus.

● STORY – The Adventures Of Fooboo Jooboo (5)

Fooboo sat there with his mouth wide open. Jesus was with him. What would he do now? The sun had set. The house was quiet. Fooboo felt very peaceful. He got into bed and went to sleep. He didn't know what would happen in class tomorrow, he didn't know if they'd laugh, but he knew that Jesus was with him. He closed his eyes and went to sleep. What would happen in class tomorrow?

The morning came only too quickly and Fooboo made his way downstairs slowly and thoughtfully. What would today bring? What would happen when he got to school? He ate his breakfast very slowly. He listened to his mum and dad shouting at each other as usual and then set off for school. He knew that Jesus was with him but he still felt uncertain. He started to talk to Jesus on the way. He was praying and he didn't even know what praying was. 'King Jesus, I know that you love me. Help me today, help them not to laugh at me and help me to be able to tell more and more people about Jesus. Also Jesus,

• See note, p. 43

can you stop my mum and dad shouting at each oher?'

Fooboo arrived at the school gates. He felt very nervous. He saw some of his friends whispering something to each other and then pointing at him. They laughed and ran off. That's what it was like all morning: people whispering and pointing. He knew that Jesus was helping him because he managed to keep being kind and nice, instead of knocking them to the ground.

During lunchtime some of the younger boys called him a Bible Basher. He just smiled at them. They soon got fed up with that game and went to play football instead. By the time lunch had finished nobody was making fun of Fooboo anymore. They'd all found something more interesting to do. But more amazing than that, Suzie and Elizabeth from Fooboo's class had come to him and asked him to explain more about becoming a Christian. He told many people about being a Christian.

But the most amazing thing was yet to happen. When Fooboo got home that evening his mum and dad said they wanted to talk with him. They wanted to know why he seemed different. Fooboo smiled. 'I've become a Christian,' he said.

'What's one of those?' they asked.

Fooboo did his best to explain. He told them how Jesus loved people so much that he died on a cross and took the punishment for all the wrong things we have done. He explained how Jesus was stronger than death and came back to life and how, if we ask him, he forgives the wrong things we've done and makes us Christians which means we can live for Jesus now and go to heaven when we die. Fooboo's mum and dad just sat there with their mouths open.

Fooboo was very excited. He prayed a little prayer and thanked Jesus.

But then something happened. The room became bright and standing before him was Asil the angel. Fooboo wasn't so afraid because now he knew who Asil was. But what Asil had come to ask him made him feel very afraid. The angel said, 'Go back to Laser City and tell the Basher Boys about Jesus.'

Fooboo remembered the kick in the ribs and the knife in the leader's hand. He was sure that he was going to die, and now he was being asked to go back. He knew that Jesus would protect him, but he was very afraid.

Tomorrow was Saturday. He would have to set off very early. Fooboo was going back to Laser City. What would happen to him? Would the Basher Boys kill him?

(To be continued...)

6 Paul Dying

	Programme	Item
Section 1	**Welcome**	
	Rules	
	Prayer	
	Praise	
	Game 1	Balance Ball
	Praise (x2)	
	Fun Item (2)	
	Game 2	Balance Cream
	Fun Item	
	Bible Text	Philippians 1:21
	Announcements	
	Interview	
	Worship (x2)	
Section 2	**Bible Lesson**	Paul Is Protected
Preaching	**Illustration 1**	If You Were To Die Today...
Time	**Illustration 2**	Fear
	Illustration 3	Death
	Story	The Adventures Of Fooboo Jooboo (6)
	Prayer	

Overview

Paul had lived the most amazing life. He met Jesus on the Damascus road; he prayed for people and saw them healed; he was lowered over the walls of cities to stop him from being killed; and, towards the end of his life, he was taken before the Roman emperor himself.

Game 1

Balance Ball

PREPARATION	A long thin tube with one end sealed and a table tennis ball for each team.
PLAYERS	Five people from each team.
SET-UP	The players line up in relay formation at A. The front person holds the tube with the table tennis ball balanced on top.
OBJECT	The player races from A to B and back without dropping the ball, and transfers the tube to the next player. If the ball drops the player must stop and replace the ball.
WINNING	The team to complete the relay and sit down first wins.

Game 2

Balance Cream

PREPARATION	A long thin tube with one end sealed and several plates of shaving foam for each team.
PLAYERS	Five people from each team.
SET-UP	The players line up in relay formation at A. The front person holds the tube with the plate of shaving foam balanced on top.
OBJECT	The player races from A to B and back without dropping the plate, and transfers the tube to the next player. If the plate drops the player must stop, pick up the plate and return to A.
WINNING	The team to complete the relay with the least number of replacement plates wins.

Preaching Time

BIBLE LESSON | **PAUL IS PROTECTED**

'If I live, it will be for Christ, and if I die, I will gain even more.' (Philippians 1:21)

Paul was eventually brought to Rome where he was put in jail while he awaited the emperor's decision. The emperor could choose to release Paul or he could order that Paul be executed.

I wonder how you'd feel knowing that the emperor could say the word and you'd be taken outside and killed? I wonder how you'd feel if you didn't know what would happen tomorrow? In fact, you wouldn't know if you'd even see tomorrow. The emperor could call for you this afternoon and that would be the end. I wonder how you'd feel about that? Maybe you'd be thinking, 'If I died today, what would happen?'

Bring up a volunteer and have them hold a sheet of paper with the words, 'What happens when I die?'

Would you be afraid? I think I might feel afraid.

Bring up a volunteer and have them hold a sheet of paper with the word, 'Fear!'

Perhaps you would wonder, 'What is death?'

Bring up a volunteer and have them hold a sheet of paper with the words 'What is death?'

If I were in Paul's position, I would have all these things racing through my mind. But Paul didn't. In fact, Paul wasn't worried about any of these things. He said, 'If I live, it will be for Christ, and if I die, I will gain even more.'

Point to the people holding the sheets as you say the appropriate lines.

- Paul wasn't worried about dying because he knew he would go straight to heaven.
- Paul wasn't afraid! He didn't need to be afraid. He knew he would go straight to be with Jesus.
- Paul knew what death was. He had nothing to worry about.

So Paul sat happily in his jail cell thinking about how great King Jesus really was. He had made a decision. If he lived then it would be so he could continue to tell people about Jesus and, if he died, that would be even better because he could be with King Jesus in an amazing place called heaven.

As it was, Paul was released from prison. He had a chance to talk to the emperor himself about King Jesus. The emperor decided that Paul had not done anything wrong and that there was nothing wrong with telling people about King Jesus.

Several years later Paul was arrested again. And this time he was killed. But Paul wasn't afraid. He'd always said, 'If I live it will be for Christ and if I die, I will gain even more.'

Leave the volunteers at the front, they will form the basis for the next three illustrations.

If You Were To Die Today...

Take the sheet of paper from the first person, send them back to their seat and begin the lesson.

People don't live very long really, on average about seventy years. Have you ever thought, 'If I were to die today what would happen?' Have you ever wondered what would happen?

When I was eight or nine I used to wonder about it a lot. Funny the things you think about! But now I don't wonder anymore. I know what will happen. God has written it in his word. The Bible teaches us that, if we are Christians, when we die we go to heaven with King Jesus. Think of your favourite place in the entire world. Heaven is like that, but even better.

So, if you are a Christian and you have asked King Jesus to forgive the wrong things you have done, then you are going to heaven and you are going to be with King Jesus one day.

Where would you go if you were to die today? If you know Jesus and you're a Christian, you would go straight to heaven. If you are not a Christian, you won't!

Fear

Object needed: *Horn.*

Walk up behind the second person and blow the horn. Take the sheet of paper from them, send them back to their seat and begin the lesson.

People are afraid of all sorts of things: some are afraid of loud noises; others are afraid of the dark; others are afraid of spiders. What are you afraid of? *(Take some answers.)*

But there is one thing we certainly don't need to be afraid of and that is dying.

Some things have a beginning and ending. Movies have a beginning and an ending: they start and a couple of hours later they finish. Days have a beginning and an ending: they begin in the morning and end in the evening. Even the world we live in has a beginning and will have an ending: it started when God created it and one day it will no longer exist. The Bible says that God is going to create a new earth. But Christians (people who love Jesus) have a beginning (they were conceived and they were born) but, even though their bodies may die, they will live with Jesus forever in heaven.

Death

Objects needed: *Flash paper* with 'Life on Earth' written on it, and matches.*

Take the sheet of paper from the third person, send them back to their seat and begin.

The Bible says that our lives are like the grass which is here today but soon disappears. Like this piece of flash paper. *(Ignite the piece of flash paper.)*

Our lives are like that. Whoosh and they're all over. We must remember two things:

• See note, p. 43

- Only lives which are lived for Jesus will really count.
- Only Christians go to heaven and live forever with King Jesus.

We all will die. If we are Christians, our bodies will die, but we will live forever with Jesus.

● STORY – The Adventures Of Fooboo Jooboo (6)

But then something happened. The room became bright and standing before him was Asil the angel. Fooboo wasn't so afraid because now he knew who Asil was. But what Asil had come to ask him made him feel very afraid. The angel said, 'Go back to Laser City and tell the Basher Boys about Jesus.'

Fooboo remembered the kick in the ribs and the knife in the leader's hand. He was sure that he was going to die, and now he was being asked to go back. He knew that Jesus would protect him, but he was very afraid.

Tomorrow was Saturday. He would have to set off very early. Fooboo was going back to Laser City. What would happen to him? Would the Basher Boys kill him?

Fooboo woke early. He was very unsure about what would happen but he knew that he had a message to bring to the Basher Boys. He knew God would protect him and he knew that, even if they killed him, he would go to be with Jesus. He sang some songs as he walked. The sun was shining brightly in the sky and he felt quite happy. He was serving King Jesus, the creator of the entire universe. He marched on towards Laser City.

By the time he reached Laser City the sun had started to set. All those exciting shops which lined the main streets were beginning to close and the people were busily making their way home. The sky was not so warm and blue now. A dark rain cloud had appeared from somewhere and, as the street continued to empty, Fooboo Jooboo didn't feel so confident anymore. It began to rain and he really wasn't dressed for rain. He was wearing his usual brightly coloured clothes but no raincoat. Before long he was wet through but the rain didn't show any sign of stopping.

He kept walking. Eventually he found the alley where he'd come so close to being killed. He walked up the alley. It was quite dark and his eyes couldn't make out anything except shadows. He prayed, 'King Jesus, I know that you are with me but I'm feeling a little bit afraid. Please help me!'

Fooboo stood still and looked around. He still couldn't see anything but he could feel many pairs of eyes staring at him. He knew he was being watched. But where were they? He started to speak, 'King Jesus has sent me to tell you something.'

Slowly the shadows started to move. One, then two Basher Boys came out of the shadows and walked towards Fooboo. Then another and another. Not just boys but girls as well. Soon there must have been fifty or so teenagers all standing around Fooboo. They held baseball bats and knives, long chains and metal bars. They looked very frightening indeed. Even the girls looked mean and nasty. Everyone was dressed in black; very different from Fooboo's brightly coloured clothes.

'Who are you? What do you want?' demanded the leader of the Basher Boys. Before Fooboo had a chance to answer, a big grin had spread across the leader's face. 'I remember you. We nearly killed you last time. We won't mess up this time. And your giant friend doesn't seem to be here to help you.' He pulled out his knife and raised it to strike Fooboo. But just then someone grabbed his wrist.

'Stop!' It was a girl's voice. She had long blonde hair, at least Fooboo thought it was blonde. It was so matted and tangled and dirty, he found it hard to tell. But she did have the most amazing blue eyes.

The leader tried to pull his arm free but the girl swung her arm around and the next thing Fooboo knew the leader was lying on the ground with the girl's foot at his throat. The piercing blue eyes looked at the leader and she said again, 'I said, stop! I mean, stop! I'll let you kill him later. But first I want to know what this King Jesus has sent him to tell us.'

She took her foot off the leader's throat and he got up slowly. Then she looked at Fooboo and demanded, 'OK, rainbow boy. Tell us the news.'

Fooboo was shaking, but he felt King Jesus helping him. He looked around at all the Basher Boys and, although they had just tried to kill him, he felt nothing but kindness towards them. He knew that living for Jesus was sometimes hard but, right now, he didn't care if they killed him. He was going to tell them what King Jesus had to say.

'King Jesus has shown me that you are all orphans or have been thrown out by your mums or dads,' he began. He wasn't sure how he knew this, he just felt King Jesus telling him.

He went on, 'I know most of you don't think anyone loves you and that's why you're all so mean and nasty. You've decided that, because nobody loves you, you won't love anyone else. You hate everyone, because you think everyone hates you. But it's not true! Someone does love you. Someone loves you so much that he was prepared to die for you. Someone loves you so much that, even though you've done all sorts of bad things, he has taken your punishment. His name is King Jesus and he loves you so much that, 2,000 years ago, he came into a world which hated him and eventually nailed him to a cross, so people like you could know that they really are loved and that, even though they've done bad things, he loves them very much. He wants you to give your lives to him, to ask him to forgive the wrong things you've done. He wants you to become Christians, because there really is someone who loves you and his name is Jesus.'

Fooboo couldn't believe how bold and strong he sounded. He knew that Jesus was helping him. He looked at the Basher Boys and said, 'Now I want you to close your eyes and think about what I've just said.'

The Basher Boys were so amazed at what Fooboo had said they closed their eyes. And, as they began to think about what had been said, many of them began to cry. Many of them had been thrown out of their homes because their mums and dads didn't love them any more.

Some of them had never met their mums and dads.

Fooboo spoke again. 'Now, who wants to know King Jesus? Who wants to be a Christian? Who wants to serve the person who died on the cross and was even stronger than death and came back to life three days later? Who wants to know King Jesus?'

Fooboo couldn't believe it. Slowly but surely one hand went up, then another, then another. Even the girl with blue eyes put her hand up. Fooboo asked them to pray with him and they all asked Jesus to forgive the wrong things they'd done.

Fooboo found them all a place to live and, every Saturday, he would travel to Laser City and hold a church meeting for all the Basher Boys. Every Saturday he would tell them all about God and about the things in God's book, the Bible. Many of the Basher Boys learnt to listen to King Jesus too. Some of them went out and started new churches and told all sorts of people about how much Jesus loved them. Fooboo led the Basher Boys' church for a few years and then he put one of them in charge: the one with the amazing blue eyes.

King Jesus had many other adventures for Fooboo. Maybe we'll hear about some more of his adventures in the future.

Letters From A King

A Series in Seven Parts

Introduction

Title	Themes covered
1 Ephesus	Love for God
2 Smyrna	No second death
3 Pergamum	Following the wrong teaching
4 Thyatira	Following the wrong way of life
5 Sardis	Obedience and disobedience
6 Philadelphia	Endurance
7 Laodicea	No commitment

Series Overview

Each church received a letter from Jesus; a letter which highlighted all the things they were doing right, but also mentioned their errors. This series will look at the letters in turn and ask, 'What can we learn from the good and bad things these churches did?'

You will need to design a chart as follows before you begin (make it as big as possible and put it on a wall):

CHURCH	Good Things	Bad Things	Promises
Ephesus			

Each week a letter (preferably in a large golden envelope) will be brought onto the stage. On its cover should be the name of the church for study on that day, and inside:

- The good things God says about the church.
- The bad things God says about the church.
- The Bible text.

These are added to the chart during the Bible Lesson. A little time can be spent explaining a bit about the church's situation. The illustrations will then look at the good things, the bad things and the promise respectively.

1 Ephesus

	Programme	Item
Section 1	Welcome	
	Rules	
	Prayer	
	Praise	
	Game 1	Rice Krispie Pick Up
	Praise (x2)	
	Fun Item (2)	
	Game 2	Rice Krispie Stick
	Fun Item	
	Bible Text	Mark 8:38
	Announcements	
	Interview	
	Worship (x2)	
Section 2	Bible Lesson	Ephesus
Preaching	Illustration 1	Degree
Time	Illustration 2	Ice Cubed
	Illustration 3	Trees
	Story	John And Jack Jones Go To Camp
	Prayer	

 **Overview** The church in Ephesus had many positive aspects. They had endured great adversity. But they also had a major flaw. They didn't have as much love as they used to.

games

Game 1

Rice Krispie Pick Up

PREPARATION	A bowl of Rice Krispies and an empty bowl for each team, and a straw for each player.
PLAYERS	Five players from each team.
SET-UP	The players line up in relay formation at A. The empty bowls are placed at A and the bowls of Rice Krispies at B.
OBJECT	The first person runs from A to B, picks up some Rice Krispies by sucking through the straw, carries the Krispies to A and places them in the empty bowl. All this happens without using their hands. The next player then goes.
WINNING	The team with the most Krispies in the empty bowl after two minutes wins.

Game 2

Rice Krispie Stick

PREPARATION	A leader from each team sits at B with Vaseline on their face. A bowl of Rice Krispies is placed three metres in front of the leader's seats.
PLAYERS	Five players from each team.
SET-UP	The players line up in relay formation at A.
OBJECT	The first person runs from A to the bowl of Rice Krispies. They have twenty seconds to throw as many Krispies, one at a time, at their leader. Only the ones that stick to the leader's face win any points. The player then returns to A where the next person sets off.
WINNING	The team whose leader has the most Krispies attached to his/her face wins.

Preaching Time

 **BIBLE LESSON** **EPHESUS**

'If you are ashamed of me, then I will be ashamed of you.' (Mark 8:38)

How many people like getting letters? I like getting letters from my friends! But a group of seven churches in the Bible actually got letters from God. Now, God didn't post these letters. He spoke to a prophet called John. Remember, a prophet is someone who hears what God is saying and tells others. John wrote God's message down and sent it to each of the seven churches. Over the next seven weeks, we will look at the seven letters to see who they were for and what they said.

All the letters had three parts:

- A good thing God said about them.
- A bad thing God said about them.
- A promise.

Just like this wallchart *(refer to the introduction)*. Each week, we will get our letter and find out who it's to and what it says. Here comes our first letter now. *(A person walks on with the golden envelope.)*

What does it say on the front? Ephesus. This was the first church to get a special letter. I'll stick this on the chart *(place the word Ephesus on the chart)*. Now I'll open the letter and find out what it says about Ephesus.

Illustration 1

Degree

Object needed: *Scroll (pretend it's a degree).*

The Ephesians did a good thing. God said they, 'Didn't give up, even when things were hard.'

This is a university degree. It's what you get if you pass a course at university. This one's a bit special. It's a teaching degree. That means the person who got it is able to teach. My friend

Pamela has one of these. But how she actually got it is very exciting.

She had been taking her A Levels and when she received her results she hadn't done very well. She didn't have enough good grades to get into university. She wanted to be a teacher but she just hadn't passed enough exams.

Lots of people said she would never be able to become a teacher, but she wasn't going to give in. She went back to school and did the exams again. Then she went to college and passed the degree. Now she has a degree just like this and teaches. She didn't give in. She kept on going!

Ice Cubed

Objects needed: *A bowl of boiling water and some ice cubes.*

The Ephesians had also done a bad thing. 'They didn't love as they used to.' *(Display this verse on the chart.)*

Let's say this bowl of boiling water was how hot the Ephesians' love for God once was. They began to love God less and less. Things began to cool their love. There are several things which make our love for God go cold. *(Drop an ice cube in as you say each of the statements.)*

- We stop meeting with other Christians.
- We never read our Bibles.
- We don't pray.
- We forget how much God loves us.

And, with every ice cube, the water gets colder; with every new item, our love gets colder.

- We make friends with people who don't like God.
- We start being ashamed of God in front of others.

All these things make our love colder. God had one problem with the Ephesians: they had stopped loving him as much as they used to.

Trees

Object needed: *An apple.*

The Ephesians were promised that, if they kept loving Jesus, 'They would eat from the tree of life.' *(Display this verse on the chart.)*

Let me explain what that means. In the garden of Eden, right back at the start of time, Adam and Eve lived in perfect harmony with all the birds and animals. But the Devil persuaded Eve, by telling her lies, to eat the fruit from a special tree, the tree of the knowledge of good and evil.

God had forbidden Adam and Eve to go near that tree. They didn't listen to God, so God punished them by throwing them out of the garden and, because they had sinned (disobeyed God), they eventually died.

But there was another special tree in the garden. It was called the tree of life. If Adam and Eve had eaten fruit from that tree, they would have lived for ever. God promised the Ephesians, 'If you keep loving me and learn to love me more then you will live for ever.'

Next week, we will learn a little bit more about what happens after we die.

● STORY – John And Jack Jones Go To Camp

John and Jack Jones were ten-year-old twins. Both of them were full of fun and mischief. They were always very excited and happy but today they were happier than usual. Tomorrow morning, very early, they were going to camp with their church. All their mates were going and they were very, very excited.

That night they packed. They put in their trousers, their trainers, their T-shirts and their warm jumpers in case it was cold. Then they put in their toilet bags with their toothbrush and soap and comb, not that they washed much on camp or combed their hair, for that matter.

Mum shouted up the stairs, 'Don't forget your Bibles.'

John packed his Bible in his suitcase and closed it.

Jack picked up his Bible but then thought,

'Won't people make fun of me if I have this Bible? I sort of like God, but I don't want people making fun of me.' He hid his Bible under the bed, closed his suitcase and came downstairs.

When John and Jack got to camp they had a great time until the time came to go to the tuck shop.

Jack went to John and said, 'Hey, John. Where's our money for tuck?'

John looked worried. 'I thought mum gave it to you!' he replied.

John and Jack looked at each other in horror, and then together said, 'Mum's forgotten. We have no money for tuck.'

John and Jack didn't have any tuck for three days but they were still enjoying camp. On Monday evening the speaker talked about how good it is to read the Bible because it proves we still love God. John and Jack listened.

At the end of the meeting John went to find his Bible and read some of his favourite verses.

He opened up his Bible. There inside his Bible was £20, with a little note saying, 'Lots of love from Mum.' And underneath mum had written, 'If you're not ashamed of God, God will not be ashamed of you.'

John rushed out of his room to find Jack. 'Jack!' he shouted. 'It's in your Bible. She's put it in your Bible.'

'She's put what in my Bible?' Jack asked.

'The money. It's in your Bible. Our tuck money was in our Bibles.'

Jack remembered he had thrown the Bible under the bed. He also remembered his mum telling him, 'Jack if you're ashamed of God, he will be ashamed of you, and you will lose out!' Jack felt like crying. But what could he do? It was too late.

Let's make sure we don't end up embarrassed. Let's keep loving God with all our hearts and souls and strength and minds.

 **Smyrna**

	Programme	Item
Section 1	Welcome	
	Rules	
	Prayer	
	Praise	
	Game 1	Box Head
	Praise (x2)	
	Fun Item (2)	
	Game 2	Box Head Two
	Fun Item	
	Bible Text	1 Corinthians 15:55
	Announcements	
	Interview	
	Worship (x2)	
Section 2	Bible Lesson	Smyrna
Preaching	Illustration 1	Walk Of faith
Time	Illustration 2	Blameless
	Illustration 3	Second Death
	Story	John Jones Gets Accused
	Prayer	

 The church in Smyrna received a very interesting letter indeed. God commends them, makes a promise, but doesn't criticise them at all. They were blameless.

games

Game 1

Box Head

PREPARATION	You will need a box for each team. The box must be small enough to be placed on the players' heads (with the open end facing up) and tied on around their chins. You will also need a balloon for each player. (Only inflate the balloons to level where five of them fit into the box.)
PLAYERS	Five players from each team.
SET-UP	The players line up in relay formation at A. The first player has the box with a balloon in it on their head.
OBJECT	The first person runs from A to B and back. The next player adds their balloon to the box, puts the box on their head and repeats the process. If the balloons fall out, that player must return to the start.
WINNING	The team that completes first and sits down wins.

Game 2

Box Head Two

PREPARATION	The boxes from above, but this time each contains five bean bags.
PLAYERS	Five players from each team.
SET-UP	Two leaders stand on chairs at B. The chairs must be one metre apart. The players stand at A. The first player has the box containing the bean bags on their head.
OBJECT	The first person runs from A to B between the two chairs. The leaders will try to take one bean bag. The player must try to avoid losing a bean bag. The player then returns to A and transfers the box to the next player who repeats the process.
WINNING	The team with the most bean bags left at the end wins.

Preaching Time

BIBLE LESSON SMYRNA

'Death has lost the battle, where is your victory, where is your sting.' (1 Corinthians 15:55)

This is our second week looking at the letters God sent to the seven churches. Remember, God didn't post them. He spoke to a prophet called John who wrote God's message down and sent it to each of the seven churches. This week's letter is to a place called Smyrna. The letters usually have three parts, but this one only has two parts.

- A good thing God said about them.
- A promise.

Here comes our second letter now. *(A person walks on with the golden envelope.)*
    What does it say here on the front? Smyrna! This was the second church to get a special letter. I'll put this on the chart *(place the word Smyrna on the chart)*. Now I'll open it and find out what it says about Smyrna.

Walk Of faith

Objects needed: *Several rolled-up pieces of paper.*

The good thing about the church at Smyrna was this: 'I know the cruel things people say about you which aren't true.'

Someone begins to walk along a pretend path from one side of the stage to the other. As he does so, rolled-up pieces of paper are thrown at him. He should cower as the missiles are thrown at him. Make the actions fit in with the narration.

As we walk our lives as Christians, lots of things try and knock us off the path. You see, the Devil doesn't like it that we are Christians, and some people don't like it either.

The person bends over and picks up the piece of paper thrown at him. He reads out loud, 'People don't like you because you're a Christian.'

When these things are thrown at us to try and knock us off the path, we need to keep going.

The person walks on when another piece lands. He reads out loud, 'You'll never get a girlfriend because you're a Christian.

Most of these things are lies that are thrown just to knock us off the path. We have to try hard to keep walking. Sometimes it gets very hard.

The person walking is bombarded with many pieces of paper.

Sometimes it's not so hard.

The person walking is bombarded lightly!

But always, it is our choice whether to keep on walking as a Christian or leave the path.

The good thing about the church at Smyrna was this: even though lies were told about them and some of them were put in prison and some of them were killed for being Christians, they never left the path. They kept walking for God.

Blameless

Objects needed: *A target covered with Velcro and several balls that stick to Velcro.*

The amazing thing about the Christians in Smyrna is that the letter has no bad thing to say about them. It seems they just didn't do things wrong. So even though people accused them, it just wasn't true.

Put an 'X' in the 'Bad Things' column on the wallchart.

They were accused of doing all sorts of bad things, but the lies wouldn't stick. *(Stand near the target and throw the first ball to miss it.)*

They were accused of cheating and stealing,

but the lies wouldn't stick. *(Throw another ball to miss the Velcro.)*

Repeat this with other accusations such as swearing, fighting, etc.

But how about us? If people said these things about us, would they stick? *(Call out your list of accusations again. This time throw the balls to stick to the target.)*

Wouldn't it be excellent, if, like the Christians at Smyrna, nothing would stick to us because we never did anything wrong?

Second Death

Object needed: *A shepherd's crook or a long stick.*

Ask for five volunteers from among the children.

The church at Smyrna was promised that, if they kept loving Jesus, 'They will not be destroyed by the second death.' *(Display this verse on the chart.)*

Let me explain what that means. Everyone dies. This is called the first death. *(Have the children fall over and pretend to die.)*

After that they go and stand before God. *(Have the children line up before an imaginary throne.)*

Now decisions are made. God asks each person in turn, 'Are you a Christian? Have you asked my son Jesus to take away your sins?'

If the answer is 'yes', you move into the place God has been preparing for you in heaven. *(Move several children to a position behind the imaginary throne.)*

If the answer is 'no', you experience what's called the second death. You are pushed away from God's presence forever.

The promise to the Christians in Smyrna was this: 'Because you are Christians, you will never experience the second death.'

● STORY – John Jones Gets Accused

John and Jack Jones were ten-year-old twins and both were full of fun and mischief. They were always very excited and happy. But, as you found out last week, Jack was a bit naughtier than John. Jack was often in trouble in the house for not making his bed, for bringing mud into the house or for not doing his chores. John was neat, tidy and always did his chores.

At school Jack spent a lot of time in the headmaster's office being told off. John was very conscientious and never did anything to be told off for. Although John behaved well in school, he was well liked. He was the captain of the school football team and had the highest goal scoring record in the history of the school. The teachers liked John and the other children liked him too.

The exception was Julian Rogers. He was sure that he should have been captain of the football team. He was much faster than John and much tougher, even if he wasn't as skilful. He didn't like John at all. He tried to pick fights with him all the time. But John would just walk away shaking his head. He thought Julian was sad and not worth the effort. Jack wanted to fight Julian, but John wouldn't let him.

Jack was always in trouble for talking in class, playing silly tricks on teachers or writing comments on the whiteboard. Once he wrote, 'Mr Thomas fancies Mrs Andrews.' That got him into lots of trouble, especially as it was the week the school inspectors were in the school. But he wasn't bad. Julian was bad. He would steal other people's things. He would get into fights and he would deliberately damage school property.

One day Julian saw his opportunity to get at John. Mrs Andrews had left her purse on the desk and Julian was the first to arrive in the classroom. He saw the purse and grabbed it. He took all her credit cards out and hid the purse under some books in John's desk.

The rest of the class came in and started to prepare for the lesson. They pulled their books out and Mrs Andrews was about to start teaching when she realised her purse was missing. She gave a shriek and then stared at the class. 'Who's taken my purse?' she asked. 'Nobody leaves this room until it's found. Now open your desks.'

She went to Julian's desk first because she knew what he was like, but the purse was not there. She searched through the desks until she came to John's. There was her purse. She couldn't believe it. She never expected to find it there. 'Everyone else may go,' she said. 'John, stay.'

Mrs Andrews called the police and it looked as if John was in serious trouble. Julian was so pleased with himself he took the credit cards and went into the city to spend some money.

John was asked all sorts of questions. But, because John had never done anything wrong, Mrs Andrews didn't really think it could be him. The headmaster didn't think it could really have been John. And when the police came, it didn't take them long to realise that the credit cards were missing.

The answer was obvious. Whoever had the credit cards was the real thief. The police soon received a call from the music shop in the city. Then it didn't take long to find Julian with the credit cards. He was in serious trouble.

But the cool thing is this: because John had never done anything wrong, even when people said bad things about him, the lies could never stick.

Let's be the type of people who love God, who never do things wrong and who never have to face the second death.

Pergamum

	Programme	Item
Section 1	**Welcome**	
	Rules	
	Prayer	
	Praise	
	Game 1	Basketball Run
	Praise (x2)	
	Fun Item (2)	
	Game 2	Table Tennis Run
	Fun Item	
	Bible Text	John 8:32
	Announcements	
	Interview	
	Worship (x2)	
Section 2	**Bible Lesson**	Pergamum
Preaching	**Illustration 1**	Don't Give Up
Time	**Illustration 2**	Heavy
	Illustration 3	It's Raining Food
	Story	Jack Lies
	Prayer	

 The church in Pergamum had suffered much but many of them kept going for God. However, they had been deceived by the lies of the Nicolaitans and Balaam.

 **games**

 **Preaching Time**

Game 1

Basketball Run

PREPARATION	A basketball (or similar) for each team.
PLAYERS	Six players from each team.
SET-UP	Five players line up in relay formation at A. The sixth player stands at B.
OBJECT	The first person runs from A to B, throws the ball to the person at B, collects it from the player and runs back to A. The next person repeats the process.
WINNING	The team that completes and sits down first wins.

 **BIBLE LESSON** **PERGAMUM**

'The truth sets us free.' (John 8:32)

This is our third week looking at the letters God sent to the seven churches. This week we will be looking at a place called Pergamum.

Like the other letters, this one has three parts:

- A good thing God said about them.
- A bad thing God said about them.
- A promise.

Here comes our third letter now. *(A person walks on with the golden envelope.)*

What does it say here on the front? Pergamum! This was the third church to get a special letter. I'll stick this on the chart *(place the word Pergamum on the chart)*. Now I'll open the letter and find out what it says about Pergamum.

Game 2

Table Tennis Run

PREPARATION	A table tennis ball and bat for each team.
PLAYERS	Six players from each team.
SET-UP	Five players line up in relay formation at A with the ball. The sixth player stands at B with the bat.
OBJECT	The first person runs from A to B, throws the ball to the person at B (who hits it back to them) and returns to A. The next player repeats the process.
WINNING	The team that completes and sits down first wins.

 **Illustration 1**

Don't Give Up

Object needed: Karate Kid *video (or Hercules or Top Gun or any other video that fits this theme).*

The good thing about the church at Pergamum was this: 'My faithful witness Antipas was taken from you and put to death. Even then you did not give up.'

Attach the words 'Didn't Give Up' to the chart.

Show the clip from Karate Kid where Daniel looks as if he will be defeated in the final competition but comes back to win, to show the rewards of not giving up.

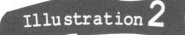 

Heavy

Objects needed: *A range of weights (talk nicely to a body builder).*

The bad thing was that the Christians in Pergamum listened to all sorts of lies and wrong things about God. *(Put the phrase 'listened to lies' in the box.)*

The lies we believe weigh us down. Let me show you what I mean. *(Bring on a leader as a volunteer.)*

Each lie about God that we listen to and believe weighs us down.

This one says, 'The world was created by accident.' *(Hand a weight with this statement on it to the leader.)*

This one says, 'We're just a bag of chemicals.' *(Hand the weight with this statement on it to the leader.)*

This one says, 'There is no heaven or hell.' *(Hand the weight with this statement on it to the leader.)*

As you can see, all these lies are getting difficult to carry. They are weighing the leader down. Here's one more, 'God doesn't exist.' *(Hand the weight with this statement on it to the leader.)*

Now these lies will stop us doing anything, if we believe them. But the truth sets us free. Let's look at these again.

The first one says, 'The world was created by accident.' But the Bible says, 'God created the world.' *(The leader drops the first weight.)*

'We're just a bag of chemicals.' But the Bible says, 'God put us together when we were in our mothers' tummies.' *(The leader drops the second weight.)*

'There is no heaven or hell.' But the Bible teaches us to pray, 'Our Father who lives in heaven.' *(The leader drops the third weight.)*

'God doesn't exist.' But the Bible says, 'The fool has said in his heart there is no God.' *(The leader drops the final weight.)*

Don't listen to the lies. They'll mess you up.

It's Raining Food

Objects needed: *Several bags of crisps, some oranges, some chocolate bars, etc.*

This promise is a bit strange. It says, 'To everyone who wins the victory, I will give some of the hidden food.' *(Place the phrase 'Hidden Food' on the chart.)*

Ask someone to throw the items of food to land near you from the top of a stepladder while you talk.

Let me explain. When God's people had left Egypt and were travelling to a country God would show them, they reached the point where they had no food and it looked like they would starve. *(Food should be dropping all around you now.)*

But God wouldn't let his people down. He always takes care of the people who love him. So he sent food from heaven to land on the ground each morning for them to eat.

Maybe God was telling the people in Pergamum who loved him that they would always have the things they needed if they stayed faithful to God. *(Pick up a chocolate bar from the ground and begin to eat it.)*

We must remember these promises are not just for these churches. We can be a part of it too. If we keep going even when things are hard, if we refuse to listen to lies about God, then God will make sure we have all we need as well.

● STORY – Jack Lies

Begin the story by asking for a volunteer to come and play the part of Jack Jones.

Jack Jones was often in trouble. But he thought that by telling lies he could get out of trouble. One day as she began their journey to the shops, Jack's mum shouted up the stairs, 'Jack, make sure you feed the dog before you go out.'

'OK, mum!' he replied. But, in the rush to get out and play football with his friends, he forgot.

Later that day when his mum asked him why the dog bowl looked so clean, Jack told a lie. He said, 'Well mum, it's because I've been teaching the dog to do his own washing up. As soon as he finished his food he must have put it in the washing bowl, washed it clean, dried it and put it back on the ground.'

Lies trap us. Let me show you what I mean. *(Wrap a layer of cotton around Jack's hands as if to tie them together.)*

But Jack's mother believed him and it seemed that his lie had worked. *(Allow Jack to snap free of the cotton.)*

But one lie doesn't usually mean the end. It usually leads to lots of other lies and then we end up really trapped. Let me show you what I mean.

One day Jack got up really early. It was his birthday and he knew what he wanted more than anything else, a new football. He rushed downstairs and there at the bottom of the stairs was his birthday present. He knew it was his football because of the shape. He pulled the wrapping paper off quickly! *(The Jack Jones character should be acting all this out.)*

Eventually the ball was free. Then Jack's dad said to him, 'Happy birthday, Jack! I hope you like your new ball. But remember, you mustn't go across to the park with it, unless I take you across. That road is too busy for you to cross alone. And if you cross that road without me Jack, I will take the ball off you. Is that clear?'

Jack nodded. But he knew that he would soon get bored with playing in the garden. The first thing he did was to write his name on the ball and then out he went to play. He stood kicking the ball against the fence for a while but that got boring very quickly. He looked across the road. All his friends were playing in the park. They waved. Jack looked round the garden. He looked towards the house. There was no sign of his father. He crept across the road and started playing football with his friends using his new ball.

That night when his dad came home he asked, 'Jack, where have you been playing?'

Jack shrugged his shoulders and replied, 'Out in the garden, of course.'

When we tell lies, we begin to trap ourselves. *(Wind the cotton once around Jack's hands.)*

'You haven't been across the road and in the park?' Jack's dad asked.

'No dad,' Jack lied. 'I've been in the garden.'

More lies. We trap ourselves even more. *(Wind the cotton around Jack's hands several times.)*

'But Mrs Smith phoned me and said you were in the park,' continued dad.

'No dad,' Jack continued to lie. 'She must have been mistaken.' *(Wind the cotton around even more times.)*

Jack's dad said no more.

The following day Jack went back across the road to play with his football and his friends. He had a great time; he scored three goals, he fouled Julian and tied the referee's shoelaces together.

But that night his dad asked him again, 'Jack, where have you been playing?'

Jack shrugged his shoulders and replied, 'Out in the garden, of course.' *(Wind the cotton around Jack's hands once.)*

'You haven't been across the road and in the park?' Jack's dad asked.

'No dad,' Jack lied. 'I've been in the garden.'

More lies. *(Wind the cotton around Jack's hands several times.)*

'But Mrs Smith came around to tell me you were in the park,' continued dad.

'No dad,' Jack continued to lie. 'She must have been mistaken.' *(Wind the cotton around even more times.)*

'But I checked in the garden and I couldn't see you anywhere.'

Jack smiled. 'I was hiding up the tree, dad. I was going to jump out on you, but you went back in too fast.' *(Wind the cotton around Jack's hands a few more times.)*

Jack's dad wasn't convinced, but said no more.

The following day, Jack went back across the road to play with his football and his friends. He didn't have such a great time: his team lost, Julian scored and, to top it all, Jack kicked his ball over Mrs Smith's fence.

That night his dad asked him again, 'Jack, where have you been playing?'

Jack shrugged his shoulders and replied, 'Out in the garden, of course.' *(Wind the cotton around Jack's hands once.)*

'You haven't been across the road and in the park?' Jack's dad asked.

'No dad,' Jack lied. 'I've been in the garden.'

More lies. *(Wind the cotton around Jack's hands several times.)*

'But Mrs Smith came around to tell me you were in the park,' continued dad.

'No dad,' Jack continued to lie. 'She must have been mistaken.' *(Wind the cotton around even more times.)*

'But Jack, she brought this ball round. It's got your name on it, Jack.'

Jack began to perspire. 'It just looks like mine, dad. Mine's outside.' *(Wind the cotton around a few more times.)*

'Fair enough,' dad continued. 'I'll take this to the police station later for lost property.'

What was Jack to do? He was trapped. *(Invite*

Jack to try and break free. The cotton should be too tight by now.)

The Bible says that the truth sets us free. Lies trap us. Truth sets us free.

Jack stood thinking for some time. Then, just as Jack's dad got to the front door, Jack shouted, 'Dad, it was me! I was over in the park! It was my ball! It was me. I'm sorry!'

Jack's dad turned around and smiled. He knew that Jack had lied. Truth sets us free. *(Cut the cotton with the scissors.)*

Jack got his ball back. He also got grounded for three weeks. He had to stay in for three whole weeks. But he got his ball back.

Lies trap us. Truth sets us free. If we tell lies, we are going to find ourselves trapped. But if we listen to lies we will also find ourselves trapped. We must learn not to tell lies and also not to listen to them.

Thyatira

	Programme	Item
Section 1	**Welcome**	
	Rules	
	Prayer	
	Praise	
	Game 1	Relay Snooker
	Praise (x2)	
	Fun Item (2)	
	Game 2	Welly Snooker
	Fun Item	
	Bible Text	Acts 4:12
	Announcements	
	Interview	
	Worship (x2)	
Section 2	**Bible Lesson**	Thyatira
Preaching	**Illustration 1**	Faith, Love And Service
Time	**Illustration 2**	Someone's Knocking On Your Door
	Illustration 3	A World To Win
	Story	Jack And John Jones (Salesman)
	Prayer	

Overview The church in Thyatira received a glowing report with regard to its love, faith and service. But the people were clearly being subjected to teachings which denied the gospel; teaching from the devil.

Game 1

Relay Snooker

PREPARATION	A snooker ball and snooker cue for each team.
PLAYERS	Three players from each team.
SET-UP	The players line up in relay formation at A.
OBJECT	The first person hits the ball with the cue (properly) and then continues to hit the ball with the cue until they have been to B and back. The only rule is that they must play the shot on their knees or lying down. On completion the cue and ball are passed to player two.
WINNING	The team that completes first and sits down wins.

Game 2

Welly Snooker

PREPARATION	A snooker cue, a ball and a wellington for each team.
PLAYERS	Three players from each team.
SET-UP	The players line up in relay formation at A. The wellingtons are placed at B.
OBJECT	The first person hits the ball with the cue (properly) and then continues to hit the ball with the cue until they have been to B and potted the ball in a wellington. They must then retrieve the ball and run back. The only rule is that they must play the shot on the knees or lying down. On completion the cue and ball are passed to player two.
WINNING	The team that completes first and sits down wins.

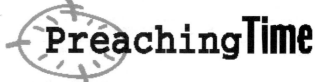

PreachingTime

BIBLE LESSON   **THYATIRA**

'Only Jesus has the power to save.' (Acts 4:12)

This is our fourth week looking at the letters God sent to the seven churches. Here comes our fourth letter now. *(A person walks on with the golden envelope.)*

What does it say here on the front? Thyatira! This was the fourth church to get a special letter. I'll put this on the chart *(place the word Thyatira on the chart)*. Now I'll open the letter and find out what it says about Thyatira.

Faith, Love And Service

Objects needed: *Two school reports (created from the tables below).*

God said of the Thyatirans, 'I know everything you have done including your love, your faith and your service.' *(Place the phrase 'love, faith and service' in the relevant box on the chart.)*

It's almost as if God had written a report on them and it said they excelled in love, faith and service.

Most of us have had school reports at one time or another. Here's *(insert a leader's name)* report. Shall I read it to you? Here we go then:

Subject	Grade	Comment
Mathematics	F	Can only count to two and only if someone helps.
Games	F	Runs very slowly. Couldn't catch a cold.
Science	F	Has blown up the classroom three times this year.

God certainly had some very good things to say about the church in Thyatira:

Subject	Grade	Comment
Love	A+	Love God very much and love other people in the same way that they love themselves.
Faith	A+	Always trust God even when things are difficult. They believe everything God says and always do what God says.
Service	A+	Will do anything they can to be helpful. They love doing things for God.

If God wrote a report on you, I wonder what he would write. What do you think he would put in the columns? Would he say that you love him and others? Would he say that you always trusted him? Would he say that you were always doing things for him?

Someone's Knocking On Your Door

Objects needed: *A front door (pretend if necessary). Costumes and basic props (e.g., a briefcase) will add colour to the drama.*

The Thyatirans had some wonderful things going for them, but they had one terrible flaw: 'They believed lies.' *(Put 'Believed lies' onto the chart.)*

There were people in Thyatira who were telling all sorts of lies. They were telling people that they didn't have to believe in Jesus to get to heaven. They were spreading lies that some of the people who loved God were beginning to believe. Now that was a long time ago, but there are still many people telling lies about God now.

Person 1 knocks on the door.

NARRATOR: Who's at the door? I'd better go and see. *(Opens the door.)* Hello!

PERSON 1: Have you ever thought about dying?

NARRATOR: Excuse me?

PERSON 1: Everyone dies. But after they die, only some of them will go to heaven.

NARRATOR: But I'm a Christian. I'm going to heaven.

PERSON 1: Not necessarily. Only 144,000 people will go to heaven. The rest have to stay on earth.

NARRATOR: *(To the audience.)* Lots of people believe this lie. But it is a lie. Everyone who believes in Jesus and has asked God to forgive the wrong things they've done, everyone who is a Christian, will be going to heaven. The Bible says so. The Bible is *all true. (To Person 1.)* Sorry sir! I don't believe a word of it! You are telling lies. The Bible says that everyone who calls on the name of the Lord will be saved. And it says, when we leave our bodies, we go to be with Jesus. God doesn't lie. But I think you do. *(Closes the door.)*

Person 2 knocks on the door.

NARRATOR: Now who? *(Opens the door.)* Hello!

PERSON 2: Lots of people are going to heaven. Thousands and millions.

NARRATOR: Yes, I agree! You should have been here earlier. You could have told the last person.

PERSON 2: I could have. Lots of people are going to heaven. I'm going to heaven.

NARRATOR: Great! So you're a Christian?

PERSON 2: Oh no! I don't believe in Jesus. I'm into New Age and yoga and meditation and stuff. I believe that everyone's going to heaven. There are lots of ways. You can be a Jehovah's Witness, a Mormon, a Buddhist or you can be like me and just chant. We're all going to heaven.

NARRATOR: *(To the audience.)* Lots of people believe this lie. But it is a lie. Everyone who believes in Jesus and has asked God to forgive the wrong things they've done, everyone who is a Christian, will be going to heaven. The Bible says so. Anyone who hasn't will not be going to heaven. The Bible is *all* true. *(To Person 2.)* Sorry sir! I don't believe a word of it! You are telling me lies. The Bible says that everyone who calls on the name of Jesus will be saved, not everyone who calls on the name of Buddha or Vishnu or who stares at crystals. Everyone who is a Christian will go to heaven. No one else. *(Closes the door.)*

You see? There are lots of lies out there. We have to be careful not to believe lies. Unfortunately, some of the Thyatirans believed the lies.

A World To Win

Object needed: *A globe or a map of the world.*

This is another strange promise. It says, 'To everyone who wins the victory, I will give them power over the nations.' *(Place the phrase 'Power over nations' on the chart.)*

Let's play 'find the country'. You call out a place name and I'll try to find it. *(As a place is mentioned, point to it.)* Let's try another place. *(Repeat the process a couple of times.)*

The Christian message isn't just for this country. It's for the whole world. God has given us power to bring the Christian message to the whole world. There are special people called missionaries who take God's word to every part of the world. *(If you have missionaries attached to your church, mention them.)*

Some of you may become missionaries to different parts of the world. Some of you may go to France or Spain; some of you may go to the Amazonian rain forests; some of you may go to the Inuit (Eskimos); some of you to China. It's exciting to know that God has given us power to take the gospel to all these places.

Let's play 'find the country' a couple more times. *(As the place is called, find it on the map and say:)* Some of you may go there as missionaries.

But that doesn't mean that you can't be missionaries right now. You can be a missionary to your school. You can tell the people there that you are a Christian, and tell them what that really means.

● STORY – Jack And John Jones (Salesman)

As we've said before, John is a bit cleverer than Jack and doesn't seem to get into too much trouble. Jack is always in trouble. And in today's story, Jack is in trouble again.

Jack had learned last week's lesson well. He knew that telling lies would keep getting him in trouble. But, unfortunately, he hadn't yet learned not to believe lies. And sometimes he was easily fooled.

Jack was woken up one morning by a loud banging on his front door. He rubbed his eyes and eventually made his way to the door. He pulled it open and still wearing his white dressing gown he looked up into a face containing more smiley teeth than Jack thought it was possible to have. Before Jack could say a word, the face began to talk. 'Good morning sir! I can see that you are a man of great intelligence.' Jack liked that so he kept listening. 'I can see that you are a young man who is going to do great things: someone who is going to be rich and famous, someone who is going to be the most popular man in town. I can see you are going to be a young man of great influence. Oh, yes. I can see it.'

Jack was waking up quickly. He liked what he was hearing. He'd always known he was destined for greatness. He knew that he'd probably be president of the entire world one day.

The man continued, 'I can see that you are going to be an amazing young man and all because you were smart enough to buy this spectacular set of books.' As if by magic, the man suddenly had a stack of very important looking books in his hands. They had leather binding. They looked very old. They looked very special.

The man started to juggle the books. Jack's mouth fell open as the ten books spun around and around in front of his face. The man kept talking, 'Young man! With these books you will fulfil your wildest dreams. These books contain everything you need to know about everything. They contain all the knowledge of all the people in all the world. There is no subject that these books can't tell you about. You need these books,'

Jack began to repeat after the salesman, 'I need the books. I need the books. I need the books.'

The salesman got to his final speech. Smiling the whole time, he said, 'And sir, these books can be yours for only £50. If you buy today.'

Jack couldn't believe it. Only £50 for all the knowledge in the world!

The man smiled. 'Young sir, if you want these books as badly as I think you do, you'll get the money. But remember, I'm only in town until 6 p.m. If you want the books, I'll be at the town hall clock at 5:45 p.m. Be there, or say goodbye to ever becoming that famous young man that I know you want to be.'

With that the man floated off down the street.

Jack was frantic. He rushed upstairs and threw John out of bed. 'John! Wake up! I need £50,' he shouted.

John pulled himself off the floor, got his blankets and jumped back into bed. He grunted, 'Well, you won't be getting it from me that's for sure.'

What was Jack going to do? He needed £50 by the end of the day. And so started the hardest day of his entire life. He dressed and thought hard about all the things he could do to gain £50 before 5:45 p.m. He thought about robbing a bank, but decided there might be a better way. He'd have to work for it. He'd have to do little jobs all over town. So off he went.

He picked up the phone and phoned his dad at work, 'Dad! I'm digging the garden and planting potatoes and sweeping the path. It will cost you £5. Thank you.' He put the phone down before dad had a chance to answer.

He worked hard at the garden. It took him nearly two hours.

'What now?' he thought. 'I still need £45.'

He knocked on Mr Smith's door and offered to clean his car for £2.50. Mr Smith agreed. He then washed Mrs Jones' car, Mrs Harold's car, Mr James' car and Mrs Pius' car (she took a bit of convincing since she had only just come back from the car wash).

Next he walked Robert Todd's dog for £3. He swept Mrs Hughes' path for another £3 and delivered all the free papers for the newsagent for £4. He carried sticks for Miss Lewis for £2 and painted Jimmy Franks' fence for £8.

It was 3:45 p.m. and Jack was exhausted. He counted his money: £4 + £2.50 + £2.50 + £2.50 + £2.50 + £3 + £3 + £4 + £2 + £8. He had £34 and

only two hours left. What could he do next? He picked blackberries and sold them to Kim Young for £8. He delivered leaflets for the hairdresser for another £2 and then he walked Robert Todd's dog again for another £3 (even though Robert really didn't want him to and the dog was still tired from the first walk). Finally he washed the butcher's car for another £2.50.

It was 4:30 p.m. and Jack was still 50p short. What was he going to do? He really wanted those books. He put his head down. He walked sadly towards the town hall clock. Maybe he could persuade the man to sell them for £49.50. But he knew that wasn't likely. He looked up and saw the man. He hung his head and slowly walked towards him, slowly enough to see something shiny on the floor in front of him. He couldn't believe it. It was a 50p piece. He picked it up and looked around. It didn't look like it belonged to anyone. He ran towards the man.

'Hello, young sir. So you've caught me have you? Let's see the money.'

Jack counted out the money. It was all there. The man handed over the books. All ten of them. Jack took them and ran all the way home. He couldn't wait to open the books. He couldn't wait to get all the knowledge in all the world.

He ran straight to his bedroom. He opened the first book and… all the pages were blank! He grabbed the next book, and the next. They were all blank! All the pages were blank in every book! The man had lied to Jack.

Jack ran out of the house and down to the town hall. But the man had gone. Jack knew that he would never see him again. He had worked so hard for nothing. He had believed the lie and worked all day long for nothing at the end. He felt very sad and walked home with tears running down his cheeks.

Jack felt very bad. But there are people in the world who spend their whole lives believing lies only to discover, when they die, that it wasn't true. The Bible is all true. Anyone who says anything which is different to the Bible is telling lies.

5 Sardis

	Programme	Item
Section 1	Welcome	
	Rules	
	Prayer	
	Praise	
	Game 1	Money Maker
	Praise (x2)	
	Fun Item (2)	
	Game 2	Grape Juice
	Fun Item	
	Bible Text	Isaiah 1:18
	Announcements	
	Interview	
	Worship (x2)	
Section 2	Bible Lesson	Sardis
Preaching	Illustration 1	White Clothes
Time	Illustration 2	Alive Or Dead
	Illustration 3	The Book Of Life
	Story	Jack Jones The Genius!
	Prayer	

Overview The church in Sardis is told that they appear alive when really they are dead. They appear to be something they are not. But there are some among them who have not sinned and these individuals are commended.

games

Preaching Time

Game 1

Money Maker

PREPARATION	An assortment of coins: 1p, 2p, 5p, 10p, 20p, 50p and a £1 coin per team (adapt this game for other countries).
PLAYERS	Six per team.
SET-UP	The teams line up in relay formation at A with the coins placed at B.
OBJECT	The leader calls out £1.86. The players in turn run from A to B, collect a coin and return. On return the next player goes. The team are trying to get the necessary coins to make £1.86. Every player goes once. The answer is to leave behind the 2p.
WINNING	First team to complete and have £1.86 and all its players sitting down wins.

Game 2

Grape Juice

PREPARATION	A bowl of grapes for each team.
PLAYERS	Six players from each team. The players should remove their shoes.
SET-UP	The players line up at A. The bowls of grapes are placed at B.
OBJECT	The first person runs from A to B, tramples the grapes for three seconds, wipes their feet and returns to A. When all the players have completed, the leader of each team pours the grape juice (excluding whole grapes) into a glass.
WINNING	The team with the most in the glass wins.

 **BIBLE LESSON** **SARDIS**

'Your sins are scarlet red, but they shall be as white as snow.' (Isaiah 1:18)

This is our fifth week looking at the letters God sent to the seven churches. Here comes our fifth letter now. *(A person walks on with the golden envelope.)*

What does it say here on the front? Sardis! This was the fifth church to get a special letter. I'll put it on the chart *(place the word Sardis on the chart)*. Now I'll open the letter and find out what it says about Sardis.

 **Illustration 1**

White Clothes

Objects needed: *White T-shirt (old), black paint.*

The good thing about the church at Sardis was this: 'You have not dirtied your clothes with sin.' *(Attach the words 'You have not dirtied your clothes' to the chart.)*

It's really easy to get your clothes dirty. You play a game of football and mud ends up on your shirt. You do some painting and paint ends up on your shirt. You slide down a hill and you get grass stains on your jeans.

But our lives can also get dirty with this thing called sin. Remember, sins are the bad things we do: the junk, rubbish and garbage in our lives.

Let's pretend this white T-shirt is our life. Let's see what happens when we sin? Let's say I steal something from a shop *(blot some paint onto the T-shirt)*, the T-shirt gets messed up. Let's say I swear at my parents *(blot some paint onto the T-shirt)*, the T-shirt gets messed up. Let's say I get into a fight *(blot some paint onto the T-shirt)*, the T-shirt gets messed up.

All the time our lives get more and more messed up. The great thing about some of the people in Sardis was that they never messed up their lives by getting involved in sin. And the older you get, the easier it becomes to get messed up in sin. Don't mess around with things that you know are wrong. It'll mess up your life.

Alive Or Dead

Object needed: *An X-ray (talk nicely to your local hospital).*

The bad thing about the church in Sardis was 'You have a reputation for being alive, but really you are dead.' *(Put onto the chart 'pretend to be something they're not'.)*

We can all pretend to be something we're not. Some of us pretend to be happy, when really we're sad. Some of us pretend to be loud, when really we're quite shy. Some of us pretend to be good, when really we're quite bad.

This is an X-ray. *(Hold up the X-ray.)* Hospitals use them to look inside people who have been in accidents. They allow us to see what damage we have inside. They allow doctors to see if we've broken any bones or swallowed anything we shouldn't have. They're very useful.

God doesn't need an X-ray machine. He can look straight inside us and see exactly what we're like. God can see our hearts. If God looked inside you today, would he be happy with what you're really like? Or would he be very disappointed?

The Book of Life

Object needed: *A big book with the words 'Book of Life' written on the cover.*

God's promise to the church at Sardis was, 'To everyone who wins the victory, I will not erase their name from the book of life.' *(Place the phrase 'Book of Life' on the chart.)*

(Open up the book and begin to read the names of some of the leaders.) This is not really The Book of Life. God himself looks after that one. It is a book which contains the names of all the people who will be going to heaven; all the people who have given their lives to Jesus; all the people who have asked Jesus to forgive the wrong things they've done; all the Christians.

What God's promise to the Christians in Sardis means is that, if they don't give up, their names will be in The Book of Life and they will be in heaven with God one day.

Is your name written in The Book of Life? I hope so! If it's not, I'll give you a chance to get it written in after today's story.

● STORY – Jack Jones The Genius!

Jack Jones hated history. He hated learning about all those dead people and all those dates. He couldn't even remember his grandfather's birthday, let alone the dates of the War of the Roses. And why were they fighting over some flowers anyway? It all seemed very bizarre.

Jack hated history. So, when Mr House announced that there would be a history test on Friday, it was no surprise that Jack nearly fell off his chair. He didn't know a thing about history.

He knew that he should probably read through his history book and find out some dates for the test, but he hated history so much he just couldn't bring himself around to doing it.

Friday came very quickly. Jack and his brother John made their way to school. Jack walked very slowly. 'What's up Jack?' asked John.

But Jack said nothing. John was the clever one who knew everything there was to know about history and Jack didn't want to admit that he knew nothing at all. Anyway, Jack was desperately trying to find an excuse for not going to the history lesson. He thought and thought until he thought his brain would explode. Then he had it. He would go to the school nurse and explain that his stomach was so painful he couldn't sit through a whole lesson.

Jack made his way to the nurse. She wasn't convinced by his strange noises and his rolling around on the ground, but she had to be careful. Yesterday she had made Harry Smith go back to his class because she didn't believe him, and he had appendicitis! She decided to let Jack spend the morning in the 'sick room' as long as he went to Mr House and explained where he would be.

Jack was so delighted he almost forgot he was supposed to be ill. He ran all the way to his classroom to tell Mr House but when he arrived Mr House wasn't there yet. Instead, lying on the desk was a copy of the history test, next to it was a copy of the answers. Jack couldn't believe his luck. He was going to pray and thank God, but thought that maybe God wouldn't like what he was about to do. Quickly, he pulled out his notebook and began to write down all the answers. He then crept out of the room as quickly as he could.

He ran back to the school nurse and announced, 'No need to worry! I'm feeling much better. I'm going to history.'

The nurse was astonished as Jack ran back down the corridor. He ran back to his class and sat ready for the test. Mr House gave out the papers. Jack pulled out his book and as quick as a flash he wrote in all the answers he had written down. He then put his hand in the air, told Mr House he had finished and made his way back to the playground.

Mr House looked at Jack's paper and marked it quickly. He then waited for the rest of the papers to come in and he placed them all in a pile to be marked.

Jack was so confident he told all his friends that he was going to get the best marks in history. 'I know more dates than a history professor! I am a genius.'

Jack was certainly pretending to be something he wasn't, but then he knew all the answers. He would certainly get away with it.

He announced to his mum and dad that they should expect an A from him for the history test because he had worked so hard. He told his granny that he was going to be the new history teacher because he was so smart. He knew everything. At the beginning of his next history lesson Mr House walked in with the results of the test. 'I'm going to give out the history tests. And there are some very good results. Well done.'

Jack couldn't contain himself. 'That'll be me sir. My brain has just started getting tuned in to history. I know more than a history professor.'

Mr House shook his head and began handing out the papers.

John had 97%. Jack felt sorry for him. 'Only 97%? I'll get 100%.'

Mr House handed Harry's paper to him. Only 65%. Jack smiled: 'I'll get nearly double that.'

And finally the moment came. Jack's paper was handed to him. There on the top was his genius grade. There was the mark that would prove how great he really was. Jack looked at the mark. Everyone else looked at the mark. It said 0%.

Jack put his hand up. 'Excuse me, sir. You've made a mistake. I got them all right.'

Mr House looked at Jack. Then he shook his head again. 'Jack, you got the mark you deserved. And, before you leave the room today, maybe you could explain to me how you managed to write down all the answers for Year Three's history test?'

'Year Three's test?' Jack began to shake. 'I thought it was… I mean… '

Jack knew he was in trouble. He had pretended to be something he was not. His friends were going to make fun of him. Mr House was going to give him detention. What a disaster! When we pretend to be something we're not, it always backfires.

When we pretend to be Christians and are not, God always knows.

6 Philadelphia

	Programme	Item
Section 1	Welcome	
	Rules	
	Prayer	
	Praise	
	Game 1	Frogs in Beans
	Praise (x2)	
	Fun Item (2)	
	Game 2	Hopper
	Fun Item	
	Bible Text	1 Samuel 15:22
	Announcements	
	Interview	
	Worship (x2)	
Section 2	Bible Lesson	Philadelphia
Preaching	Illustration 1	Don't Give Up
Time	Illustration 2	Strong
	Illustration 3	Christian
	Story	Jack Jones Partly Obeys
	Prayer	

Overview The Christians in Philadelphia were not very strong, but God still commended them for their obedience. To obey is better than sacrifice, Isaiah tells us. Through their adversity they had learnt to obey.

games

PreachingTime

Game 1

Frogs in Beans

PREPARATION	Five frogs (gems – 1p each from sweet shops) and a bowl of beans for each team.
PLAYERS	Five players from each team.
SET-UP	The players line up in relay formation at A. The frogs have been placed in the bowls of beans at B.
OBJECT	The first person runs from A to B, without using their hands they rescue a frog. The person then returns to A where the next person sets off.
WINNING	The first team to complete and sit down wins.

BIBLE LESSON **PHILADELPHIA**

'Obedience is better than sacrifice.' (1 Samuel 15:22)

This is our sixth week looking at the letters God sent to the seven churches. Remember, God didn't post these letters. He spoke to a prophet called John and John wrote his message down and sent it to each of the seven churches.

Here comes our sixth letter now. *(A person walks on with the golden envelope.)*

What does it say here on the front? Philadelphia! This was the sixth church to get a special letter. I'll stick this on the chart *(place the word Philadelphia on the chart)*. Now I'll open the letter and find out what it says about Philadelphia.

Illustration 1

Don't Give Up

Objects needed: *Two light bulbs connected to an electric current, one with an on/off switch and one with a dimmer control. If your venue has both types of switches, so much the better.*

Game 2

Hopper

PREPARATION	None needed.
PLAYERS	Six players from each team.
SET-UP	The players line up in relay formation at A.
OBJECT	The first person hops 'like a frog' from A to B and back. The next person then sets off.
WINNING	The first team to complete and sit down wins.

The good thing about the Christians of Philadelphia was this, 'You kept on obeying.' *(Attach the word 'Obedience' to the chart.)*

I have two different types of switch here.

This first one is a dimmer switch. I can make it dark, brighter, brighter still and bright. I can have different amounts of light depending upon how I feel. Obedience is not like this type of switch. We either obey: 'on'. Or we disobey: 'off'. There is no such thing as obeying a little bit. We either obey or we don't obey. There is no middle ground.

This second type of switch is a straight on/off switch. I can switch it on and off and that is all. Obedience is like this type of switch. We either obey or we don't obey. There is no middle ground.

We either do what God wants or we don't.

There is no in between. God was pleased with the church in Philadelphia because they obeyed all the time. If you obey God today but you disobey him tomorrow (you go and do something you know he wouldn't want you to do) then you haven't really obeyed God at all.

Strong

Object needed: *A weightlifting bar (talk nicely to a body builder).*

The bad thing about the Philadelphian Christians was that they were not very strong. *(Put the words 'Not very strong' on the chart. Then try to lift the weightlifting bar. Struggle with it and fail to do it! This is a great chance for overacting.)*

We imagine that not being very strong is a major flaw. Sometimes I think I'm not a very good Christian. I don't feel strong enough to tell my friends about Jesus. I don't feel able to pray and read my Bible every day. I think I'm a very weak Christian. I think that, because I'm not strong, I'm a failure.

But God thinks differently from us. He promises that when we feel weak he will make us strong. It's very exciting to be able to say to God, 'Look God! I can't do this. I don't feel strong enough to tell people about Jesus! Can you help me?'

When we do that, the creator of the entire universe, the great God who has incredible power and strength, shares some of that strength with us. He makes us strong. So being weak isn't always a bad thing. Sometimes God gets a chance to do amazing things through us just because we feel weak and know that we need his strength.

Christian

Object needed: *The word 'Christian' written on two sheets of paper so it reads 'Christ' 'ian'.*

God's promise to the Philadelphian church was 'To everyone who wins the victory, I will give them a new name.' *(Place the phrase 'New name' on the chart.)*

Everyone who has given their life to Jesus has a special name. The name is 'Christian'. It is divided into two parts: the first part is 'Christ' and the second part 'ian'. It literally means **'CHRIST'S ONE'**.

It means that we belong to Jesus. It is a very special name. You don't get it by going to church; you don't get it by being nice; you don't even get it because your mum and dad are Christians. You only get it if you ask Jesus to take away all the wrong things you've done, say sorry to Jesus for hurting him by doing wrong things and promise to live for him. In other words, to be called a Christian you must give your life to Jesus. That's what the name means.

Now, are you Christ's ones or not? Remember, it means doing your best, with God's help, to obey God all the time.

● STORY – Jack Jones Partly Obeys

Jack's mum was very kind to him. She loved him very much and always gave him as many things as she could. She wasn't very strict. But she was strict about one thing. 'Jack! I don't want you playing near the canal. Have you got that?'

Jack would always nod. He liked to humour his mother and give himself a peaceful life.

One morning Jack woke up ready for fun. After breakfast he went off to find some of his friends to play with. He walked over to Nigel's house. Nigel was always a whole lot of fun to be with. He knocked on the door. But Nigel was in bed with the flu.

'I know. I'll try James,' Jack thought. He walked all the way to James' house. It was quite a walk. He knocked on the door but, when James' mother answered, all she could say was that he was already out somewhere.

'Maybe Tom will be in,' Jack thought. But, after walking all the way back to the other side of town, he discovered that Tom had gone camping with his dad.

'What am I going to do?' wondered Jack.

He thought for some time. Eventually he decided to walk over to Mary's house. He didn't really want to do it: it wasn't that she was horrible, it was just that she was a girl and he wasn't sure that boys should be playing with girls. He couldn't think of a reason why not, so he walked to Mary's house and knocked on the door.

All sorts of strange ideas were flying through Jack's mind as he stood there. 'Will she make me wear dresses? Will I have to put make-up on? Will I have to play with dolls?'

He told himself to stop being stupid and waited for Mary to answer. But all the worrying had been pointless. Mary was out. Then, to his horror, Mary's mum told him where she was. Jack couldn't believe it: James playing with girls! Then again, only two minutes earlier, he had been ready to play with a girl.

A strange thought occurred to him. 'What if they are boyfriend and girlfriend?' He began to chuckle at the thought. Mary was really tall and James was quite small. But secretly he was a bit concerned. He liked Mary himself though he would never admit it.

Jack walked slowly away from Mary's. What was he going to do now? It seemed that nobody wanted to play today. He walked back down the road. At the bottom of the road a sign said, 'Canal this way'. Jack remembered his mum's warnings not to play near the canal. Jack thought about this but then he said to himself, 'Just walking along the side of the canal isn't the same as playing by the canal, is it?' Deep down, he knew his mother didn't want him near the canal at all. But he was going anyway.

Jack wandered down the path. Lovely flowers were growing on either side of the path. They were green, red and yellow. The sun had come out from behind the clouds and light sparkled on the water in the canal. 'It would make a lovely postcard. I wonder why mum doesn't want me to come down here?' Jack asked himself.

He walked on. Just then some of the bushes ahead of him began to move and the sun went behind a cloud. Suddenly Jack felt chilly. 'I'm sure it's just a rabbit or something,' he thought.

He kept going but just as he reached the bushes someone jumped out and grabbed him. Then more people appeared. They were all wearing masks. It was very frightening. Jack could tell they were teenage boys but he didn't know who they were. They started pushing him back and forth and laughing. He thought they might be drunk.

Suddenly they grabbed his arms and legs and lifted him off the ground. They began swinging him backwards and forwards over the canal. 'Stop!' Jack shouted. 'Let me go!'

Just then James and Mary came up the path from the opposite direction. As soon as they saw what was happening and realised Jack was in trouble they started shouting, 'Put him down! Let him go!' They ran towards the teenagers.

The teenagers had had their fun. They meant to put Jack back on the path but one of them slipped. Jack flew into the air and landed in the canal with a mighty splash! The teenagers disappeared back into the bushes.

Jack could swim fairly well but he couldn't get back up the sides of the canal. They were too steep. He splashed about for a few minutes but soon got tired.

'Hold on!' shouted James. 'We'll get you out.' He ran back down the path to fetch a lifebelt he had seen earlier. It was still there. He grabbed it and ran back.

'Catch!' he shouted to Jack as he threw him the lifebelt.

Jack grabbed it and held on.

'I'll go and get help,' called James. He ran back down the path until he found some adults walking a dog.

'Come and help!' he shouted. 'My friend's in the canal.'

The adults came quickly and very soon they had Jack back on dry ground. He was shaking, very cold and very afraid, but at least he was out of the canal.

Mary bent down and gave Jack a big hug. Then the adults gave him a lift home in their car.

Needless to say, Jack's mum was furious and certainly wasn't interested in some silly excuse about not playing near the canal, just walking. She made him go have a hot bath and then grounded him for a whole month. He wasn't allowed out, he couldn't play on his computer and he couldn't watch television for a whole month. But he knew it could have been worse. He knew he could have drowned. He felt bad about disobeying his mum.

That night in bed one good thing about the incident occurred to him. 'At least I got a hug off Mary!' And with that he went to sleep.

You see, partly obeying is the same as disobeying. God gives us rules to protect us in just the same way that Jack's mum gave him a rule to protect him. But remember, we have to obey totally. There's no such thing as partly obeying. Partly obeying is the same as disobeying.

7 Laodicea

	Programme	Item
Section 1	**Welcome**	
	Rules	
	Prayer	
	Praise	
	Game 1	Water Balloons
	Praise (x2)	
	Fun Item (2)	
	Game 2	Water Balloons With Leaders
	Fun Item	
	Bible Text	Joshua 24:15
	Announcements	
	Interview	
	Worship (x2)	
Section 2	**Bible Lesson**	Laodicea
Preaching	**Illustration 1**	Accident
Time	**Illustration 2**	Horlicks
	Illustration 3	Heaven
	Story	John The Football Expert
	Prayer	

 **Overview** The church in Laodicea is a great church for us to finish our year on. It presents us with a warning to ensure that we're on fire for God. God warns us that, if we are neither hot nor cold, he will spit us out of his mouth!

games

Game 1

Water Balloons

PREPARATION	Six water balloons and a bucket for each team.
PLAYERS	Six players from each team.
SET-UP	The players line up in relay formation at A. The buckets are placed at B and a line is drawn two metres in front of them.
OBJECT	The first person runs from A to the line, throws the water balloon at the bucket and returns to A. The next player repeats the process.
WINNING	The team that gets the most water balloons in their bucket wins.

Game 2

Water Balloons With Leaders

PREPARATION	Six water balloons and a bucket for each team.
PLAYERS	Six players and a leader from each team.
SET-UP	The players line up in relay formation at A. The leaders stand at B with the buckets behind them. A line is marked two metres in front of B.
OBJECT	The first person runs from A to the line, throws the water balloon to the leader and returns to A. If the leader catches the balloon and it doesn't burst, it is placed in the bucket. When the first player reaches A the next player begins.
WINNING	The team that gets the most water balloons in the bucket wins.

PreachingTime

BIBLE LESSON — ## LAODICEA

'Choose today whom you will serve, as for me and my family we will serve God.' (Joshua 24:15)

This is our final week looking at the letters God sent to the seven churches. God spoke to a prophet called John. Remember, a prophet is someone who hears what God is saying and tells others. John wrote God's message down and sent it to each of the seven churches.

Like most of the others, today's letter has three parts:

- A good thing God said about them.
- A bad thing God said about them.
- A promise.

Here comes our final letter now. *(A person walks on with the golden envelope.)* What does it say here on the front? Laodicea! This was the seventh church to get a special letter. I'll stick this on the chart *(place the word Laodicea on the chart)*. Now I'll open the letter and find out what it says about Laodicea.

Illustration 1

Accident

The good thing about the church at Laodicea was this: 'They had been punished.'

That sounds strange. How can being punished be a good thing? How can being disciplined be good? I'll try and explain:

Several months ago I was driving my car up a side street. Cars were parked on both sides of the street and I was going fairly slowly. As I drove along a young boy ran out from between the cars and right in front of me. I slammed on the brakes and the car screeched to a stop. When it stopped it was literally touching the boy's legs.

I opened the window to ask if he was all right. Before he had a chance to speak, his mother rushed over, looked at him and told me he was fine (much to my relief). Then she marched him over to the pavement and smacked his bottom very hard!

I felt a bit sorry for the poor boy. He was still shaken from being nearly run over by my car and now he was being smacked by his mother. But then I realised something. The mother wasn't hitting him because she liked hitting him. She was punishing him because she loved him. She wanted to make sure that he didn't do anything so foolish again. She loved him, so she disciplined him.

God is exactly the same. If he didn't care about us, he would never discipline us. But, because he cares about us, he disciplines us. God punished the people of Laodicea so that they would know that he loved them very much.

Put the phrase 'discipline those he loves' on the chart.

Horlicks

Objects needed: *A jar of Horlicks and a can of Coca-Cola.*

The bad thing about the Laodicean Christians was that they were neither hot nor cold. *(Put the word 'Lukewarm' on the chart.)*

I like Horlicks made with hot milk at the end of the day, just before I go to bed. *(Pick up the Horlicks.)* I warm the milk and pour it into my favourite mug. It is delicious and it helps me sleep.

I like freezing cold Coca-Cola after a game of basketball or football. *(Pick up the Coke.)* When I'm really thirsty and just a little bit tired, I like to drink cold Coke.

Sometimes I forget about my Horlicks after I've made it. It goes cold and a skin forms on top of it. It tastes disgusting! Lukewarm Horlicks is probably the most disgusting taste there is.

Sometimes instead of putting my Coke in a fridge, I leave it in the sunshine. It gets lukewarm and when I try to drink it after the basketball game it tastes horrible.

Hot is good. Cold is good. Lukewarm is horrible.

Christians can be like that. God likes it when we're hot for him, when we're excited about how great he is and we're telling our friends about him. He hates it when sometimes we're hot and other times we're cold. It's as if we were lukewarm. In fact, God says this to the Laodiceans: 'Because you are neither hot, nor cold, but lukewarm, I will spit you out of my mouth.'

Let's be hot for God.

Heaven

God's promise to the Laodicean Christians was 'To everyone who wins the victory, they will be with God in heaven.' *(Place the phrase 'Be with God' on the chart.)*

This is a very important promise. God is saying, if we truly believe in him and follow him, we will be with him forever. If we don't, then we won't.

I want every single one of you to be with God in heaven one day. I want you to be with the rest of us Christians, celebrating and having a great time before God. Let's make sure we're there. I will be deeply saddened if every one of you isn't in heaven with King Jesus one day.

● STORY – John The Football Expert

John had never been to a football match before. He was very excited as he stood with the rest of the people in the queue. But he was also a bit nervous. Some of the other lads looked very tough indeed. Jack was a committed Manchester United fan and they were waiting to watch a Manchester United game. Man U was playing Newcastle. The ground was packed to capacity. Thousands of fans were there. Jack led John over to the Manchester United end of the stadium and they waited for the game to begin.

John joined in with all the songs before the players came out. And the roar when the teams did come out was deafening. Everyone began to cheer as the players ran back and forth on the pitch. They were having a wonderful time. John wasn't sure about the things they were shouting at the referee, he seemed such a nice man, but apart from that he was having a great afternoon.

His brother Jack was going wild, waving his

scarf, jumping up and down, and shouting at the players. It was a sight to see. Then ten minutes before half-time Manchester United scored. The fans went crazy. A woman in front of them was so excited that she turned round and gave John a big kiss. He blushed! Before half-time had arrived, John was completely into it. He had his own red-and-white scarf out, he was dancing about with Jack and he was beginning to believe that maybe the referee wasn't so nice after all.

The whistle for half-time came at last.

'Go and get the drinks and hot dogs,' Jack said to him. 'It's over there.'

John stood in a long queue for what seemed like hours. In fact, it was only ten minutes. At last he got to the front and placed his order. He took his hot dogs and cans of pop and headed back to the stadium. As he began to walk back to his seat he began to sing one of the songs. 'Man United, Man United, Man United are the best. Man United are the best.'

So many people were pushing and shoving that it took John a long time to get back to his seat or what he thought was his seat. He wasn't surprised that Jack wasn't there. Jack was probably looking for his mate James. Only when the whistle went for the start of the second half did John realise what he'd done. This time, when the Manchester United team came out, all the people around him started to boo loudly.

John looked around quickly. He was surrounded by people wearing black-and-white scarves. They were singing different songs. He was on the wrong side of the stadium. What was he going to do? He thought quickly. He pushed his red-and-white scarf deep into his pocket and began to sing the new songs.

Ten minutes after half-time Newcastle scored and this time all the Newcastle fans started dancing. John didn't know what to do, so he started dancing as well. This time a woman in front wearing a black-and-white hat gave him a kiss. Before long, John was enjoying himself again. He'd learnt all the new songs and was singing along with the Newcastle fans.

Then Newcastle scored again! John danced and shouted. He was having a lot of fun. The final whistle went and Newcastle had won 2–1.

John made his way back across to Jack. It took some time to find him.

'Now stay close to me,' Jack warned. 'Sometimes there's trouble after these games.' Sure enough, as they left the stadium, small fights were breaking out and the police were everywhere.

They hadn't been walking long when a gang of skinheads turned around and stared at them. They were wearing black-and-white scarves. One of them shouted, 'Get them! They're Manchester boys.'

Jack shouted, 'Run!' And together they ran as fast as they could in the other direction.

'Come on! Down this way,' Jack commanded. 'This is the way the Man United guys go.'

Just when they thought they'd lost them, they turned a corner and ran straight into a gang of skinheads wearing red-and-white scarves. 'It's OK!' said Jack. 'They're on our team.'

But Jack was in for a big surprise. One of the skinheads stared at John and whispered to his friends, 'I saw him over at the Newcastle end.'

Jack looked at the skinheads. He couldn't hear what they were saying, but he knew there was trouble. He glanced at John and asked, 'John, where were you after half-time?'

John shrugged, then replied, 'I was over at the Newcastle end. I supported them for the second half.'

Jack couldn't believe it. 'You're crazy!' he shouted. 'You can't be on both sides.' He looked at the skinheads again and then shouted, 'Run!'

They took off as fast as they could. John had tried to be on both sides and now both sides hated him. They ran back down the street and straight into the Newcastle skinheads.

'Back the other way!' shouted Jack.

But the Manchester skinheads were waiting for them. They were trapped. They hid behind a nearby car and began to pray very hard. Fortunately, as soon as the Manchester skinheads saw the Newcastle skinheads, both gangs lost interest in Jack and John.

John and Jack watched as the gangs started fighting. It wasn't long before the police turned up and arrested them all but it was long enough for the skinheads to have hurt each other quite badly.

When they had all gone, Jack looked at John and said, 'I am never taking you to a football game again until you decide whose side you're on. You can't be on both sides. You have to decide, John! Or you'll get us beaten up by both sides.'

We too must learn to make decisions. If we pretend to be Christians one day and the next we're something else, we will never please God. We'll be hot one day, cold the next and God will spit us out of his mouth.

John and Jack walked home slowly. John would certainly never forget his first football match. As he walked, he began to think about which team he would support.

You too must think about who you will support. Joshua said something amazing which is written in the old part of the Bible. He told the Israelites that they could do whatever they wanted but he was going to serve God. Will you serve God too?

Special Events

 # Teletubbies' Christmas

	Programme	Item
Section 1	Welcome	
	Rules	
	Prayer	
	Praise	
	Game 1	Christmas Cake
	Praise (x2)	
	Fun Item (2)	
	Game 2	Christmas Wrap
	Fun Item	
	Bible Text	Matthew 2:2
	Announcements	
	Interview	
	Worship (x2)	
Section 2	Bible Lesson	The Wise Men Bring Gifts
Preaching	Illustration 1	Where's Jesus?
Time	Illustration 2	What's Christmas All About?
	Illustration 3	The Battle
	Story	Dipsy's Birthday
	Prayer	

verview The only historical basis for the celebration of Christmas is the birth of Jesus Christ.

games

PreachingTime

Game 1

Christmas Cake

PREPARATION	For each team you will need a cup of flour, a cup of water, a small bowl containing four beaten eggs, a cup of currants and a cup of sugar.
PLAYERS	Five players from each team.
SET-UP	The players line up in relay formation at A. Big bowls are placed at B for each team.
OBJECT	Each person takes an item and runs to B, drops the item into the bowl and returns to A to tag the next team person.
WINNING	The first team to take all items to B and put them in the bowl, return to A and sit down. For extra fun, put the mixture in a tray, place in the oven for forty minutes and give bonus points on a taste test.

Game 2

Christmas Wrap

PREPARATION	Lots of wrapping paper, tape, tinsel, Christmas tree decorations, etc.
PLAYERS	A leader and three players from each team.
SET-UP	The leader stands on a chair.
OBJECT	To wrap as much of the leader as possible in the items provided.
WINNING	The team with the most attractively wrapped leader after three minutes.

BIBLE LESSON

THE WISE MEN BRING GIFTS

'Where is the child born to be King?' (Matthew 2:2)

The wise men were called wise men because – yes, you guessed it – they were wise. They saw the special star in the sky and knew something important was happening. The star meant something. It meant a king had been born.

'Where is the child born to be King?' asked one of the wise men. 'Let's go and search.'

They followed the star for a long time. Eventually they came to a palace. They were sure they would find the king inside. But he wasn't there.

We also look for the meaning of Christmas in all the wrong places. We think Christmas is only about presents or chocolates or television or our new toys. But we will not find the meaning of Christmas in any of these things. You won't find the king in your presents or your food or even on your television.

The wise men looked in the wrong place. The palace belonged to Herod. He pretended that he wanted to meet the new king himself but he really want to kill King Jesus so that nobody would ever find him.

It is not wrong to watch television over Christmas or have presents or eat lots of chocolates. But sometimes the Devil uses these things to stop us finding out the true meaning of Christmas and that's when it becomes wrong.

The wise men kept on searching and eventually they found King Jesus. We too will find out what Christmas is all about and we will find the king, if we don't give up. He's the most important part of Christmas. Don't let the Devil stop you seeing the true meaning of Christmas. Don't let the Devil make you forget about the king. Christmas is about King Jesus being born as a baby. It's about God coming to earth.

Illustration 1

Where's Jesus?

Objects needed: *Crib with baby doll in, Christmas present (big box wrapped up), Christmas tree (smallish), a song book, television, Christmas cards.*

Position the crib in the centre of the stage but slightly to the back.

NARRATOR:	We celebrate Christmas because 2,000 years ago Jesus, the Son of God, the king of all creation, became a human being and was born as a baby in Bethlehem. But many years have passed since then and many things have come to stop us remembering what Christmas is all about.
SANTA CLAUS:	Ho! Ho! Ho! Christmas is all about great big presents. *(Santa places the Christmas present in front of the crib so that it obscures part of the crib.)*
	Ho! Ho! Ho! Christmas is all about Christmas trees. *(Santa places the tree in front of the crib.)*
	Ho! Ho! Ho! *(Sings)* 'When Santa got stuck up the chimney, he began to shout...' Christmas is all about singing carols. *(Santa places a song book in front of the crib.)*
	Ho! Ho! Ho! Christmas is all about Christmas cards. This one's from Rudolph. *(Santa places the card in front of the crib.)*
	Ho! Ho! Ho! Christmas is all about television. I can't wait for the Christmas films. They are so good this year. *(Santa places a television in front of the crib.)*
	Ho! Ho! Ho! Me! That's what Christmas is all about! Me! Ho! Ho! Ho! I really like Christmas!

Illustration 2

What's Christmas All About?

Objects needed: *The items must be left in position from Illustration 1.*

This next section involves Mr Geeky, so follow carefully the directions in the section in the introduction entitled characterisations.

GEEKY:	So what is Christmas all about? I don't understand. There's just so much to it. Is it about this? *(Holds up television.)*
NARRATOR:	No, sorry! That was invented over 1,900 years after the first Christmas.
GEEKY:	Well Christmas is about this then? *(Holds up Christmas card and reads 'To Santa from Rudolph'.)*
NARRATOR:	No, sorry! A man called Henry thought of those 1,843 years after the first Christmas.
GEEKY:	What about this? *(Holds up a song book and sings 'When Santa got stuck up the chimney...')*
NARRATOR:	Sorry! That is 1,800 years too late.
GEEKY:	Then this? *(Holds up the tree.)*
NARRATOR:	No! That's 1,850 years too late.
GEEKY:	Well it has got to be this one! Santa Claus brings these. *(Holds up the Christmas present.)*
NARRATOR:	Well, presents were given on the very first Christmas but not by Santa Claus. He didn't turn up until 1,300 years after the first Christmas.
GEEKY:	The only thing left is this crib with a baby in.
NARRATOR:	But this is no ordinary baby. We celebrate Christmas because 2,000 years ago Jesus, the Son of God, the king of all creation, became a human being and was born as a baby in Bethlehem

The Battle

The narrator stands in the middle. Santa Claus stands on a chair on one side and the crib is on the other side.

NARRATOR:	So many things try and stop you remembering what Christmas is all about. It's hard to remember that it's about Jesus, the Son of God, being born in Bethlehem when so many other things are happening.
SANTA CLAUS:	It's about television.

Narrator walks towards Santa, muttering about great movies, then stops and thinks.

NARRATOR:	No it's not. It's about Jesus. *(Walks towards the crib.)*
SANTA CLAUS:	It's about singing. 'When I got stuck up the chimney, I began to...'

Narrator walks towards Santa, muttering about chimneys, then stops and thinks.

NARRATOR:	No it's not. It's about Jesus. *(Narrator walks towards the crib.)*
SANTA CLAUS:	It's about trees and decorations and Christmas lights.

Narrator walks towards Santa, then stops and thinks.

NARRATOR:	No it's not, it's about Jesus. *(Narrator walks towards the crib.)*
SANTA CLAUS:	It's about presents.

Narrator walks towards Santa, muttering about Playstations, then stops and thinks.

NARRATOR:	No it's not. It's about Jesus. *(Narrator walks towards the crib.)*
SANTA CLAUS:	It's about me! It's all about me! I am Christmas. *(Keeps talking in this vein.)*
NARRATOR:	It is really hard. I know what Christmas is all about but it's easy to forget. It's quite a battle to keep your mind fixed on Jesus. It's quite hard to keep remembering Jesus at this time of the year. But that's what Christmas is all about. Santa! Christmas isn't about you. It's about Jesus.

Santa stops talking and looks shocked. He gets down from his chair and walks off.

NARRATOR:	We celebrate Christmas because 2,000 years ago Jesus, the Son of God, became a human being and was born as a baby in Bethlehem.

● STORY – Dipsy's Birthday

You will need a Teletubby costume. If you have no idea who the Teletubbies are, make sure you watch the popular television show before the day. If the Teletubbies are no longer in vogue, feel free to update the story with whoever is in vogue.

One day in Teletubby Land Dipsy was very excited.

DIPSY:	Very excited, very excited.
NARRATOR:	It was the night before Dipsy's birthday and he really was very, very excited.
DIPSY:	Very, very excited.
NARRATOR:	He paced up and down the house doing noisy walking. He went in and out, in and out, sat down, stood up, sat down, went back out, came back in. He really couldn't wait for his birthday to come. He was so looking forward to his birthday that, as soon as Children's BBC finished, he ate some Tubby custard.
DIPSY:	Some Tubby custard.
NARRATOR:	He ate some Tubby toast.
DIPSY:	Tubby toast, Tubby toast.
NARRATOR:	And he went off to bed. He thought that if he went to bed early, the morning would come

quicker and he'd get his birthday presents quicker. He lay in his bed, but do you think he could sleep?

No, he couldn't. He turned this way, then that way. He tried sleeping where his feet should be. He tried sleeping without the blanket. He just couldn't get to sleep.

At nine o'clock, when Tinky Winky, Po and Laa Laa went to bed, he was still awake. He tried and tried to sleep but he was just too excited. And he could hear Po snoring next door. Eventually at about two in the morning he fell asleep.

The following morning he was awake and very, very excited.

DIPSY: Very excited, Dipsy birthday!

NARRATOR: He rushed to the door to look for the cards the postman should have delivered. Nothing! He didn't worry. He thought, 'Noo Noo must have taken them in and left them on the table with my presents.'

He rushed into the kitchen. Tinky Winky was eating his breakfast, mum was eating her breakfast, the dog was even having his breakfast. But where were his cards? Where were his presents? Nowhere to be seen! He sat down but nobody said 'Happy birthday'. He waited. But still no cards or presents.

Eventually Dipsy set off for school, feeling a little bit fed up. 'Never mind,' he thought. 'At least my friends in school will remember my birthday.'

DIPSY: Friends remember Dipsy birthday!

NARRATOR: Dipsy arrived at school and walked into the playground. Nobody said 'Happy birthday'. Nobody gave him any cards. Billy asked if he wanted to play football, but he didn't say, 'Happy birthday.' His teacher didn't say, 'Happy birthday.' His headmaster didn't say, 'Happy

birthday.' Nobody said anything. They'd all forgotten. Then Dipsy thought, 'Maybe they've arranged a surprise party for me after school and they're all keeping it a secret.'

DIPSY: Surprise party!

NARRATOR: At the end of the day Dipsy rushed home as fast as he could. But when he arrived, everyone had got there before him. All his friends were there. His mum and dad were there. They were all there...

But Dipsy couldn't believe what he was seeing. Everyone was giving presents to each other. Tinky Winky was giving presents to Laa Laa. Laa Laa was giving presents to Po. Po was giving presents to Noo Noo. But nobody was giving presents to Dipsy. Everyone had forgotten his birthday. Dipsy couldn't believe it. He stood on the kitchen table and began to shout, 'What about me? What about me?'

DIPSY: It's my birthday! What about me? What about me? What about me? What about me? What about?

NARRATOR: The next thing Dipsy felt was somebody shaking him. 'Dipsy! Wake up! Wake up!'

It was Po. Dipsy had been dreaming it all. It was only four in the morning and his birthday hadn't even arrived.

The next morning Dipsy woke up and there were loads of cards waiting for him at the door. Laa Laa and Po gave him presents and there was even one from Noo Noo. All his friends at school said 'Happy birthday' as did the teacher and headmaster. And when he got home that night there was a surprise party just for him. He went to bed that night feeling very, very happy.

But do you know whose birthday it is at Christmas?

Sometimes I think Jesus is shouting on Christmas day, 'What about me? What about me? It's my birthday! What about me?'

2 The Story Of Easter

	Programme	Item
Section 1	**Welcome**	
	Rules	
	Prayer	
	Praise	
	Game 1	Egg Catch
	Praise (x2)	
	Fun Item (2)	
	Game 2	Egg Find
	Fun Item	
	Bible Text	John 3:16
	Announcements	
	Interview	
	Worship (x2)	
Section 2	**Bible Lesson**	The Cross
Preaching	**Illustration 1**	Shovels
Time	**Illustration 2**	Choices
	Illustration 3	Eggs
	Story	The Train Driver's Son
	Prayer	

Overview Jesus died a substitutionary death. He died in our place. He took our punishment.

games

PreachingTime

Game 1

Egg Catch

PREPARATION	You will need a hardboiled egg for each team.
PLAYERS	Two players from each team.
SET-UP	Players face each other one metre apart.
OBJECT	The first player throws the egg to the second. If the second player catches the egg, they must take a step backwards. The second player then throws the egg back to the first person. This goes on until one player drops the egg.
WINNING	The team that throws the egg furthest without dropping it wins.

 **BIBLE LESSON** **THE CROSS**

'God loved the people of this world so much he sent Jesus.' (John 3:16)

Show the Crucifixion scene from a video such as *Jesus of Nazareth* or *Jesus*.

Illustration 1

Shovels

Object needed: *A shovel.*

You may have heard the true story of the British prisoners of war who were forced to build the bridge over the River Kwai during the last war. Many of these men died in the process. They were literally treated as slaves and made to work long hours with very little food.

At the end of one of these impossibly hard days the demoralised prisoners were dragged out into the courtyard and the camp commander announced that a shovel was missing. He went on to explain that, unless the man who had stolen the shovel was found, every one of them would be shot. Nobody moved, but the prisoners knew the commander would shoot them all.

After what seemed like an eternity, a big Scots Guardsman stepped out of the line. The Japanese guards gathered around him and battered him to death with the butts of their guns. Later that day it was found that there had been a miscount and there wasn't a shovel missing at all. This man had given his life for his friends.

Two thousand years ago Jesus did exactly the same. He died on a cruel cross. He had never done a thing wrong but he knew that, if he took the punishment, we wouldn't have to be punished, we could be forgiven all the wrong that we've done and that we could go to heaven when we die.

Game 2

Egg Find

PREPARATION	Thirty cream eggs.
PLAYERS	Five players from each team.
SET-UP	The players line up in standard relay pattern at A. The eggs are hidden so that the teams can tell where they are, but the players cannot.
OBJECT	The first person runs from A, finds an egg and returns. Player two then runs. This continues until one of the teams has ten eggs.
WINNING	The first team with ten eggs and every player sitting down wins.

Choices

Object needed: *A see-through container full of dirty water with a pound coin at the bottom.*

If I asked for a volunteer to put their hand in here, I know a few of you would do it, in spite of the water being dirty. If I told you there was a pound coin at the bottom, many more of you would volunteer. Because of the reward you would be prepared to put your hand in the dirty water.

The Bible says that what Jesus did was similar. He knew that by dying, he would take the punishment for our sins. We would be able to have all our sins forgiven. All that junk and garbage could be taken away.

God the Father would never have let Jesus die for no reason. He let Jesus die so that we could one day be with him in heaven.

Eggs

Object needed: *A picture of a chick coming out of an egg.*

I think most people think about eggs at Easter time. They think about eggs for many different reasons.

I like to think about eggs and about little fluffy yellow chicks hatching from them at Easter time because they remind me of something. They remind me that, although Jesus died on the cross and was buried in that dark cave, he was stronger than death and, just like the chicks who burst out of the egg into the light, Jesus burst out of the grave and came back to life. Amazing stuff!

● STORY – The Train Driver's Son

David Evans was a very happy man. His life revolved around two things: his work and his son. And he loved both dearly.

David worked in a signal box near the railway line where it crossed a long bridge. His job was quite easy but also very important. Every couple of hours two trains would approach the bridge from opposite directions. One would come up the track from Swansea going towards London and the other would come down the track from London going towards Swansea. When he saw a train coming, it was his job to pull one of the levers in his box to stop one of the trains, allowing the other train to travel safely across the bridge. When that train had passed he would push the lever back and let the other train pass.

It was a very easy job but if David fell asleep or wasn't paying attention when the trains came it could be disastrous. What could happen? *(Allow the children to respond, they'd crash.)*

Trains never crashed because David took his job very seriously and never fell asleep or forgot to look out for the trains.

Every day David would arrive home from work at 5:30 p.m. and his little son John would be waiting for him. David really loved John. John looked a little bit like his dad. He had blond hair and blue eyes. He was a lot shorter because John was only five, but apart from that, they looked very similar.

Every night when David walked through the door John would run across to him, jump into his arms and proclaim, 'Dad, I've been ever so good today. Ever so good!'

David knew that John probably hadn't really been 'ever so good' because John was probably the most mischievous five-year-old in the world.

One day David went into the kitchen because he could hear the cat miaowing like crazy. He followed the sound into the bathroom and there was John trying to put the cat down the toilet. The cat was going wild and John was trying to pull the chain. 'What are you doing, John?' David demanded.

John smiled at his dad and replied, 'Dad. Snowy was dirty, so I was washing her.'

On another occasion David was in the garden painting the fence when John came out to join him. 'Can I help dad? Blue is my favourite colour. Can I help?' he asked over and over again?

His Dad knew it wasn't a good idea and said, 'Sorry John, you can't.'

John nagged and nagged and eventually said,

'Oh come on, dad. I'll be ever so good. Because I'm always ever so good.'

David still wouldn't give in. Next door's Labrador puppy jumped up on the wall and started barking. 'Look dad,' said John, 'even Toby wants me to paint.'

John wouldn't give up so eventually David gave him a paintbrush and said, 'Do it slowly and carefully or I'll take the brush away from you.'

John just laughed. 'I'll be excellent, because I'm ever so good. Ain't I, dad?'

John really did look as if he was going to do a good job. He painted slowly and carefully and made sure that no drips fell on the grass. John was doing so well that his Dad said, 'John, I'll go in and make us a cup of tea.'

John replied, 'OK, Dad. I'll just keep painting, because I'm ever so good at this. Ain't I, dad?'

David had only been gone about two minutes when he heard next door's dog barking wildly. He rushed into the garden, but too late. John was standing in the middle of the garden laughing loudly. 'Look, dad!' he said, pointing to next door's dog. 'I've painted Toby.' Sure enough, next door's golden Labrador was blue. John thought it was brilliant. He laughed and laughed and laughed. 'I'm ever so good. Ain't I, dad? Ever so good!'

David didn't think so, and neither did the neighbours, who spent the next ten days washing Toby in paint remover to get him back to his usual colour. John was always getting into trouble, but David couldn't help loving him.

Every morning before work David would sit down to eat his breakfast. John would come down five minutes later, still wearing his Power Ranger pyjamas, and sit opposite his Dad. John would pour his Rice Krispies into his dish. Some of them went into his dish, but most went on the table. Then he would pour the milk on top and most of that ended up on the table too. After breakfast, he would look at his Dad and say, 'Can I come with you to work today, please?'

David would always say 'no', but John kept asking. 'Oh please, dad. I'll be ever so good.'

'No!' David would reply. 'You have to go to school.'

Then John would look at his Dad and say, 'But dad, I don't want to go to school. I want to come to work with you and get money and buy more toys. Can I come please?'

This happened every single morning: nag, nag, nag. But David wouldn't give in and John had to go to school.

David refused to give in until one Saturday morning when John came rushing downstairs and started nagging. He did his best to ignore his son. He thought, 'If I pretend to be reading this newspaper, maybe he'll go and play.'

John asked again, 'Dad, can I come? Please!'

David turned the page and kept reading. John jumped off his chair and walked over to his Dad. He looked underneath the paper and straight up at his Dad. David lowered the paper so he couldn't see John. John jumped on a chair and looked down on David. David lifted the paper up so he couldn't see John again. This time John had had enough, he threw his arms into the newspaper and tore it in two. David was left there with the daily newspaper in two halves. 'John! What do you want?'

John asked the usual questions and David said 'no'. John nagged and nagged and nagged until eventually he said, 'Dad, if you let me come to work with you today, I'll never ask you ever again for the rest of my life, even when I'm really old like granny.'

David thought this opportunity was too good to be missed, so he gave in. John couldn't believe it. He rushed upstairs and put his jeans on. Then he remembered he still had his pyjamas on, so he took his jeans off again, took his pyjamas off, then put on his jeans, his warm jumper, his big coat and, of course, his green wellington boots. Then he was ready to go. So they set off down the street, whistling as they went. John was really excited. He waved to all the neighbours and shouted 'Hello! I'm going to work to get money to buy toys. I'm going to work and I'm going to be ever so good.'

At last they arrived at the signal box. David climbed up the ladder first and John followed him. He made John sit in the corner where he could see all the trains go past and gave him some paper and pens to do some colouring. 'I'm ever so good, ain't I dad?' called John. 'Ever so good!'

At nine o'clock the train from Swansea went past. All the people waved and John waved back. Then the train from London passed and John waved some more. 'I'm ever so good, ain't I dad? Ever so good.'

Ten o'clock came, the trains went past and John said, 'I'm ever so good, ain't I dad? Ever so good.'

At eleven o'clock the trains went past and John said, 'I'm ever so good ain't I dad? Ever so good.'

Twelve o'clock came and John said, 'I'm ever so good, ain't I dad? Ever so good.'

At one o'clock John said, 'I'm ever so good, ain't I dad? Ever so good.'

Two o'clock came… and nothing… not a sound. David looked around and John had gone. He looked out the window and there was John, happily playing in the puddles by the railway track. Jump! Splash! Jump! Splash! David banged on the window and shouted at John, but John was having too much fun to stop. This was what green wellies were meant for. Jump! Splash! Jump! Splash! Jump! Oh, no! John had caught his foot in one of the rails! He couldn't get it free. He pulled and pulled, then he looked up at his Dad and shouted, 'Stuck! It's stuck!'

John looked down at the track and saw the train from Swansea approaching very quickly. He looked up the track and saw the train from London. He looked up at his Dad and screamed, 'Stuck! Stuck!'

There was no way David could get to him in time. He had to make a decision. If he pulled back his lever the train would go across the bridge safely but John would be run over. If he didn't, all the people on the train would die but John would be safe. What should he do? Should he let hundreds of people die and save his son or should he save the people and let John die? What a decision!

Two thousand years ago at Easter God the Father faced the same decision. Should he let Jesus die on the cross so that all the wrong things people had ever done could be forgiven or should he forget about the people and send an army of angels to rescue Jesus? God the Father decided to let Jesus die so that the entire world could be forgiven of all the wrong things they had ever done.

David decided that he needed to save the people. He pulled the lever and the trains went past. The London train passed, the people saved, but nobody saw the tears in David's eyes. Then the Swansea train passed and nobody saw the tears in David's eyes. When the trains had gone, David looked down and all that was left was a small green wellington boot still trapped in the tracks.

Several minutes passed, then a small voice called out, 'Dad! Why are you crying?' David turned and stared at John. 'Are you crying because I lost my welly?'

David couldn't believe it. 'No,' he sobbed. 'I'm crying because I thought you were dead!'

John thought about this for a while and then said, 'I guess that's a pretty good reason to cry.'

That night at bedtime, David tucked John into bed. He was just on his way out of the room when John shouted, 'Dad, I've been ever so good today. Haven't I, dad? Ever so good!'

Unlike John, Jesus really did die. He died for all the wrong things we've done. Jesus was stronger than death and came back to life but what he did took courage and great, great love. He loved us so much that he died for us. Jesus wants to forgive all the wrong things you've ever done. If you want him to forgive you, then stand right now. Let this be the Easter that King Jesus forgives all the wrong things you've done and you become a Christian.

Resources
To Reach A New Generation

MUSIC

Children of the Cross, Jim Bailey (Kingsway)
God's Gang, Jim Bailey (Kingsway)
King of Heaven, Doug Horley (Kingsway)
The Stonkin' Christmas Mix, Jim Bailey (Kingsway)
On Eagles' Wings, Doug Horley (Kingsway)
Whoopah! Wahey!, Doug Horley (Kingsway)
Any of Ishmael's Collections (Kingsway)
Soul Survivor Collections, Compilation (Survivor Records)

PUPPETS, 'ILLUSIONS' AND TEACHING MATERIALS

Mr Paul Morley, 91 Green Street, Middleton, Manchester M24 2TB (telephone: 01706 649921; e-mail: www.tricksfortruth.com or paul@morley54.freeserve.co.uk).
For a spectacular range of professional puppets go to www.armslength.com

BOOKS

Angels With Dirty Faces, Ishmael (Kingsway)
Devil Take the Youngest, Winkie Pratney (Bethany House)
Fire on the Horizon, Winkie Pratney (Renew Books, Gospel Light)
Streets of Pain, Bill Wilson (Word)
Reclaiming a Generation, Ishmael (Kingsway)
Streets of Pain, Bill Wilson (Word)
A Theology of Children's Ministry, Lawrence O. Richards (Zondervan)
77 Talks for 21st Century Kids, Chris Chesterton (Monarch)
52 Ideas for Junior Classroom Assemblies, Chris Chesterton & Pat Gutteridge (Monarch)
52 Ideas for Infant Assemblies (with songs), Chris Chesterton & Elaine Buckley (Monarch)

VIDEOS

The Toy That Saved Christmas, Veggie Tales (Word)
Jonah, Testament Series (Bible Society)
Elijah, Testament Series (Bible Society)
David and Saul, Testament Series (Bible Society)
Creation and the Flood, Testament Series (Bible Society)
Miracle Maker (Bible Society)

WEBSITES THAT SELL EXCELLENT CHILDREN'S RESOURCES

www.kingdomcreative.co.uk
www.duggiedugdug.co.uk
www.ishmael.org.uk
www.kidzblitz.com
www.Jubilee-kids.co.uk

(Websites correct at time of going to press.)

Blank Lesson Plan

	Programme	Item
Section 1	Welcome	
	Rules	
	Prayer	
	Praise	
	Game 1	
	Praise (x2)	
	Fun Item (2)	
	Game 2	
	Fun Item	
	Bible Text	
	Announcements	
	Interview	
	Worship (x2)	
Section 2	Bible Lesson	
Preaching	Illustration 1	
Time	Illustration 2	
	Illustration 3	
	Story	
	Prayer	

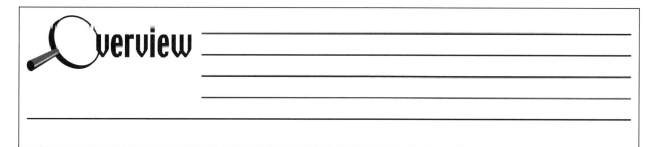

Overview

Bible Texts To Photocopy Onto Acetate

NOTE

The following pages contain biblical quotations mentioned in the curriculum material. They may be freely photocopied onto acetates.

All biblical quotations are taken from the Contemporary English Version (CEV) and are used by permission. They are arranged in biblical sequence.

I am the Lord!
There is nothing
too difficult for
me.

Genesis 18:14

Choose today whom you will serve, as for me and my family we will serve God.

Joshua 24:15

Obedience is better than sacrifice.

1 Samuel 15:22

People judge others by what they look like, but I [God] judge people by what is in their hearts.

1 Samuel 16:7

In the times of trouble you will protect me.

Psalm 27:5

Even if my mother and father should desert me, you will take care of me.

Psalm 27:10

Discover for
yourself that God
is kind.

Psalm 34:8

You [God] love justice and hate evil.

Psalm 45:7

If I were to climb to the highest heavens you would be there, if I were to dig down to the world of the dead you would also be there.

Psalm 139:8

Your sins are scarlet red, but they shall be as white as snow.

Isaiah 1:18

When I was in trouble I prayed to you and you listened to me.

Jonah 2:2

God said 'Don't depend on your own power or strength, but on my Spirit.'

Zechariah 4:6

Where is the child born to be King?

Matthew 2:2

Come with me! I will show you how to bring in people instead of fish.

Matthew 4:19

God blesses
people whose
hearts are pure.
They will see God!

Matthew 5:8

Do not worry...

Matthew 6:31

If you tell others that you belong to me, I will tell my father in heaven that you are my followers.

Matthew 10:32

I will be with you always even until the end of the world.

Matthew 28:20

If you are
ashamed of me,
then I will be
ashamed of you.

Mark 8:38

The Lord's Spirit has come to me, ... to free everyone who suffers.

Luke 4:18

Anyone who starts ploughing and keeps looking back isn't worth a thing to God's Kingdom.

Luke 9:62

God loved the people of this world so much that he gave his only son, so that everyone who has faith in him will have eternal life and never really die.

John 3:16

The water I give is like a flowing fountain that gives everlasting life.

John 4:14

The truth sets us free.

John 8:32

Only Jesus has the power to save.

Acts 4:12

If you belong to Jesus Christ you won't be punished.

Romans 8:1

God will accept
you and save you,
if you truly
believe AND TELL
OTHERS.

Romans 10:9

Whatever we build will be tested by fire on the day of judgement.

1 Corinthians 3:13

Our first duty is to be faithful to the one we work for.

1 Corinthians 4:2

Death has lost the battle, where is your victory, where is your sting?

1 Corinthians 15:55

God's Spirit
makes us loving,
happy, peaceful,
patient, kind,
good, faithful,
gentle, and
self-controlled.

Galatians 5:22-23

If I live, it will be for Christ, and if I die, I will gain even more.

Philippians 1:21

Christ gives me
the strength to
face anything.

Philippians 4:13

It is only natural for us to thank God for you. God chose you to be the first ones to be saved.

2 Thessalonians 2:13

We know that the law is good if it is used in the right way.

1 Timothy 1:8

I will never leave you or forsake you.

Hebrews 13:5

The prayer of an innocent person is powerful and it can help a lot.

James 5:16

He who has Jesus
has life.

1 John 5:12